THE WORKS OF SHAKESPEARE

EDITED FOR THE SYNDICS OF THE
CAMBRIDGE UNIVERSITY PRESS
BY
JOHN DOVER WILSON

JULIUS CÆSAR

JULIUS CÆSAR

CAMBRIDGE UNIVERSITY PRESS

Published by the Syndics of the Cambridge University Press
Bentley House, 200 Euston Road, London, NW1 2DB
American Branch: 32 East 57th Street, New York, N.Y. 10022

ISBNS:
0 521 07539 4 hard covers
0 521 09482 8 paperback

First published 1949
Reprinted 1956 1964
First paperback edition 1968
Reprinted 1970 1971 1974

First printed in Great Britain at the University Press, Cambridge
Reprinted in Great Britain by Hazell Watson & Viney Ltd,
Aylesbury, Bucks

CONTENTS

Places where slight editorial changes or additions introduce variants from the first edition are, when possible, marked by a date [1955] in square brackets.

To

PERCY SIMPSON

INTRODUCTION

Popular in English schools and colleges on account of its simple style and classical theme, *Julius Cæsar* has probably appeared in a larger number of editions than any other of Shakespeare's plays, though, as it happens, the most interesting edition of all was prepared for Indian university students and is little known in this country.[1] The name of Sir Mark Hunter, a distinguished Indian Civil Servant who was also a good Elizabethan student, stands on the title-page, while he confesses in a preface that he is much indebted to Dr Percy Simpson 'for many scholarly notes, not all of which are expressly acknowledged'. In fact, Dr Simpson, who a year earlier had succeeded, as will presently appear, in establishing the true date of the play for the first time, virtually acted as his assistant editor; and I have frequently found myself treading in his steps, as I traced my own path through the play. For which reason, and also because there is special fitness in associating this most Roman of Shakespeare's Roman plays with the veteran scholar who has devoted half a lifetime to the most Roman of Shakespeare's friends and rivals, admiration has combined with friendship to inspire the dedication on the opposite page.

[1] *The Tragedy of Julius Cæsar*, ed. by Mark Hunter, 1900 ('College Classics', Madras: Srinivasa, Varadachari and Co.). It contains, for example, a valuable essay on 'Double Time' in *Julius Cæsar* (Introduction, pp. cviii–cxxi), a matter which pressure of space has obliged me to ignore below.

I. *Date and Contemporary Allusion*

Shakespeare's *Julius Cæsar* was first produced in the autumn of 1599. The evidence is twofold. In 1601 John Weever, who had already in 1599 addressed a respectful epigram to 'Honie-tong'd Shakespeare', published a poem called *The Mirror of Martyrs*, containing the following lines which clearly refer to the Forum scene:[1]

> The manie-headed multitude were drawne
> By *Brutus* speach, that Cæsar was ambitious,
> When eloquent *Mark Antonie* had showne
> His vertues, who but *Brutus* then was vicious?

First detected by Halliwell-Phillipps,[2] the allusion was taken as dating the play 1600 or 1601 until Dr Percy Simpson pointed to a passage in the Dedication which states that the poem 'some two yeares agoe was made fit for the Print', and implies therefore that Weever must have seen a performance in 1599. Dr Simpson published his discovery in 1899;[3] and in the same year a second piece of evidence came to light, confirming the date 1599 and narrowing it down to the autumn. The travel-book of a Swiss gentleman, Thomas Platter, covering the years 1595 to 1600, and including a visit to England in 1599, was found at Basle and printed in *Anglia*.[4] Platter witnessed two plays in London, one

---

[1] For the two references v. Chambers, *William Shakespeare: Facts and Problems*, II, 199.

[2] V. Halliwell-Phillipps, Introduction to *Julius Cæsar* in *Works of Shakespeare* (1853–65). The date 1600–1 was still accepted by MacCallum in 1910, Furness in 1913, and Sidney Lee in 1916 (*Life of Shakespeare*, new and enlarged edition, pp. 333–4).

[3] *Notes and Queries*, 11 Feb. 1899 (9th series, III, 105).

[4] G. Binz, *Anglia*, XXII, 456–64.

of them evidently Shakespeare's *Julius Cæsar*, which he refers to as follows:

After lunch on 21 September, round about 2 o'clock, I went with my companions across the water, and in the straw-thatched house saw the tragedy of the first emperor, Julius Cæsar, excellently performed by some fifteen persons. At the end of the play, according to custom, they danced with much grace and in wonderful combination, two clad in men's clothes and two in women's.[1]

Like Polonius the worthy Switzer seems to have found the jig more interesting than the tragedy, perhaps because he could not follow English very easily. But a play on Julius Cæsar in 1599 can only have been Shakespeare's,[2] while the 'straw-thatched' Globe, which his company began building in January or February 1599 and took some seven months to complete, cannot have been ready for regular performances much before the autumn, so that *Julius Cæsar* will have been one of the first plays to be seen there. It is even possible that Shakespeare wrote it expressly for the opening. His references in the Prologue of *Henry V* to the cramped conditions of 'this cockpit' and 'this wooden O', often taken as pointing to the Globe, would have been an oddly inauspicious welcome to patrons attending the fine new house, of which he was no doubt as proud as his fellows. Besides, *Henry V*, as I have

---

[1] I translate from the German text as printed in Chambers, *Elizabethan Stage*, II, 364–5. The words 'in the straw-thatched house' ('in dem streüwinen Dachhaus', which Chambers strangely renders 'in the strewn roofhouse') evidently refer to the shining straw of the new Globe roof, easily picked out across the river from the older thatched roofs of other buildings on Bankside.

[2] For further evidence see Chambers, *William Shakespeare: Facts and Problems*, I, 397.

shown,[1] was probably several months too early for the
Globe. In any case, *Julius Cæsar* was certainly performed at the newly opened theatre on Bankside, was
the next play Shakespeare undertook after *Henry V*,[2]
and like *Henry V* belongs to 1599.

With the establishment of this date a number of
other contemporary parallels and allusions fall into
place. On the one hand, the similarity in thought and
phrase of 3. 1. 112–14 with a stanza of Daniel's
Musophilus, registered under *Poetical Essays* on 9
January 1599, and of 1. 2. 52 with lines in Sir John
Davies' *Nosce Teipsum*, registered on 14 April following,
indicate that Shakespeare was pretty certainly reading
both poems as he wrote the play.[3] On the other hand,
we can now feel equally confident that Ben Jonson was
making fun of two of its passages in his *Everyman out
of his Humour*, produced by Shakespeare's company in
1599, and was borrowing from another in his *Cynthia's
Revels* of 1600.[4] But that a play on Julius Cæsar should

[1] V. p. x, *Henry V* ('New Shakespeare') and the note on
1 Prol. 13, together with Chambers, *Elizabethan Stage*, II, 415.

[2] That Shakespeare was studying Plutarch's *Antonius*
when writing *Henry V* seems proved by 5 Prol. 26–8:

> 'Like to the Senators of th'antique Rome,
> With the Plebeians swarming at their heels,
> Go forth and fetch their conqu'ring Cæsar in,'

which echoes 'Now when Cæsar was returned from his
last war in Spain, all the chiefest nobility of the city rode
many days' journey from Rome to meet him' (Skeat,
Shakespeare's Plutarch, p. 163), while the additional touch
about the swarming plebeians suggests that the opening
scene of *Julius Cæsar* was already present in Shakespeare's
mind, if not already on paper.

[3] V. below notes on 3. 1. 112–14 and 1. 2. 52–8.

[4] V. below notes on 3. 1. 77 (*ad fin.*); 3. 2. 105–6
5. 5. 73–5.

have been undertaken by his unlearned friend, and have scored a success, was a standing offence in Jonson's eyes. He was still girding at it in 1626, and his animosity has even left traces in the Folio text.[1]

II. *Style and Characters*

Yet, whether Jonson liked it or not, Shakespeare's first dramatic essay on a classical theme has all the proportion, simplicity and restraint which are characteristic of classical art. Not that there is anything of neo-classic rigidity about it; still less does its success depend on sheer virtuosity, as does the intricate mechanism of Ben Jonson's plots. Indeed, mechanism is the last thing it suggests. 'The action moves forward with a varied rhythm, upon an ebb and flow of minor event that is most lifelike. The whole play is alive...in every line.'[2] Neither sub-plot nor digression distracts the mind from the central theme.[3] The lack of a clown may be due to Kempe's defection from the company early in 1599; but in any case the absence of all comic matter—it contains not a single note of bawdy, a rare thing in Shakespeare—is entirely in keeping with the tone of this sober, streamlined drama.

As for style, a sparing use of metaphor and word-play, coupled with a remarkable economy and directness of speech by all the characters, secures the 'dignified and unadorned simplicity—a Roman simplicity, perhaps', which, as Bradley says, and Sir Edmund Chambers

[1] V. note on 3. 1. 47–8, 'Note on the Copy', pp. 93–4, and an article on 'Ben Jonson and *Julius Cæsar*' in *Shakespeare Survey*, II (1949).

[2] Granville-Barker, *Prefaces to Shakespeare*, 1st series, p. 90.

[3] On the alleged irrelevance of the quarrel-scene v. below, § IV, pp. xix–xx.

agrees, is the distinguishing feature of the play.[1] Some, indeed, detect a certain lack of ease. Dr Johnson remarks that Shakespeare's 'adherence to the real story, and to Roman manners, seems to have impeded the natural vigour of his genius'. And Mr Van Doren, who is always worth hearing on questions of style, after noting the 'perfection of form', adds:

But...the perfection is of that sort that limits rather than releases poetry. ...Its persons all have something of the statue in them, for they express their author's idea of antiquity rather than his knowledge of life. They have the clarity and simplicity of worked marble, and are the easiest of Shakespeare's people to understand, if one...is innocent of the distinction between men and public men. The characters of *Julius Cæsar* are public men....But Shakespeare's deepest interest is in the private man.[2]

He also notes that all the characters 'tend to talk alike', 'in speeches that have tangible outlines like plastic objects', with phrasing 'invariably flawless from the oral point of view' and full 'of the music of monosyllables', of 'which no play of Shakespeare has so many, so superbly used'. Suggestive and true enough up to a point, it is after all true in some degree of every play by the mature Shakespeare, since each has its own special atmosphere, creating a distinctive style to which the characters must conform.[3]

And the critic quite misses the mark when he passes from style to character. Public affairs are, of course,

[1] *Shakespearean Tragedy*, by A. C. Bradley, p. 85 n., and *William Shakespeare: Facts and Problems*, by E. K. Chambers, I, 399.

[2] Mark Van Doren, *Shakespeare*, pp. 180–1.

[3] This similarity of speech is not to be confused with the monotony of the speeches by the Greeks in *Troilus*, which is designed to convey an impression of commonplace stupidity.

the chief preoccupation of all the persons in the play;
what is at stake is the future of Rome (and of the world),
not as in later tragedies, the hero's soul (and our own).
But that they are still 'private' men is the secret of the
play's success. *Julius Cæsar* is the greatest of political
plays, not by reason of its political theme, nor even of
its shapely form and transparent style, but because, by
making its public men convincingly private persons also,
it brought the affairs and men of Rome in 44 B.C. home
to the business and bosoms of the Elizabethans of
London in A.D. 1599—and of men in all countries and
generations since. This is in fact the main reason why
the unscholarly *Julius Cæsar* is still read by scholars
and unlearned alike, while the scholarly *Sejanus*, which
recreates the public life of the same period far more
accurately, gives pleasure to none but scholars. True,
we know Brutus less well than Hamlet, for his disposition is shaken by perplexities of public conduct, not

> With thoughts beyond the reaches of his soul.

But we know him better than any character of Jonson
or of Shaw. We love him, too; has anyone ever felt
love for a character in Jonson or Shaw? To some degree
this is true also of Cassius; while all the other leading,
and most of the minor, characters are people we feel
we have met, the fifth Act being, as Granville-Barker
notes, 'a galaxy of such creations'. For Shakespeare's
imagination was becoming increasingly prolific at this
date, and *Julius Cæsar* teems with living persons.

III. *The Source*

Moreover, his source was Plutarch, an author all
but as fertile in character as himself; from whom, too,
though he read him at two removes, in Sir Thomas

North's always workmanlike and often vivid translation
of Jacques Amyot's French translation of the Greek, he
'acquired more essential history...than most men
would from the whole British Museum'.[1] Plutarch
and Seneca were the predominant stars in the classical
sky of late sixteenth century Europe. Montaigne confesses he had not seriously studied anything solid except
the writings of these two,[2] and almost every page of
the *Essaies* bears witness to the pre-eminent influence
of Plutarch. Of Amyot's version he speaks in the language of religious devotion: 'it is our breviary', without
which, he says, unlearned folk like himself would have
been lost souls.[3] Precisely similar tribute is paid by
Henri Quatre, who confesses that Plutarch (again read
only in Amyot) 'has been like my conscience, whispering
in my ear good deeds and admirable principles both for
my private life, and for the conduct of affairs'.[4] The
last words stress a point then taken for granted, though
now easily overlooked: the book's political significance,
its value for rulers. Amyot in his Preface declares,
'history is the schoolmistress of princes', while North's
title emphasizes the fact that Plutarch's *Lives* are, not
of ordinary, but of 'noble Grecians and Romans'. In
a word the book was 'a mirror for magistrates'.

Yet this was really subsidiary to a larger aim, that of
displaying 'the virtues and vices' of the makers of
history in the past for the instruction of makers of history
in the present. And this surely was the primary purpose
of Shakespeare also; or if not, at any rate what he
achieved. The history of England is reflected in his
English history plays from a quite definite point of

[1] T. S. Eliot, *Selected Essays*, p. 17.
[2] V. *Essaies*, I, 25.   [3] *Essaies*, II, 4.
[4] Letter to his wife, quoted by MacCallum (*Shakespeare's
Roman Plays*, p. 127); translation mine.

view.[1] And when he turned from English to Roman
history he did not lay aside his own mirror. On the
contrary, equipped with an understanding and aware-
ness learnt from ten years' brooding on the provincial
scene of England before the rise of the Tudor monarchy,
and surveying, as he now did from the shoulders of
Plutarch, a scene wider, more central, and of more
abiding interest, that of Rome on the eve of becoming
an empire, he produced in *Julius Cæsar* what is perhaps the most brilliant and most penetrating artistic
reflection of political realities in the literature of the
world.

Yet art is not life; still less can the moralist be expected to preserve a true historical perspective. Moral
Plutarch was often compelled to pass lightly over
matters of great historical importance; for example,
Cæsar's nine years' campaigns in Gaul. And his six-
teenth-century translators, anxious to attract as many
readers as possible to this great storehouse of human
wisdom, carried on the process; they set vigour and
point above verbal accuracy, and the illusion of actuality
before a strict adherence to the facts as they received
them. Thus, to a large extent without realizing it, they
transposed the whole into the key of their own time.
Before they swam into Shakespeare's ken in the pages
of North, 'the noble Grecians and Romans' had put
on the doublet and hose of French and English gentlemen,[2] and Rome had become a neo-classic 'commonwealth'. Finally, under pressure of contemporary

[1] Explained in my Introduction to *Richard II*. This does
not mean that he was a political propagandist, as recent
writers on the history plays seem to imply. Separate Burke's
wisdom from Burke's party politics, and you find Shakespeare with the former, though he is, of course, more of
a poet.

[2] See note on 1. 2. 266.

political assumptions unconsciously held, and subject
to the necessity of appealing to prentice-boy and Inns-
of-Court student alike, Shakespeare was himself driven
to assign motives impossible to ancient Romans,[1] and to
create characters Plutarch would hardly have recognized.

What then did Shakespeare take from Plutarch,
and how did he remould it? Archbishop Trench represented the relation as one of absolute dependence,
and found in the incidents of *Julius Cæsar* 'almost
nothing which he does not owe to Plutarch'.[2] Subsequent writers (e.g. Aldis Wright, Gollancz, and even
Herford)[3] modified this verdict but slightly, if at all,
till we come to MacCallum,[4] who gives a whole
chapter to 'Shakespeare's transmutation of his material'
—without, however, carrying us very far. Yet the
truth is quite simple. Shakespeare used Plutarch
exactly as he had used Holinshed. Apart, that is, from
two compelling desires—the dramatist's to make as good
a stage-play as possible, and the poet's to present history
in a form judged at once to be substantially accurate[5]
and ideally true[6] by the judicious in his audience—he
felt free to manipulate his source at pleasure, altering

[1] Cf. Gustave Lanson, *Histoire de la Littérature Française*
(ed. 1909), p. 273.

[2] *Plutarch*, by R. C. Trench (1873), p. 66.

[3] v. Introd. Clarendon ed., pp. xliii–xlv; *Temple Shakespeare*. Preface to *Julius Cæsar*; *Eversley Shakespeare*,
vol. viii, Introd., p. 9.

[4] *Shakespeare's Roman Plays*, by M. W. MacCallum
(1910), pp. 187–211.

[5] I.e. in general accord with what they remembered of
Suetonius and Plutarch.

[6] Cf. Sidney's *Apology for Poetry* on the relation between
History and Poetry, e.g. 'The Poet nameth Cyrus or
Aeneas no other way than to show what men of their
fames, fortunes and estates *should* do.'

or adding as his purposes required. He does, indeed, seem to follow Plutarch more closely; but only because Plutarch's material was already rough-hewn to his hand, while that of the English compiler resembles nothing so much as haphazard heaps of rude boulders accumulated at the confluence of glaciers. North's prose, too, was at once more vivid and of finer quality than Holinshed's. Thus from time to time in *Julius Cæsar* we come upon patches of almost direct transference, like this oft-quoted parallel in the speech of Lucilius to Antony:

Plutarch's *Life of Brutus*[1]

I dare assure thee that no enemy hath taken nor shall take Marcus Brutus alive, and I beseech God keep him from that fortune: for wheresoever he be found, alive or dead, he will be found like himself.

Julius Cæsar, 5. 4. 21–5

I dare assure thee that no enemy
Shall ever take alive the noble Brutus:
The gods defend him from so great a shame!
When you do find him, or alive or dead,
He will be found like Brutus, like himself.

Yet that such occasional lifting in no way proves absolute dependence a rapid survey of the first two scenes will show. Shakespeare's 1. 1 is a brilliant overture introducing the fundamental fact of the situation: the fickle populace, with its love of a strong man, be he Pompey or Cæsar. It combines a couple of hints taken from separate incidents in Plutarch, and uses them to convey a totally new impression. In detail, too, the differences are many. In Plutarch the clash of tribunes and crowd takes place after, not before, the Lupercalia; the tribunes are adherents of Brutus, not Pompey; the crowds come to rejoice at the insult to Cæsar's images, not at his

[1] Shakespeare's *Plutarch*, ed. by W. W. Skeat, p. 149.

triumph; while finally the images are adorned with diadems for the proposed coronation, not, as in Shakespeare, with trophies for the triumph. In 1.2 Shakespeare *seems* to take fewer liberties than in 1.1. The 'facts' of the Soothsayer, the Lupercalia, and Antony's offer of the crown are much the same in both accounts; Cassius's conversation with Brutus is closely related to a paragraph in Plutarch's *Brutus* headed 'Cassius incenseth Brutus against Cæsar'; and Cæsar's comments upon the two men are similarly inspired by a passage in the *Life of Cæsar*.[1] Yet how different is the presentation! Shakespeare merely reports the 'holy chase' and the offer of the crown. It was impracticable to represent the former in the theatre, and to show the latter would have blunted the edge of Antony's Forum speech. But the reporting serves to illuminate character—that of Cæsar, Brutus and Cassius in the main, but giving glimpses also of Antony, Calphurnia, Cicero, and above all Casca. The procession, gay with music on the way to the ceremony, but returning 'like a chidden train', is Shakespeare's invention; Plutarch mentions none. So, too, is the fine stroke by which the offer of the crown is synchronized with the talk between Brutus and Cassius, so that Cassius's hints of death to the tyrant are punctuated by the crowd's shouts symbolizing death to liberty. Thus, while the material for the framework of the scene comes in the main from Plutarch, the frame itself is planned and fitted together by Shakespeare, after first picking and shaping his stones with the trained eye of a master-builder.

So with the rest of the play. Everywhere we find the stage craftsman and dramatic poet at work, selecting and rejecting, sometimes splicing together incidents not even remotely connected in the original, sometimes

---

[1] V. head-note (iv) to 1. 2.

pouncing on a chance phrase, or mistranslation by North which, transfigured in imagination, takes life and blossoms out as something rich and strange.[1] And all this is made subject to the larger design of the total composition. Perhaps the best single illustration of Shakespeare's attitude towards his source is the speeches in the Forum. 'He read in Plutarch', writes a modern classical scholar in a book just to hand,[2]

that Antony was a distinguished orator in the Asiatic, and Brutus in the Attic, style. These remarks are made quite by the way, except that Plutarch does dwell a little upon the style of Brutus and makes a few quotations from his letters which exhibit his bare, thin, excessively antithetic manner. Now in *Julius Cæsar* we have the great funeral oration of Antony, entirely the work of Shakespeare, for it is not in Plutarch:[3] and if it is hardly so florid as a speech in the Asiatic style might be expected to be, it sufficiently develops all the resources of rhetoric. Contrast the speech of Brutus, which is also entirely the work of Shakespeare. It is in prose, and the imitation of the Attic style as Roman orators practised it is so perfect that unless we knew it was Shakespeare's, we might suppose it was a translation.

To say with Trench[4] that Shakespeare 'resigns himself into the hands' of Plutarch is to talk of the clay controlling the potter.

IV. *Cæsar and Cæsarism*

Two criticisms have been directed against the structure of the play. First, the Quarrel scene is alleged by Bradley to be a mere 'episode, the removal of which would not affect the actual sequence of events', and

---

[1] See notes 2.1.173–4; 3.1.106–11; 3.2.190; 5.1.100–7.
[2] J. A. K. Thomson, *The Classical Background of English Literature* (1948), p. 185.
[3] But v. p. 159 for hints.
[4] *Op. cit.* p. 66.

therefore dramatically indefensible.[1] It might be replied, and Bradley would hardly deny, that it increases
our knowledge of and love for both Brutus and Cassius,
and so by incalculably deepening our pity for them
raises the play to the heights of tragedy. Yet the real
answer is different, viz. that the main issue of the play is
not the conspirators' fate but the future of Rome, of
liberty, of the human race, to which their fate is
incidental. Though Brutus is a tragic hero whom we
pity as a man, the heart of his tragedy is the defeat of
his cause. His death is but a symbol of a greater
disaster, the death of liberty. And the defeat is brought
about, not at Philippi, but through the corruption and
instability of human nature.

Viewed in this wider perspective, the Quarrel scene
is discovered to possess a more than personal meaning.
The cause of the quarrel is a fellow, 'condemned and
noted' by Brutus, for whom Cassius had interceded.
Pella's taking of bribes, to Cassius a trivial offence, is to
Brutus a sin against Justice itself, the very sin for which
Cæsar had been slain; and here was his friend, and
chief comrade as 'purger' of the state, countenancing
corruption, and even, it was commonly reported, selling
and marting offices himself! In the end anger is drowned
in pledges of reconciliation, and its occasion is blotted
from the mind of Brutus by thoughts and talk of Portia.
But *we* do not, or should not, forget. For the attitude
of Cassius means that the cause is utterly lost; nobody
except Brutus believes in it or truly understands it. And
Shakespeare makes his point by a studied rearrangement
of the 'facts' in Plutarch.[2] The Quarrel scene therefore
is one of the pillars of the dramatic structure, since it
reinforces our growing sense of the inevitability of
Cæsarism.

[1] *Op. cit.* p. 60.   [2] See pp. 171–2.

We shall grasp this more fully by examining the second point of criticism—the play's supposed lack of unity, a criticism which has actually given rise to theories of two earlier separate dramas, culminating respectively in the death of Cæsar, and in the defeat and death of Brutus.[1] But more wrong-headed than any such theory is the impression of a break in continuity, expressed, for example, by Chambers[2] even as he rebuts the notion of a double origin:

> *Julius Cæsar* has two peaks, one in the Capitol and the other at Philippi, and the psychological interest is at least as much in Brutus as in Cæsar. The effect of a double theme is thereby given.

Taken as it stands this ignores the 'idea' of the play, misses the point of the title, and suggests a certain balance of interest in the characters of Cæsar and Brutus which is, I think, entirely misleading. And these misunderstandings are in fact all one: a misunderstanding of the impression which Shakespeare intended the figure of his Julius to convey, an impression which it indubitably did convey to the spectators of his theatre.

Written in our day the play might have been called *Cæsar and Cæsarism*; but abstract words were not then in vogue, and this particular one was not invented till 1857.[3] Yet Shakespeare's title was adequate enough in view of what the name of Julius stood for in 1599.[4] For the play's theme is the single one, Liberty *versus*

---

[1] See *The Shakespeare Canon*, vol. 1 (1922), by J. M. Robertson, who supposes that two plays by Marlowe, successively revised first by Drayton and others, and then by Shakespeare, were made into our single play by Jonson!

[2] *William Shakespeare*, 1, 399.

[3] V. O.E.D. 'Cæsarism', which attributes it to the American writer, Orestes A. Brownson [1955].

[4] See MacCallum, *op. cit.* p. 232.

Tyranny, which implies on the one hand a diagnosis of the situation confirmed by modern historians, viz. the necessity of absolutism for the Rome of Cicero; and on the other a sense of the greatness of Rome and the Empire, never more powerfully realized than in Shakespeare's day. That greatness is symbolized by one aspect of the character of Shakespeare's Cæsar, who stands not only for the man who died in March 44 B.C., but also for the semi-mythical Colossus who 'doth bestride the narrow world' both of Cassius and of Shakespeare, and whose spirit still, from time to time, as we know to our cost, 'walks abroad' and 'turns our swords In our own proper entrails'.[1] When Brutus exclaims

> We all stand up against the spirit of Cæsar,

he sums up the play in one line. For the spirit of Cæsar, which was the destiny of Rome, is the fate against which Brutus struggles in vain. And his failure to do so is his tragedy (and ours), inasmuch as Cæsarism is a secular threat to the human spirit, and the living 'Julius', as Shakespeare shows him, is the mouthpiece of that threat. Some[2] think Shakespeare's Cæsar adumbrates Mommsen's, a being 'of mighty creative power and... most penetrating judgment',[3] a historical superman; Shaw, on the other hand, complains that Shakespeare was incapable of rising to Mommsen's conception.[4] But Shakespeare, who had read neither Mommsen nor Nietzsche, had before him a different kind of myth altogether, the classico-medieval image, seen through

---

[1] Cf. the 'double plane of vision' in *Richard II*; see my Introduction to that play, p. xxxvii.

[2] E.g. E. K. Chambers in *Shakespeare; a Survey*, pp. 146–54.

[3] *History of Rome*, by T. Mommsen (Engl. trans. 1901) v, 313.

[4] *Three Plays for Puritans* (1901), p. xxix. Cf. *Dramatic Opinions* (1898), II, 398.

renaissance eyes, of an almost supernatural conqueror who out of lust for power ruined the Roman republic. In other words the paradox of Shakespeare's Cæsar is a paradox of renaissance thought, which combined a well-nigh religious awe for Rome and Cæsar with sympathy for Brutus and his fellows as Rome's liberators from a tyrant. Dante in thrusting the liberators into his lowest hell[1] is a Ghibelline and imperialist exception; all republicans and most literary and artistic circles in Italy honoured Brutus as a saint.[2] As for French and English opinion, let Montaigne speak. Having praised Cæsar's greatness, 'the wonderful parts wherewith he was indued', his sobriety, his gentleness, his clemency, and 'the incomparable grandeur' of his soul, he continues in this wise:

But all those noble characteristics were stifled in this furious passion of ambition by which he allowed himself so far to be controlled that it might be called the very helm and rudder of all his actions....He was so drunk with vanity that in the presence of his fellow-citizens he dared... to say that his decisions should thenceforth serve as laws and ...suffered himself to be worshipped as a god in person. To conclude, it was this vice alone, in my opinion, that destroyed the finest and richest character that ever was, and has rendered his memory abhorrent to all men of good will, inasmuch as he sought his own glory in the ruin of his country and in the destruction of the mightiest and most flourishing commonwealth that the world will ever see.[3]

Behind this judgement lie Suetonius's *Lives of the Cæsars* and Lucan's *Pharsalia*, two favourite books in

---

[1] *Inferno*, xxxiv, 61–7.

[2] Burckhardt, *Renaissance in Italy* (Engl. trans. 1904), pp. 59–60. MacCallum's dictum (*op. cit.* p. 27)—'At the Renaissance the characteristic feeling was enthusiasm for Cæsar and his assassin alike'—seems to me entirely wrong.

[3] Florio's *Montaigne*, II, ch. 33 (my own translation).

the medieval world and after.[1] Lucan burns with hatred
for tyranny in general, and for Cæsar, destroyer of the
Republic, in particular.[2] Shakespeare pretty certainly
knew *Pharsalia*, Book I, from Marlowe's verse translation,[3] if not in the original, and may have known
Suetonius too. At any rate he adopts—as one would
expect—the traditional renaissance view derived from
them. I do not in fact know any sixteenth- or seventeenth-
century play which did not.[4] Cæsar is generally shown
as mighty, awe-inspiring, semi-divine; but never held
up for admiration. This is true both of popular drama
and learned. Chapman's *Cæsar and Pompey* and
Jonson's *Sejanus* alike embody this view. Perhaps,
indeed, contemporary opinion on the matter is best
expressed in the speech of Arruntius, a character in the
latter play, whom Herford describes as 'the voice and
exponent of the irrepressible critic and censor in Jonson
himself'.[5] Contrasting the immunity of Tiberius with
the fate of the tyrant Julius Cæsar, Arruntius asks:

> Where is now the soul
> Of god-like Cato? he that durst be good
> When Cæsar durst be evil: and had power
> As not to live his slave, to die his master?
> Or where the constant Brutus that (being proof
> Against all charm of benefits) did strike
> So brave a blow into the monster's heart,
> That sought unkindly to captive his country?

and concludes:

> Brave Cassius was the last of all that race.[6]

[1] Sandys, *Hist. of Class. Scholarship*, 1903, pp. 196 and 617.
[2] See esp. *Pharsalia*, I, 146–57. 'Acer et indomitus' it
begins.
[3] See note on 2. 2. 17–25.
[4] Addison's *Cato* shows it still very much alive in 1713.
[5] *Ben Jonson*, ed. Herford and Simpson, II, 13.
[6] *Ibid.* IV, p. 358; *Sejanus*, Act I, ll. 89–104.

Jonson might laugh at this or that point in Shakespeare's play; he had, and could have, nothing to urge against his friend's delineation of the principal characters.

A Roman Tamburlaine of illimitable ambition and ruthless irresistible genius; a monstrous tyrant who destroyed his country and ruined 'the mightiest and most flourishing commonwealth that the world will ever see' —one feature remained to add before the sixteenth century stage-figure of the great dictator was complete, that of a braggart, of the 'thrasonical Cæsar', to whom Shakespeare refers more than once.[1] This, as Ayres has shown, was mainly due to the subjection of renaissance tragedy to Seneca. The first known European play on Cæsar is a Latin play by Muretus (Muret) in 1544, which, following the lines of Seneca's *Hercules Oetaeus*, presents (as Seneca does) the apotheosis of a world conqueror, who boasts of his mighty deeds in the style of Hercules.[2] Next, in 1559, Muret's disciple Grévin produced a vernacular *César*, and the hero of this is likewise a braggart. Still more clearly related to Shakespeare was Garnier's *Cornélie* in 1574. Hostile throughout to the tyrant Cæsar,[3] and claiming sympathy for Pompey, it provides a Cassius who is an 'exact prototype', as Dr Boas claims,[4] of the Cassius of our play, and in its dialogue between Cassius and Brutus a close parallel with that in the second scene of *Julius*

[1] See *Cymb.* 3. 1. 23; *As You Like It*, 5. 2. 30; and also 2 *Henry IV*, 4. 3. 41.

[2] See H. M. Ayres, *P.M.L.A.* (1910), xxv, 183–227. A valuable article to which all subsequent critics of *Julius Cæsar* are much indebted.

[3] It was actually used as a republican manifesto when Henri Quatre was assassinated; see: MacCallum, *op. cit.* p. 27, n. 1.

[4] *Works of Kyd*, ed. F. S. Boas, p. lxxxiii. Cf. below, note on 1. 3. 90.

Cæsar.[1] Shakespeare must have known *Cornélie* from Kyd's translation (1595), and his debt to it seems indubitable. Garnier gives Cæsar a long bombastic speech in the vein of Seneca's Hercules, and constantly makes him speak of himself pompously in the third person. On the other hand, following Plutarch closely as it does, his portrait of the man is the most sympathetic of this period.

Only one pre-Shakespearian English play on the Cæsar theme has survived, though performances of what seem to have been four or five others are recorded.[2] The anonymous *Cæsar's Revenge*, a poor play, written in imitation of Marlowe and Kyd at some date, it would seem, between 1592 and 1596, has one striking link with Shakespeare's play: the 'evil spirit', as Plutarch merely calls it, which appears to Brutus before Philippi is identified as Cæsar's ghost, and like Andrea's in the *Spanish Tragedy*, becomes the symbol and mouthpiece of the revenge.[3] We may be sure then that the ghost reached Shakespeare from an earlier English tradition. Again the cry which this unknown dramatist gives his dying Cæsar—

> What, Brutus too! Nay, nay, then let me die;
> Nothing wounds deeper than ingratitude,

comes very close both to 'Et tu, Brute',[4] and to Antony's

> Ingratitude, more strong than traitor's arms,
> Quite vanquished him.

---

[1] V. Bernage, *Étude sur Garnier*, 1880 (cited MacCallum, p. 60).

[2] See Chambers, *Elizabethan Stage*, II, 15, 143–4, 179; iii, 309; iv, 216 for particulars.

[3] V. edition (1939) by G. L. Kittredge (p. xi) who was, I think, the first to note this point. See also note 4. 3. 272.

[4] Cf. H. M. Ayres, *loc. cit.* 225, n. 2.

On the whole, however, his Cæsar, modelled on Tamburlaine and 'the conquering Hercules'[1] of tradition, is less like Shakespeare's than is Garnier's.

In short, Shakespeare was following both established dramatic tradition and the historical scholarship of his age when he gave his Cæsar that 'strut', that habit of self-deification which annoys many modern readers. We may also agree with Kittredge that at the end of his career Cæsar 'has become the victim of infatuation' and 'lost that sense of values which alone could maintain him in equilibrium', and that Shakespeare legitimately made the most of this to produce the effect of nemesis. Never was ἄτη more insensate or more magnificently expressed than in this mortal aspiring to divine honours, and boasting, as he stalks blindly to his doom,

> Cæsar shall forth; the things that threatened me
> Ne'er looked but on my back; when they shall see
> The face of Cæsar, they are vanishéd.[2]

Yet when all is said, Shakespeare's Cæsar is his own portrait and more 'caustic' than any other of the age. The word is Herford's, who has well brought out the exhibition of Cæsar's physical and moral weaknesses, his superstition, his 'vacillation' on the fatal morning, and 'above all' the profession of immovable constancy which that vacillation so ironically refutes.[3] Shakespeare

---

[1] *Cæsar's Revenge* (Malone's Society reprint), l. 253.

[2] That Shakespeare knew, and is here consciously applying, the doctrine of ἄτη seems clear from *Antony and Cleopatra*, 3. 13. 111–15. Cf. also Sir Thomas Elyot's application of the notion to Cæsar in *The Book of the Governour* (1531), bk. II, cap. 5 ('Of affabilitee'.) For Shakespeare's familiarity with this book, cf. my note on *Henry V*, I. 2. 180 ff.

[3] V. *Eversley Shakespeare*, VIII, 14.

adds to the infirmities in Plutarch a deafness in one ear; and makes 'the falling sickness', which Plutarch does mention, seize him at the most awkward and humiliating moment—when being offered a crown. Worse still, he substitutes for the pluck, resolution, and endurance often praised by Plutarch, a 'feeble temper';[1] and derives the three examples of this from passages in North which show the exact opposite. Cassius is here, indeed, the speaker, and the points illustrate his malice; but Brutus does not reply to the charge, and it is fully borne out by stroke after stroke later. Cassius begins by hinting at the great man's sensitiveness to 'the winter's cold', whereas Plutarch, while admitting a delicate constitution, gives instances of his hardiness in ignoring it.[2] Cassius tells a story of a swimming match in which Cæsar has to cry to him for help; Plutarch on the contrary stresses his strength and skill in swimming and tells of a wonderful aquatic feat.[3] Lastly, of Cæsar's 'fever in Spain', when according to Cassius his 'coward lips' cried out for water 'as a sick girl', Plutarch writes:

Yet therefore [he] yielded not to the disease of his body, to make it a cloak to cherish him withal, but contrarily took the pains of war as a medicine to cure his sick body, fighting always with his disease, travelling continually, living soberly, and commonly lying abroad in the field.[4]

Or take our impressions as Shakespeare brings him first on to the stage. Even John Palmer, who sees the dictator clearer than any other modern critic, though through eyes not sufficiently accustomed to use Elizabethan spectacles, has failed to observe the full signi-

[1] Kittredge's gloss 'bodily weakness' (p. 101) will not do for this; v. G. 'temper'. The whole burden of Cassius's speech is that Cæsar lacks 'guts'.

[2] See for example Skeat's *Shakespeare's Plutarch*, p. 58.

[3] *Ibid.* p. 86.   [4] *Ibid.* p. 57.

ficance of this entry.[1] Picture a great concourse of
people; a ceremonial procession, consisting of priests and
other persons bound for the Lupercalia, among them
Antony and a number of young men stripped for the
chase; then, from the distance and drawing ever nearer,
the sound of music such as Elizabethans were wont to
associate with royalty; and lastly, the great man himself,
surrounded with all the pomp of an oriental monarch,
and borne in, as I think, upon a litter:[2] a figure haughty,
ageing, infirm. And, if this be set down as in part the
creation of editorial fancy, it cannot be denied that
Shakespeare makes Cæsar ride or walk alone, so that
when he desires to lay his commands upon Calphurnia,
she has to hurry up from the rear; or that those commands at once express his anxiety for an heir and
publicly brand her as the barren party responsible for
his childlessness,[3] words upon which Elizabethans
would be quick to set their own interpretation. Thus
in stroke after stroke, as is shown further in my
notes, Shakespeare builds up a portrait of the man for
his spectators; and all this, the contemptible side of the
character, is solely of his own making.

What then? Are we not left to conclude that, faced
with the problem of Julius, Shakespeare made up his
own mind about him? Long before, when called upon
to depict a very different sort of dictatorship, he had
shown that he knew how the system worked. 'When
I am king,' declares Jack Cade, 'all shall eat and drink on

---

[1] See his *Political Characters of Shakespeare*, pp. 34–46.

[2] In North (see below, 3. 1 head-note, *Plutarch* (iv))
Cæsar rides to the Senate House in a litter on the Ides of
March, a point which Shakespeare might well have utilized
here for stage purposes. Cf. *K. John*, 5. 3. 16; *Lear*, 3. 6. 97,
for the use of a litter.

[3] Both inventions, v. notes 1. 2 *Plutarch* (i).

my score, and I will apparel them all in one livery, that they may agree like brothers and worship me their lord'.[1] Such is Cæsarism, including 'panem' if not 'circenses', with the equality of all in one classless mob, united in reverence before a semi-divine being, whether Napoleon, Führer, or general secretary of the communist party. But Cade was a comic figure; and ' Julius' must be taken seriously; for Shakespeare has now to exhibit on the stage the effects of Cæsarism on the soul of Cæsar himself. Having written, or taken a large share in, eight history plays before 1599, he had been contemplating, almost continuously for eight years or more, men struggling for power by fair means or foul, and exercising it fairly or foully. Chambers points out that *Julius Cæsar*, written just after *Henry V*, shows 'the same preoccupation with a political problem in the relations of leader and mob'.[2] I agree, while wholly dissenting from his further deduction that both leaders are 'supermen'. Rather, as it seems to me, having written of a hero who, singing 'Non nobis' in the hour of victory, preserves his integrity, Shakespeare turns to consider the sort of conqueror whose appetite grows by what it feeds on, who, having become the 'foremost man of all this world', begins to think and speak of himself as more than mortal; in a word, the Man of Success, as the Elizabethans understood him.

For what he thought of such a man we have in evidence not only the portrait in the first three Acts, but the soliloquy of Brutus at the beginning of the second, which has puzzled all the critics, including Coleridge and Granville-Barker. Brutus's theme is the effect of power upon character, and his conclusion is

[1] *2 Henry VI*, 4. 2. 77–83.
[2] *Shakespeare: A Survey*, pp. 146–7.

that to crown Cæsar would endow him with that absolute power which, as Acton notes, corrupts absolutely.[1]
So far, Brutus admits, Cæsar had not shown himself the
tyrant; but then he has not yet attained 'the upmost
round' of the ladder. Once thus high he will scorn
'the base degrees by which he did ascend'. Once
crowned, all barriers will be down; and, human nature
being what it is, 'the bright day will bring forth the
adder', since absolute rulers have no use for mercy
('remorse'). What is there 'perplexing' (Coleridge)
or 'pedantic' (Verity) or 'confused' (Palmer) or
'fumbling' (Granville-Barker) in this, or why should
it be described as 'a marvel of fanatical self-deception'
(Herford)? That Brutus believes the end, of which he
confesses he has at the moment no proof, justifies the
means, which is murder, or that the means turn out to
be entirely mistaken, has of course an important bearing
upon his character and on the political issue of the play
as a whole. But Shakespeare does all he can to show
us that the reading of Cæsar's character in the soliloquy
is correct. Had he represented Cæsar as 'the perfect
statesman' of Mommsen, or the clear-eyed realistic
opportunist of a living historian,[2] or the magnaminous,
genial and wise, if over-ambitious, dictator whom
Plutarch draws, he would have given us a very different
play, at once far less tragic and less profound. And we
who have come to know what dictators look like when
the façade of their synthetic magnificence is down and
their myth exploded, can feel nothing but astonishment
at a genius which lacking our experience could so
penetrate to their secret.[3]

[1] Acton, *Historical Essays and Studies*, p. 504.
[2] *The Roman Revolution*, by Ronald Syme (1939).
[3] See pp. xliv, xlvi for stage-productions in 1937 and 1939
which turned this to account.

But this, I shall be told, was an accident. Shakespeare, Bernard Shaw declares, wrote 'Cæsar down for the merely technical purpose of writing Brutus up'. He might have added that he wrote Brutus down for a like purpose in the Forum scene, and Antony down in the Proscription scene immediately after, and then wrote Brutus and Cassius up again more and more from that moment until the catastrophe. Shakespeare is always busy adjusting his dramatic scales, making bids for the sympathies of the audience on behalf, now of this character, then of that; now of this side, then of the other. These things are of the essence of his craft, and by such means he creates that final impression of dramatic justice which all allow to be one of his chief claims to greatness. Moreover, he had a technical reason of special weight for disparaging Cæsar while still alive, namely, that his assassination scene was an extraordinarily difficult corner for an Elizabethan playwright to turn. Cæsar was not a crowned head, nor the anointed of the Lord, as were Richard of Bordeaux and, implicitly, Duncan of Scotland. But he was 'the first emperor', and to the Elizabethans, as we have seen, a being of almost superhuman stature, so that the spectacle of his being hacked to pieces by assassins would inevitably strike them as something appalling, if not sacrilegious. The purpose of 'the royal airs which Cæsar gives himself in this scene', notes Kittredge, 'is to justify the act of the conspirators, which if our sympathies are not on their side will appear to be a cowardly assassination'.[1] If that be true of readers in 1939, how much more must it have been true of spectators in 1599.

But what is dramatically convenient, is not necessarily false. On the contrary, at any rate in Shakespearian

[1] Kittredge, *op. cit.* note 3. 1. 32.

tragedy, it is likely to be truer than history itself. For 'poetry is a more philosophic and a finer thing than history, since poetry speaks of universals and history only of particulars'.[1] The Gaius Julius who fell in the Curia Pompeiana on the Ides of March, 44 B.C. was a 'particular' man over whose character and schemes historians will continue to dispute; the Cæsar who falls on Shakespeare's Capitol is the universal Dictator. Yet when we turn and 'look upon Cæsar' in our frontispiece, which reproduces a contemporary, or almost contemporary, portrait in stone, we are left wondering whether, in this play at any rate, the truth of poetry may not be the truth of history also. For what confronts us is a *divus Julius* indeed, but one who has long since disjoined 'remorse from power', if he ever felt it.

J. D. W.

January, 1948

---

[1] Aristotle, *Poetics*, §9.

THE STAGE-HISTORY OF
JULIUS CÆSAR

Popularity tempered with recurrent neglect is the mark of *Julius Cæsar* as a stage play. London witnessed it almost every year from the late seventeenth to the last quarter of the eighteenth century; yet three of our most famous actors never appeared in it, and twice over for an extended period (1780–1812 and 1851–98) its stage history is a virtual blank. Part of the explanation may be that it hardly provides actors with a supremely tragic role, while it offers even less scope for great actresses. But its opportunities for pageantry made it one of Tree's most resounding triumphs, when he ended its longest eclipse with nine successful revivals at His Majesty's Theatre from 1898 to 1913.

The earliest notice of it, as already shown,[1] is by a Swiss traveller, Thomas Platter, who witnessed a performance at The Globe on 21 September 1599.[2] Thereafter till the closing of the theatres in 1642 it seems to have been a popular favourite. Thus Leonard Digges in his *Verses Commendatory* to Shakespeare's *Poems* (1640) writes:

> So have I seen when Cæsar would appeare,
> And on the Stage at half-sword parley were,
> Brutus and Cassius; Oh how the audience,
> Were ravished, with what wonder they went thence;

and he contrasts this reception with the impatience shown at Ben Jonson's 'tedious (though well-laboured)' Roman plays. It was also presented several times at

[1] V. Introd. pp. viii–ix.
[2] V. Clare Williams, *Thomas Platter's Travels in England* (1937), p. 166.

Court—for example, at the festivities for the marriage of Princess Elizabeth and the Elector Palatine in the winter of 1612–13,[1] and again as late as 31 January 1637, and 13 November 1638.[2]

From the Restoration to the rise of Garrick the play was constantly shown. It is in Downes's list of the fifteen principal old stock plays revived at Theatre Royal, Drury Lane, after its opening in May 1663; and it was one of the twenty-one plays allotted to the King's Company by a Royal Warrant early in 1669.[3] Downes gives the cast for a performance dated '*about* 1671' by Genest:[4] Hart played Brutus, Mohun Cassius, Kynaston Antony, and Bell Cæsar, with Mrs Marshal and Mrs Corbet as Calphurnia and Portia. A warrant of 1 June 1677 proves a performance before Royalty in December 1676.[5] After the amalgamation of the two Companies it was again revived in Drury Lane in 1684, Betterton playing Brutus, which Hart ceased to act henceforth, while Smith was Cassius and Goodman Cæsar. The 1684 Quarto of the play, 'as it is now acted at Theatre Royal', shows the Folio text followed closely, except for some change of minor parts, as when Casca takes Marullus's speeches in 1. 1, a change which lasted till Kemble's productions. When Betterton again formed a separate Company in 1695, he continued to present the play—in Lincoln's Inn Fields, February 1704, and at the Haymarket, March 1706 and 14 January

---

[1] This assumes, with Sir Edmund Chambers and most scholars, that *Cæsar's Tragedye* named in the Warrant of 20 May 1613 for payment to John Heminges, is our play.

[2] J. Q. Adams, *The Dramatic Records of Sir Henry Herbert*, pp. 57, 76, 77.

[3] Allardyce Nicoll, *History of the Restoration Drama*, pp. 315, 316.

[4] J. Genest, *Some Account of the English Stage*, 1660–1830 (1832), I, 339.   [5] Allardyce Nicoll, *op. cit.* pp. 307, 308.

1707. This last was a grand performance by subscription under the patronage of Lord Halifax, with a cast of unusual strength: Betterton Brutus, Verbruggen Cassius, Wilks Antony, Barton Booth Cæsar, and Mrs Barry and Mrs Bracegirdle as Calphurnia and Portia. The play was repeated the next day, and on 1 April, when, so the *Daily Courant* tells us, Mrs Bradshaw and Mrs Bowman took the women's parts, and Cibber was brought in as an extra fifth citizen.

After the reunion of the companies in 1708 *Julius Cæsar* was one of the earliest Shakespeare plays put on at Drury Lane, but now without Betterton. In his place on 22 December 1709, Booth acted Brutus to Powell's Cassius. Betterton's Brutus had undoubtedly been a great creation. Cibber in his *Apology* adduces as proof of his versatility the contrast between 'the un-ruffled temper' in his acting of the Quarrel scene and the 'fierce and flashing fire' of his Hotspur.

His steady look alone supplied that terror which he disdained an intemperance in his voice should give rise to.[1] It would seem that Betterton abandoned the tradition of a quarrel threatening a duel, which Digges's phrase, 'half-sword parley', points to, and which Quin seems to have revived.[2]

Though Betterton died in 1710, Drury Lane con-tinued to show the play every year (except 1711) down to 1728.[3] The Booth-Powell partnership lasted till

[1] Colley Cibber, *Apology for His Life* (ed. R. W. Lowe), I, 103–4.

[2] See *Peregrine Pickle*, ch. 51. The actor described is said to be Quin (v. A. C. Sprague, *Shakespeare and the Actors*, p. 324).

[3] In Genest 1724 is also a blank; but Mr C. B. Hogan of Yale, who is engaged on researches into the history of eighteenth-century Shakespeare revivals, has kindly sent me a list which shows performances in January and September that year.

1715, when Elrington took Powell's place as Cassius; Wilkes played Antony; and Mills, at first Cæsar, after 1721 took over Cassius from Elrington. Genest names both Wilkes and Mills in the cast for 26 April 1721, and notices a revival for Mills's benefit in May 1723, with a further performance in September. In March 1716 Booth chose the play for his own benefit, and went on acting Brutus at Drury Lane till 1728.

Meanwhile the rival theatre in Lincoln's Inn Fields had put on *Julius Cæsar* in eleven different seasons from 1716 to 1729. The part of Brutus was first taken by Keen, a deserter from Drury Lane, in October 1716, and again in March 1718, when Quin was Antony and Ryan Cassius. Thereafter Quin took over Brutus and became Booth's great rival in the part. Davies contrasts the two men's acting of the quarrel—Quin's 'look of anger approaching to rage', with Booth's steadfast look, and speech 'not much above a whisper', but producing 'a stronger effect than the loudness of Quin'.[1] In November 1720, Boheme appeared as Cæsar, but from 1722 the part was given successively to Leigh and Ryan. In 1732 at Goodman's Fields Delane appeared as a new Brutus for twelve nights running. In 1734 Quin returned to Drury Lane, where our play was once again seen for six nights from 4 November; Quin acted Brutus to Mills's Cassius and Milward's Antony, while Cibber junior was Casca, and Macklin one of five citizens (in September 1738, he played the second citizen). Further revivals followed in 1736 and each year from 1738 to 1741 (in 1740 three). Davies declared that Milward was the only man in his memory 'whose powers were perfectly suited to' Antony's Forum speech, and he praises his Antony, Quin's Brutus, and the Cassius and Cæsar of the two Mills as four parts never since

[1] T. Davies, *Dramatic Miscellanies* (1783), II, 248–9.

'equally presented'.[1] He never mentions Milward in any other part; yet for revivals in 1738, 1739 and 1740 the cast gives Cassius to him and Antony to Wright; and Genest, though puzzled, accepted this.[2] Genest records five separate revivals at Drury Lane in 1738; Mr Hogan[3] adds a sixth. That of 28 April was given in aid of the fund for a monument to Shakespeare and by 5 June had realized £170, with £30 still to come in for tickets taken.[4] Several different actresses took the women's parts during these forty years, but Mrs Thurmond was most frequent as Portia (1721–34), and Mrs Horton as Calphurnia (1721 and 1725), both at Drury Lane.

Under Garrick Drury Lane never saw the play. Davies says Garrick once had the idea of acting Cassius, and suggests he gave it up for fear 'he should swell the consequence of Quin as Brutus'.[5] The latter had now transferred his talents to Covent Garden, where *Julius Cæsar* was shown in eleven different years from 1742 to 1758, and three more times in the sixties and seventies. Quin gave Brutus there in 1742, 1747, 1748 and 1750, with Sheridan taking his place in 1744 and 1755. In 1748 Delane (the Brutus of the previous year's revival in Drury Lane), played Antony to Quin's Brutus, and Ryan came back (after thirty years) as Cassius; later, when well over sixty (in 1755 and 1758), Ryan again played this part. Meanwhile, from 1750, Quin's last recorded year as Brutus, Barry had taken over Antony from Delane, having previously acted the part in the 1747 production. In 1744 and 1747 Mrs

---

[1] Davies, *op. cit.* ii, 244–5, 212.

[2] Genest, *op. cit.*, III, 526.

[3] V. note 3 on p. xxxvi above.

[4] v. Allardyce Nicoll, *History of the Early Eighteenth Century Drama*, p. 69.

[5] Davies, *op. cit.* II, 213.

Pritchard, in 1748 and 1750 Peg Woffington, was Portia.

The last revivals of the period (1766, 1767 and 1773) are chiefly interesting because Bell's stage version (1773), printed from the Covent Garden prompt-book, gives the text they used. An edition of 1719, absurdly claiming to be the play 'as altered by Davenant and Dryden', had put into Brutus's mouth after the ghost's exit in 4. 3 the following:

> Sure they have raised some devil to their aid,
> And think to frighten Brutus with a shade;
> But ere the night closes this fatal day,
> I'll send more ghosts thy visit to repay.

It also made him die exclaiming:

> Scorning to view his country's wrongs,
> Thus Brutus always strikes for liberty.
> Poor slavish Rome! Now farewell.

Bell's text retains both interpolations, proving that they were used in 1773; while Walker is reported as having spoken the first in 1766. Bell also shows some doubling of minor parts, Casca now absorbing Titinius[1] as well as Marullus,[2] and Decius Brutus taking some of Flavius's and Trebonius's speeches; while minor episodes, such as Ligarius's entry in 2. 1 and the killing of the poet Cinna, are omitted.

Only one more production in this century is recorded —at Drury Lane for six nights in January and February 1780. The cast was as a whole undistinguished; but on 15 February, Bensley took Cassius. It was left to

---

[1] This change goes back to earlier revivals, since Davies (*op. cit.* II, 212) says that 'many years since', Titinius's part was added to Casca for lack of enough actors for the many characters; and other remarks of Davies point to the 1736 or the 1738 productions.

[2] See above, p. xxxv.

J. P. Kemble to restore the play to favour, but after
he had left Drury Lane for Covent Garden. There on
29 February 1812, and in each later year till 1817, he
staged the play with unprecedented splendour, paying
such attention to historical accuracy in scenery and
costume that one young spectator felt as if he 'had been
transported to the very heart of the Julian Forum'.[1]
The Times of 2 March, however, qualified its praise by
complaining of the wrongly shaped Rostrum and the
smallness of the crowd.[2] The cast was hardly less effective than the stage equipment, Kemble proving a fine
Brutus to C. M. Young's perhaps even more impressive
Cassius; Charles Kemble was Antony, Egerton Cæsar,
Fawcett Casca, Mrs Powell Portia, and Mrs Weston
Calphurnia. Kemble doubled minor characters much
as the 1773 version had done, and changed the names
of speakers rather perplexingly. He followed Bell also
in omitting Ligarius in 2. 1, and Cinna the poet; and
he further omitted 4. 1. But he rejected the pre-
posterous lines of Brutus at the end of the ghost scene,
and he kept the addition to his dying speech only in an
improved form:[3]

> Disdaining life, to live a slave in Rome,
> Thus Brutus strikes his last for liberty.
>
> *(Stabs himself)*
> Farewell,
> Beloved country! Cæsar, now be still, [etc.].

[1] J. C. Young, *Memoir of Charles Mayne Young, Tragedian*
(1871) p. 38; v. quotation in A. C. Ward, *Specimens of
English Dramatic Criticism*, p. 89.

[2] Quoted by Prof. G. C. D. Odell, *Shakespeare from
Betterton to Irving*, II, 105.

[3] Cf. Odell, *op. cit.* II, 65. Harold Child's 'he did not
let Brutus speak' the lines added to 'his last speech' (*Shakespearian Productions of J. P. Kemble*, p. 17) is somewhat
misleading in its phrasing.

After Kemble till nearly the end of the century only three great actors, C. M. Young, Macready, and Samuel Phelps, concerned themselves with the play. Young acted Brutus in Covent Garden in five seasons between 1819 and 1827, and is last recorded as playing the part in October 1829 in Drury Lane. 'In all probability', says Genest, 'there never was a better Brutus.'[1] It was to his Brutus that Macready first acted in the play as Cassius in June 1819, at Covent Garden, and then nine times more before 1822; in 1836 he played the part to Sheridan Knowles's Brutus with Charles Kemble as Antony (a part he had acted since 1822). In October 1836 Macready changed to his henceforward most frequent role of Brutus, and played in the new part thirteen times in 1836–7, and ten times subsequently.[2] Yet he himself declared Cassius the part in which during his whole career he had 'taken a peculiar pleasure'.[3] In February 1850 he appeared as Brutus before Queen Victoria and Prince Albert in Windsor Castle, with Charles Kean as Antony (Kean's only appearance in *Julius Cæsar* in England). His last rendering was at the Haymarket in January 1851, when he wrote in his diary: 'I acted Brutus as I never, no never, acted it before.'[4] Three weeks before he had here reverted once more to Cassius with Howe as Antony. Phelps first acted in the play as Cassius to Macready's Brutus, in Covent Garden in 1838 and 1839, and at Drury Lane in 1843. On this last occasion Sheridan Knowles was Casca and Miss Faucit Portia, while Antony, played by Vandenhoff in 1839, was now J. R. Anderson, previously

[1] J. Genest, *op. cit.* IX, 121.
[2] Figures given in W. Archer, *W. C. Macready*, p. 30.
[3] W. C. Macready, *Reminiscences*, ed. Sir F. Pollock, I, 179.
[4] *Ibid.* II, 365.

Octavius. As Manager of Sadlers Wells, Phelps produced the play there in 1846 and 1847, choosing it for his
benefit in May 1846, and showing it nine times in the
1846–7 season. From now on he took the part of
Brutus. He again chose the play for his final farewell
to Sadlers Wells on 6 November 1862, when Edmund
Phelps was Antony and Creswick Cassius.

But in spite of Phelps's efforts the play was in total
eclipse in London (except for a performance by the Saxe-
Meiningen actors at Drury Lane in 1881 and Edmund
Tearle's revival at the Olympic in 1892) till the turn
of the century. Then, in 1898, began the revivals by
Sir Herbert (then Mr) Tree at His Majesty's Theatre.
For a hundred nights from 22 January the play was
shown to enthusiastic audiences. The next year saw
another revival, and from 1905 to 1913 only one year
(1912) was without one. The staging of 1898, designed
and supervised by Alma-Tadema, outdid in magnificence even Tree's usual efforts. *The Times* spoke of
its 'succession of scenes of unexampled beauty'; and
Dr Percy Simpson wrote: 'the Rome of 2000 years
ago lives before us'. The Forum scene, he declared, 'for
its moving effect has probably never been surpassed on
the stage'.[1] The play was shown in three Acts, the first
to the end of 3. 1, the second the rest of Act 3, and the
third from 4. 2 to the end. The proscription scene (4. 1)
was cut out as by Kemble, though Ligarius's entry in
2. 1 and the killing of Cinna were now restored. The
cast was impressive; Tree took Antony (and made him,
says Dr Simpson, 'the central figure in the play'),
Lewis Waller was Brutus, Franklin McLeay Cassius,
while Casca and Cæsar fell to Louis Calvert and Charles

[1] See the whole critique in Furness, *Variorum* edition of
the play, pp. 441–3, and in Appendix E of Mark Hunter's
edition.

Fulton, and Portia and Calphurnia to Evelyn Millard
and Lily Handbury. Both Professor Odell and Mr
Gordon Crosse judge McLeay's Cassius to be the most
effective thing in the play, while the latter says also of
Waller's Brutus: 'I have never seen anyone play it
better.'[1]

After Tree, the play in the twentieth century regained
its old vogue. The Tercentenary celebrations reached
their high watermark in a matinée at Drury Lane on
2 May 1916 before Their Majesties, when between
the Acts King George knighted Benson in the Royal
Box with a sword hurriedly procured from a theatrical
costumier.[2] Sir Frank had been playing Cæsar to
Arthur Bouchier's Brutus, H. B. Irving's Cassius, Henry
Ainley's Antony, Basil Gill's Octavius and Lilian
Braithwaite's Portia; and the cast included a crowd
numbering over one hundred. In 1920 Basil Gill
played Brutus to Ainley's Antony at St James's Theatre.
The Old Vic has given four separate revivals—in 1926
by Robert Atkins with Baliol Holloway as Cassius and
Edith Evans as Portia; in 1930 with Harcourt Williams
Brutus, Donald Wolfit Cassius and John Gielgud
Antony; in 1932 with 'the best Brutus since Waller'[3]
in Ralph Richardson, playing to Robert Speaight's
Cassius; and in 1935, when Ion Swinley was Antony,
and the Brutus and Cassius of Leo Genn and William
Devlin provided a specially spirited quarrel. 1932 saw
three separate theatres presenting the play in January
and February, when besides the Old Vic production

[1] Odell, *op. cit.* II, 390; Gordon Crosse, *Fifty Years of
Shakespearean Playgoing*, pp. 49–52.
[2] For a fuller account see M. C. Day and J. C. Trewin,
The Shakespeare Memorial Theatre (1932), pp. 143–5, and
W. J. Macqueen Pope, *Theatre Royal, Drury Lane* (1945),
p. 303.
[3] Gordon Crosse, *op. cit.* p. 29.

and another at the 'Q' Theatre (Basil Gill the Brutus), His Majesty's renewed the past glories of Tree. The producer, Oscar Asche, staged the play, as he explained in a speech from the stage, on Tree's own principles with spectacular magnificence; ingenious devices included a realistic downpour of rain in 2. 1. In 1934 Sir Oswald Stoll's production at the Alhambra had Godfrey Tearle for Antony and Basil Gill as Brutus. In 1937, Robert Atkins gave the play in the Regent's Park Open-air Theatre. In November 1939 it was played in modern dress at The Embassy Theatre in a way that harmonized with the topical relevance aimed at—the drama showed, said *The Times* of 30 November, 'that Shakespeare knew all there was to be known about the problem of the dictator'.[1]

At Stratford the play has been shown sixteen times in the old Theatre, three times after the 1926 fire in the adapted cinema, and in four different years in the new Theatre. Stratford, indeed, anticipated Tree with the play, giving it first in 1889 with Osmond Tearle as producer in the absence of Benson: and then in the Festivals of 1892, 1896 and 1898 under Benson's direction. Of this last revival he tells us that he had prepared the play for presentation in London, but was forestalled—clearly by Tree; Benson's scenery, like Tree's, being designed by Alma-Tadema.[2] Benson acted Antony, as always, and his rendering of the part rivalled, if it did not surpass, Tree's; Louis Calvert was Brutus, and Oscar Asche Casca. A single passage (Brutus with Portia) was given during the Tercentenary; and on 9 November 1926, the Quarrel scene by Godfrey Tearle (Brutus) and Basil Gill (Cassius) formed the crowning item in a special programme which raised £2000 towards the rebuilding of the theatre.

[1] Cf. Introd. § IV.
[2] F. R. Benson, *My Memoirs*, pp. 300–2.

In America, after a slow start (with only four revivals before 1817) the play became a marked favourite; fifty-one different years in the nineteenth century saw it staged in New York, while it was revived fifteen times in twenty years in Philadelphia.[1] In the first half of the century Hamblin, in the second half Davenport and Edwin Booth, were the outstanding players of Brutus, while J. B. Booth and Eddy were the chief figures as Cassius till eclipsed towards the end of the century by Laurence Barrett, 'the perfect Cassius', according to Professor Odell. The early thirties had seen Hamblin and J. B. Booth in constant partnership at the Bowery, with Cooper as Antony; in the late eighties a similar partnership was Edwin Booth's and Barrett's, in extended runs in different theatres. New York saw both Macready (in 1827 as Cassius, and in 1848 as Brutus) and Kean (1839) in our play. On 25 November 1864 the three Booths acted together in the Winter Garden in the Tercentenary effort to raise money for a statue to the dramatist in Central Park; J. Wilkes Booth, Lincoln's assassin six months later, acted Antony. In 1871–2 a most spectacular production held Booth's Theatre for 85 nights, Edwin Booth playing Brutus and Barrett Cassius; while in 1875–6 the play ran for 101 nights, with Davenport now as Brutus. In the present century, New York has witnessed seventeen separate revivals, but none since 1937.[2] Of these 'the most notable' were Richard Mansfield's

[1] G. C. D. Odell, *Annals of the New York Stage* (14 vols. to 1892); A. H. Wilson, *History of the Philadelphia Theatre*, 1835–55.

[2] I owe this information and all that follows to the kindness of Mr C. B. Hogan, who has sent me a detailed record of all twentieth-century New York performances, noting that in most cases the Companies carried the production on to the other chief cities of the United States. Inverted commas indicate quotations from his accompanying letter.

(1902), William Faversham's (1912), 'a very elaborate performance', and Orson Welles's (1937)—157 times. 'Welles's brilliant production, done completely without scenery, in modern dress, and tinged with Fascism,'[1] Mr Hogan regards as one of the best Shakespearian performances he has ever seen. In 1907 and 1910 Ben Greet's Company, with Sybil Thorndike as Portia, presented the play in The Garden Theatre, New York.

C. B. YOUNG

July 1947

[1] Cf. the London revival of 1939; see above, p. xliv.

TO THE READER

The following is a brief description of the punctuation and other typographical devices employed in the text, which have been more fully explained in the *Note on Punctuation* and the *Textual Introduction* to be found in *The Tempest* volume:

An obelisk (†) implies corruption, or emendation not yet generally accepted, and suggests a reference to the Notes.

A single bracket at the beginning of a speech signifies an 'aside'.

Four dots represent a *full stop* in the original, except when it occurs at the end of a speech, and they mark a long pause. Original *colons* or *semicolons*, which denote a somewhat shorter pause, are retained, or represented as three dots when they appear to possess special dramatic significance. Similarly, significant *commas* have been given as dashes.

Round brackets are taken from the original, and mark a significant change of voice; when the original brackets seem to imply little more than the drop in tone accompanying parenthesis, they are conveyed by commas or dashes.

Single inverted commas (' ') are editorial; double ones (" ") derive from the original, where they are used to draw attention to maxims, quotations, etc.

The reference number for the first line is given at the head of each page. Numerals in square brackets are placed at the beginning of the traditional acts and scenes.

JULIUS CÆSAR

The Scene: Rome; the neighbourhood of Sardis;
the neighbourhood of Philippi

CHARACTERS IN THE PLAY

JULIUS CÆSAR

OCTAVIUS CÆSAR
MARCUS ANTONIUS } *triumvirs after the death of*
M. ÆMILIUS LEPIDUS } *Julius Cæsar*

CICERO
PUBLIUS } *senators*
POPILIUS LENA

MARCUS BRUTUS
CASSIUS
CASCA
TREBONIUS
LIGARIUS } *conspirators against Julius Cæsar*
DECIUS BRUTUS
METELLUS CIMBER
CINNA

FLAVIUS *and* MARULLUS, *tribunes*

ARTEMIDORUS of Cnidos, *a teacher of Rhetoric*

A Soothsayer

CINNA, *a poet*

Another poet

LUCILIUS
TITINIUS
MESSALA } *friends to Brutus and Cassius*
YOUNG CATO
VOLUMNIUS

VARRO
CLITUS
CLAUDIUS
STRATO
LUCIUS   } *servants to Brutus or his officers*
DARDANIUS
LABEO
FLAVIUS

PINDARUS, *bondman to Cassius*

CALPHURNIA, *wife to Cæsar*

PORTIA, *wife to Brutus*

    Senators, Citizens, Officers, Attendants, etc.

JULIUS CÆSAR

[I. 1.]   *Rome. A street*

FLAVIUS, MARULLUS, and certain commoners

Flavius. Hence! home, you idle creatures, get
        you home:
Is this a holiday? what! know you not,
Being mechanical, you ought not walk
Upon a labouring day without the sign
Of your profession? Speak, what trade art thou?

1 Commoner. Why, sir, a carpenter.

Marullus. Where is thy leather apron and thy rule?
What dost thou with thy best apparel on?
You, sir, what trade are you?

2 Commoner. Truly, sir, in respect of a fine workman, 10
I am but as you would say a cobbler.

Marullus. But what trade art thou? answer me
directly.

2 Commoner. A trade, sir, that I hope I may use with
a safe conscience, which is indeed, sir, a mender of bad
soles.

Marullus. What trade, thou knave? thou naughty
knave, what trade?

2 Commoner. Nay, I beseech you, sir, be not out with
me: yet if you be out, sir, I can mend you.   20

Marullus. What mean'st thou by that? mend me, thou
saucy fellow!

2 Commoner. Why, sir, cobble you.

Flavius. Thou art a cobbler, art thou?

2 Commoner. Truly, sir, all that I live by is with the
awl: I meddle with no tradesman's matters, nor women's
matters; but withal I am indeed, sir, a surgeon to

old shoes; when they are in great danger, I recover
them. As proper men as ever trod upon neat's leather
30 have gone upon my handiwork.

Flavius. But wherefore art not in thy shop to-day?
Why dost thou lead these men about the streets?

2 *Commoner.* Truly, sir, to wear out their shoes, to get
myself into more work. But indeed, sir, we make holiday, to see Cæsár and to rejoice in his triumph.

Marullus. Wherefore rejoice? What conquest brings
he home?

What tributaries follow him to Rome,
To grace in captive bonds his chariot-wheels?
You blocks, you stones, you worse than senseless
things!
40 O you hard hearts, you cruel men of Rome,
Knew you not Pompey? Many a time and oft
Have you climbed up to walls and battlements,
To towers and windows, yea, to chimney-tops,
Your infants in your arms, and there have sat
The live-long day with patient expectation
To see great Pompey pass the streets of Rome:
And when you saw his chariot but appear,
Have you not made an universal shout,
That Tiber trembled underneath her banks
50 To hear the replication of your sounds
Made in her concave shores?
And do you now put on your best attire?
And do you now cull out a holiday?
And do you now strew flowers in his way
That comes in triumph over Pompey's blood?
Be gone!
Run to your houses, fall upon your knees,
Pray to the gods to intermit the plague
That needs must light on this ingratitude.

Flavius. Go, go, good countrymen, and for this fault 60
Assemble all the poor men of your sort;
Draw them to Tiber banks and weep your tears
Into the channel, till the lowest stream
Do kiss the most exalted shores of all.
        [*the crowd melts away*
See, whe'r their basest mettle be not moved;
They vanish tongue-tied in their guiltiness.
Go you down that way towards the Capitol;
This way will I: disrobe the images,
If you do find them decked with ceremonies.
 Marullus. May we do so?   70
You know it is the feast of Lupercal.
 Flavius. It is no matter; let no images
Be hung with Cæsar's trophies. I'll about,
And drive away the vulgar from the streets:
So do you too, where you perceive them thick.
These growing feathers plucked from Cæsar's wing
Will make him fly an ordinary pitch,
Who else would soar above the view of men
And keep us all in servile fearfulness.   [*they go*

[1. 2.] *Enter in solemn procession, with music,* CÆSAR,
reclining in his litter, ANTONY, *stripped for the course,*
CALPHURNIA, PORTIA, DECIUS, CICERO, BRUTUS,
CASSIUS, CASCA, *a Soothsayer, aud after them*
MARULLUS *and* FLAVIUS, *with a great crowd following*

 Cæsar. Calphurnia!   [*the procession halts*
 Casca.   Peace, ho! Cæsar speaks.
 Cæsar.   Calphurnia!
 Calphurnia [*comes forward*]. Here, my lord.
 Cæsar. Stand you directly in Antonius' way,
When he doth run his course. Antonius!
 Antony. Cæsar, my lord?

Cæsar. Forget not, in your speed, Antonius,
To touch Calphurnia; for our elders say,
The barren, touchéd in this holy chase,
Shake off their sterile curse.

Antony.   I shall remember:

10 When Cæsar says 'do this,' it is performed.

Cæsar. Set on, and leave no ceremony out.

                                      [*music again*

Soothsayer. Cæsar!

Cæsar. Ha! who calls?

Casca. Bid every noise be still: peace yet again!

Cæsar. Who is it in the press that calls on me?
I hear a tongue, shriller than all the music,
Cry 'Cæsar.' Speak, Cæsar is turned to hear.

Soothsayer. Beware the ides of March.

Cæsar.   What man is that?

Brutus. A soothsayer bids you beware the ides
    of March.

20 *Cæsar.* Set him before me, let me see his face.

Cassius. Fellow, come from the throng, look
    upon Cæsar.

Cæsar. What say'st thou to me now? speak once again.

Soothsayer. Beware the ides of March.

Cæsar. He is a dreamer, let us leave him: pass.

            [*Sennet; the procession moves forward
                        and passes out of sight*

Cassius. Will you go see the order of the course?

Brutus. Not I.

Cassius. I pray you, do.

Brutus. I am not gamesome: I do lack some part
Of that quick spirit that is in Antony.

30 Let me not hinder, Cassius, your desires;
I'll leave you.

Cassius. Brutus, I do observe you now of late:

I have not from your eyes that gentleness
And show of love as I was wont to have:
You bear too stubborn and too strange a hand
Over your friend that loves you.

Brutus.　　　　　　　　　　　Cassius,
Be not deceived: if I have veiled my look,
I turn the trouble of my countenance
Merely upon myself. Vexéd I am
Of late with passions of some difference,　　　　　40
Conceptions only proper to myself,
Which give some soil perhaps to my behaviours;
But let not therefore my good friends be grieved
(Among which number, Cassius, be you one),
Nor construe any further my neglect
Than that poor Brutus with himself at war
Forgets the shows of love to other men.

Cassius. Then, Brutus, I have much mistook
　　　your passion,
By means whereof this breast of mine hath buried
Thoughts of great value, worthy cogitations.　　　50
Tell me, good Brutus, can you see your face?

Brutus. No, Cassius; for the eye sees not itself
But by reflection, by some other things.

Cassius. 'Tis just,
And it is very much lamented, Brutus,
That you have no such mirrors as will turn
Your hidden worthiness into your eye,
That you might see your shadow. I have heard
Where many of the best respect in Rome
(Except immortal Cæsar), speaking of Brutus,　　　60
And groaning underneath this age's yoke,
Have wished that noble Brutus had his eyes.

Brutus. Into what dangers would you lead
　　　me, Cassius,

That you would have me seek into myself
For that which is not in me?
  Cassius. Therefore, good Brutus, be prepared to hear:
And since you know you cannot see yourself
So well as by reflection, I your glass
Will modestly discover to yourself

70 That of yourself which you yet know not of.
And be not jealous on me, gentle Brutus:
†Were I a common laughter, or did use
To stale with ordinary oaths my love
To every new protester; if you know
That I do fawn on men and hug them hard,
And after scandal them; or if you know
That I profess myself in banqueting
To all the rout, then hold me dangerous.

                              [*flourish and shout*

  Brutus. What means this shouting? I do fear,
    the people
Choose Cæsar for their king.

80 *Cassius.*   Ay, do you fear it?
Then must I think you would not have it so.
  Brutus. I would not, Cassius, yet I love him well...
But wherefore do you hold me here so long?
What is it that you would impart to me?
If it be aught toward the general good,
Set honour in one eye and death i'th'other,
And I will look on both indifferently:
For let the gods so speed me as I love
The name of honour more than I fear death.

90 *Cassius.* I know that virtue to be in you, Brutus,
As well as I do know your outward favour.
Well, honour is the subject of my story...
I cannot tell what you and other men
Think of this life; but, for my single self,

I had as lief not be as live to be
In awe of such a thing as I myself.
I was born free as Cæsar, so were you;
We both have fed as well, and we can both
Endure the winter's cold as well as he.
For once, upon a raw and gusty day,   100
The troubled Tiber chafing with her shores,
Cæsar said to me 'Dar'st thou, Cassius, now
Leap in with me into this angry flood,
And swim to yonder point?' Upon the word,
Accoutréd as I was, I plungéd in
And bade him follow: so indeed he did.
The torrent roared, and we did buffet it
With lusty sinews, throwing it aside
And stemming it with hearts of controversy.
But ere we could arrive the point proposed,   110
Cæsar cried 'Help me, Cassius, or I sink!'
I, as Æneas our great ancestor
Did from the flames of Troy upon his shoulder
The old Anchises bear, so from the waves of Tiber
Did I the tired Cæsar: and this man
Is now become a god, and Cassius is
A wretched creature, and must bend his body
If Cæsar carelessly but nod on him.
He had a fever when he was in Spain,
And when the fit was on him, I did mark   120
How he did shake: 'tis true, this god did shake;
His coward lips did from their colour fly,
And that same eye whose bend doth awe the world
Did lose his lustre: I did hear him groan:
Ay, and that tongue of his that bade the Romans
Mark him and write his speeches in their books,
Alas, it cried, 'Give me some drink, Titinius,'
As a sick girl...Ye gods! it doth amaze me

A man of such a feeble temper should
130 So get the start of the majestic world,
And bear the palm alone.   [*shout; flourish*

  Brutus. Another general shout!
I do believe that these applauses are
For some new honours that are heaped on Cæsar.
  Cassius. Why, man, he doth bestride the
    narrow world
Like a Colossus, and we petty men
Walk under his huge legs and peep about
To find ourselves dishonourable graves.
Men at some time are masters of their fates:
140 The fault, dear Brutus, is not in our stars,
But in ourselves, that we are underlings.
Brutus and Cæsar: what should be in that 'Cæsar'?
Why should that name be sounded more than yours?
Write them together, yours is as fair a name;
Sound them, it doth become the mouth as well;
Weigh them, it is as heavy; conjure with 'em,
Brutus will start a spirit as soon as Cæsar.
Now, in the names of all the gods at once,
Upon what meat doth this our Cæsar feed,
150 That he is grown so great? Age, thou art shamed!
Rome, thou hast lost the breed of noble bloods!
When went there by an age, since the great flood,
But it was famed with more than with one man?
When could they say, till now, that talked of Rome
That her wide walls encompassed but one man?
Now is it Rome indeed, and room enough,
When there is in it but one only man.
O, you and I have heard our fathers say
There was a Brutus once that would have brooked
160 Th'eternal devil to keep his state in Rome
As easily as a king.

Brutus. That you do love me, I am nothing jealous;
What you would work me to, I have some aim:
How I have thought of this and of these times,
I shall recount hereafter; for this present,
I would not (so with love I might entreat you)
Be any further moved. What you have said
I will consider; what you have to say
I will with patience hear, and find a time
Both meet to hear and answer such high things.   170
Till then, my noble friend, chew upon this:
Brutus had rather be a villager
Than to repute himself a son of Rome
Under these hard conditions as this time
Is like to lay upon us.
     Cassius. I am glad that my weak words
Have struck but thus much show of fire from Brutus.

Re-enter CÆSAR *and his train*

     Brutus. The games are done, and Cæsar is returning.
     Cassius. As they pass by, pluck Casca by the sleeve,
And he will (after his sour fashion) tell you   180
What hath proceeded worthy note to-day.
     Brutus. I will do so: but, look you, Cassius
The angry spot doth glow on Cæsar's brow,
And all the rest look like a chidden train:
Calphurnia's cheek is pale, and Cicero
Looks with such ferret and such fiery eyes
As we have seen him in the Capitol,
Being crossed in conference by some senator.
     Cassius. Casca will tell us what the matter is.
     Cæsar. Antonius!   190
     Antony. Cæsar?
     Cæsar. Let me have men about me that are fat,

J.C. – 4

Sleek-headed men, and such as sleep a-nights:
Yond Cassius has a lean and hungry look;
He thinks too much: such men are dangerous.

   Antony. Fear him not, Cæsar; he's not dangerous;
He is a noble Roman, and well given.

   Cæsar. Would he were fatter! but I fear him not
Yet if my name were liable to fear,
200 I do not know the man I should avoid
So soon as that spare Cassius. He reads much;
He is a great observer, and he looks
Quite through the deeds of men; he loves no plays,
As thou dost, Antony; he hears no music;
Seldom he smiles, and smiles in such a sort
As if he mocked himself and scorned his spirit
That could be moved to smile at any thing.
Such men as he be never at heart's ease
Whiles they behold a greater than themselves,
210 And therefore are they very dangerous.
I rather tell thee what is to be feared
Than what I fear; for always I am Cæsar.
Come on my right hand, for this ear is deaf,
And tell me truly what thou think'st of him.

                [Sennet. Cæsar and his train pass on

   Casca. You pulled me by the cloak, would you speak
with me?

   Brutus. Ay, Casca, tell us what hath chanced to-day,
That Cæsar looks so sad.

   Casca. Why, you were with him, were you not?

220   *Brutus.* I should not then ask Casca what had chanced.

   Casca. Why, there was a crown offered him: and being
offered him, he put it by with the back of his hand, thus:
and then the people fell a-shouting.

   Brutus. What was the second noise for?

   Casca. Why, for that too.

Cassius. They shouted thrice: what was the last cry for?

Casca. Why, for that too.

Brutus. Was the crown offered him thrice?

Casca. Ay, marry, was't, and he put it by thrice, every 230 time gentler than other; and at every putting-by mine honest neighbours shouted.

Cassius. Who offered him the crown?

Casca. Why, Antony.

Brutus. Tell us the manner of it, gentle Casca.

Casca. I can as well be hanged as tell the manner of it: it was mere foolery, I did not mark it. I saw Mark Antony offer him a crown, yet 'twas not a crown neither, 'twas one of these coronets: and, as I told you, he put it by once: but for all that, to my thinking, he would 240 fain have had it. Then he offered it to him again; then he put it by again: but, to my thinking, he was very loath to lay his fingers off it. And then he offered it the third time; he put it the third time by: and still as he refused it, the rabblement hooted and clapped their chopped hands and threw up their sweaty night-caps and uttered such a deal of stinking breath because Cæsar refused the crown, that it had almost choked Cæsar; for he swooned and fell down at it: and for mine own part, I durst not laugh, for fear of opening 250 my lips and receiving the bad air.

Cassius. But, soft, I pray you: what, did Cæsar swoon?

Casca. He fell down in the market-place and foamed at mouth and was speechless.

Brutus. 'Tis very like: he hath the falling-sickness.

Cassius. No, Cæsar hath it not; but you, and I, And honest Casca, we have the falling-sickness.

Casca. I know not what you mean by that, but I am sure Cæsar fell down. If the tag-rag people did not clap

260 him and hiss him according as he pleased and displeased them, as they use to do the players in the theatre, I am no true man.

Brutus. What said he when he came unto himself?

Casca. Marry, before he fell down, when he perceived the common herd was glad he refused the crown, he plucked me ope his doublet and offered them his throat to cut. An I had been a man of any occupation, if I would not have taken him at a word, I would I might go to hell among the rogues. And so he fell. When he
270 came to himself again, he said, if he had done or said any thing amiss, he desired their worships to think it was his infirmity. Three or four wenches, where I stood, cried 'Alas, good soul!' and forgave him with all their hearts: but there's no heed to be taken of them; if Cæsar had stabbed their mothers, they would have done no less.

Brutus. And after that, he came, thus sad, away?

Casca. Ay.

Cassius. Did Cicero say any thing?

280 *Casca.* Ay, he spoke Greek.

Cassius. To what effect?

Casca. Nay, an I tell you that, I'll ne'er look you i' th'face again: but those that understood him smiled at one another and shook their heads; but for mine own part, it was Greek to me. I could tell you more news too: Marullus and Flavius, for pulling scarfs off Cæsar's images, are put to silence. Fare you well. There was more foolery yet, if I could remember it.

Cassius. Will you sup with me to-night, Casca?

290 *Casca.* No, I am promised forth.

Cassius. Will you dine with me to-morrow?

Casca. Ay, if I be alive, and your mind hold, and your dinner worth the eating.

Cassius. Good; I will expect you.

Casca. Do so: farewell, both.   [*he goes*

Brutus. What a blunt fellow is this grown to be!
He was quick mettle when he went to school.

Cassius. So is he now in execution
Of any bold or noble enterprise,
However he puts on this tardy form.   300
This rudeness is a sauce to his good wit,
Which gives men stomach to digest his words
With better appetite.

Brutus. And so it is....For this time I will leave you:
To-morrow, if you please to speak with me,
I will come home to you; or, if you will,
Come home to me and I will wait for you.

Cassius. I will do so: till then, think of the world.

                              [*Brutus goes*

Well, Brutus, thou art noble; yet I see
Thy honourable metal may be wrought   310
From that it is disposed: therefore it is meet
That noble minds keep ever with their likes;
For who so firm that cannot be seduced?
Cæsar doth bear me hard, but he loves Brutus:
†If I were Brutus now and he were Cassius,
He should not humour me. I will this night,
In several hands, in at his windows throw,
As if they came from several citizens,
Writings, all tending to the great opinion
That Rome holds of his name, wherein obscurely   320
Cæsar's ambition shall be glancéd at:
And after this let Cæsar seat him sure;
For we will shake him, or worse days endure. [*he goes*

[I. 3.]   *The same; midnight*

Thunder and lightning. Enter, from opposite sides,
CASCA, with his sword drawn, and CICERO

Cicero. Good even, Casca: brought you Cæsar home?
Why are you breathless? and why stare you so?
  Casca. Are not you moved, when all the sway
    of earth
Shakes like a thing unfirm? O Cicero,
I have seen tempests, when the scolding winds
Have rived the knotty oaks, and I have seen
Th'ambitious ocean swell and rage and foam,
To be exalted with the threat'ning clouds;
But never till to-night, never till now,
10 Did I go through a tempest dropping fire.
Either there is a civil strife in heaven,
Or else the world too saucy with the gods
Incenses them to send destruction.
  Cicero. Why, saw you anything more wonderful?
  Casca. A common slave—you know him well by sight—
Held up his left hand, which did flame and burn
Like twenty torches joined, and yet his hand
Not sensible of fire remained unscorched.
Besides—I ha' not since put up my sword—
20 Against the Capitol I met a lion,
Who glazed upon me and went surly by
Without annoying me: and there were drawn
Upon a heap a hundred ghastly women
Transforméd with their fear, who swore they saw
Men all in fire walk up and down the streets.
And yesterday the bird of night did sit
Even at noon-day upon the market-place,

Hooting and shrieking. When these prodigies
Do so conjointly meet, let not men say
'These are their reasons: they are natural:'   30
For, I believe, they are portentous things
Unto the climate that they point upon.

Cicero. Indeed, it is a strange-disposéd time:
But men may construe things, after their fashion,
Clean from the purpose of the things themselves.
Comes Cæsar to the Capitol to-morrow?

Casca. He doth; for he did bid Antonius
Send word to you he would be there to-morrow.

Cicero. Good night then, Casca: this disturbéd sky
Is not to walk in.

Casca.   Farewell, Cicero. [*Cicero hurries home* 40

     CASSIUS *comes along the street*

Cassius. Who's there?
Casca.   A Roman.
Cassius.   Casca, by your voice.
Casca. Your ear is good. Cassius, what night is this!
Cassius. A very pleasing night to honest men.
Casca. Who ever knew the heavens menace so?
Cassius. Those that have known the earth so full
    of faults.
For my part, I have walked about the streets,
Submitting me unto the perilous night,
And thus unbracéd, Casca, as you see,
Have bared my bosom to the thunder-stone;
And when the cross blue lightning seemed to open   50
The breast of heaven, I did present myself
Even in the aim and very flash of it.

Casca. But wherefore did you so much tempt
    the heavens?
It is the part of men to fear and tremble

When the most mighty gods by tokens send
Such dreadful heralds to astonish us.

Cassius. You are dull, Casca, and those sparks of life
That should be in a Roman you do want,
Or else you use not. You look pale and gaze
60 And put on fear and cast yourself in wonder,
To see the strange impatience of the heavens:
But if you would consider the true cause
Why all these fires, why all these gliding ghosts,
Why birds and beasts from quality and kind,
Why old men, fools, and children calculate,
Why all these things change from their ordinance,
Their natures and preformèd faculties,
To monstrous quality, why, you shall find
That heaven hath infused them with these spirits
70 To make them instruments of fear and warning
Unto some monstrous state.
Now could I, Casca, name to thee a man
Most like this dreadful night,
That thunders, lightens, opens graves, and roars
As doth the lion in the Capitol;
A man no mightier than thyself or me
In personal action, yet prodigious grown
And fearful, as these strange eruptions are.

Casca. 'Tis Cæsar that you mean; is it not, Cassius?
80 *Cassius.* Let it be who it is: for Romans now
Have thews and limbs like to their ancestors;
But, woe the while! our fathers' minds are dead,
And we are governed with our mothers' spirits;
Our yoke and sufferance show us womanish.

Casca. Indeed they say the senators to-morrow
Mean to establish Cæsar as a king;
And he shall wear his crown by sea and land,
In every place save here in Italy.

Cassius. I know where I will wear this dagger then:
Cassius from bondage will deliver Cassius.   90
Therein, ye gods, you make the weak most strong;
Therein, ye gods, you tyrants do defeat.
Nor stony tower, nor walls of beaten brass,
Nor airless dungeon, nor strong links of iron,
Can be retentive to the strength of spirit;
But life, being weary of these worldly bars,
Never lacks power to dismiss itself.
If I know this, know all the world besides,
That part of tyranny that I do bear
I can shake off at pleasure.   [*thunder still*

  Casca.   So can I: 100
So every bondman in his own hand bears
The power to cancel his captivity.
  Cassius. And why should Cæsar be a tyrant then?
Poor man! I know he would not be a wolf
But that he sees the Romans are but sheep:
He were no lion were not Romans hinds.
Those that with haste will make a mighty fire
Begin it with weak straws: what trash is Rome,
What rubbish and what offal, when it serves
For the base matter to illuminate   110
So vile a thing as Cæsar! But, O grief,
Where hast thou led me? I perhaps speak this
Before a willing bondman; then I know
My answer must be made. But I am armed,
And dangers are to me indifferent.
  Casca. You speak to Casca, and to such a man
That is no fleering tell-tale. Hold, my hand:
Be factious for redress of all these griefs,
And I will set this foot of mine as far
As who goes farthest.   [*they clasp hands*
  Cassius.   There's a bargain made.   120

Now know you, Casca, I have moved already
Some certain of the noblest-minded Romans
To undergo with me an enterprise
Of honourable-dangerous consequence;
And I do know, by this they stay for me
In Pompey's porch: for now, this fearful night,
There is no stir or walking in the streets,
And the complexion of the element
In favour's like the work we have in hand,
130 Most bloody-fiery and most terrible.

Cinna is heard approaching

Casca. Stand close awhile, for here comes one in haste.
Cassius. 'Tis Cinna; I do know him by his gait;
He is a friend. Cinna, where haste you so?
Cinna. To find out you. Who's that? Metellus Cimber?
Cassius. No, it is Casca, one incorporate
To our attempts. Am I not stayed for, Cinna?
Cinna. I am glad on't. What a fearful night is this!
There's two or three of us have seen strange sights.
Cassius. Am I not stayed for? tell me.
Cinna.   Yes, you are.
140 O Cassius, if you could
But win the noble Brutus to our party—
Cassius. Be you content. Good Cinna, take this paper,
And look you lay it in the prætor's chair,
Where Brutus may but find it; and throw this
In at his window; set this up with wax
Upon old Brutus' statue: all this done,
Repair to Pompey's porch, where you shall find us.
Is Decius Brutus and Trebonius there?
Cinna. All but Metellus Cimber; and he's gone
150 To seek you at your house. Well, I will hie,
And so bestow these papers as you bade me.

Cassius. That done, repair to Pompey's theatre.

          [Cinna goes

Come, Casca, you and I will yet ere day
See Brutus at his house: three parts of him
Is ours already, and the man entire
Upon the next encounter yields him ours.

 Casca. O, he sits high in all the people's hearts;
And that which would appear offence in us
His countenance, like richest alchemy,
Will change to virtue and to worthiness.   160

 Cassius. Him and his worth and our great need of him
You have right well conceited. Let us go,
For it is after midnight, and ere day
We will awake him and be sure of him.   *[they go*

[2. 1.] *An orchard beside the house of Brutus*

BRUTUS *comes forth, paces to and fro in deep thought,*
 and then calls through the door open behind him

 Brutus. What, Lucius, ho!
I cannot, by the progress of the stars,
Give guess how near to day. Lucius, I say!
I would it were my fault to sleep so soundly.
When, Lucius, when? awake, I say! what, Lucius!

     LUCIUS *appears*

 Lucius. Called you, my lord?
 Brutus. Get me a taper in my study, Lucius:
When it is lighted, come and call me here.
 Lucius. I will, my lord.

   [goes in; Brutus falls to meditation again
 Brutus. It must be by his death: and, for my part, 10
I know no personal cause to spurn at him,
But for the general—he would be crowned:

How that might change his nature, there's the question.
It is the bright day that brings forth the adder;
And that craves wary walking...Crown him!—that!
And then, I grant, we put a sting in him,
That at his will he may do danger with.
Th'abuse of greatness is when it disjoins
Remorse from power: and, to speak truth of Cæsar,
20 I have not known when his affections swayed
More than his reason. But 'tis a common proof,
That lowliness is young ambition's ladder,
Whereto the climber-upward turns his face;
But when he once attains the upmost round,
He then unto the ladder turns his back,
Looks in the clouds, scorning the base degrees
By which he did ascend: so Cæsar may;
Then, lest he may, prevent. And, since the quarrel
Will bear no colour for the thing he is,
30 Fashion it thus: that what he is, augmented,
Would run to these and these extremities:
And therefore think him as a serpent's egg
Which hatched would as his kind grow mischievous,
And kill him in the shell.

LUCIUS returns

  Lucius. The taper burneth in your closet, sir.
Searching the window for a flint I found
This paper thus sealed up, and I am sure
It did not lie there when I went to bed.

                            [*gives him the letter*

  Brutus. Get you to bed again, it is not day.
40 Is not to-morrow, boy, the ides of March?
  Lucius. I know not, sir.
  Brutus. Look in the calendar and bring me word.
  Lucius. I will, sir.   [*goes in*

Brutus. The exhalations whizzing in the air
Give so much light that I may read by them.

                            [*opens the letter and reads*
'Brutus, thou sleep'st: awake and see thyself.
Shall Rome, &c. Speak, strike, redress....'
'Brutus, thou sleep'st: awake.'
Such instigations have been often dropped
Where I have took them up.
'Shall Rome, &c.' Thus must I piece it out: 50
Shall Rome stand under one man's awe? What, Rome?
My ancestors did from the streets of Rome
The Tarquin drive, when he was called a king.
'Speak, strike, redress.' Am I entreated
To speak and strike? O Rome, I make thee promise,
If the redress will follow, thou receivest
Thy full petition at the hand of Brutus!

Lucius returns

Lucius. Sir, March is wasted fifteen days.   [*knocking*
Brutus. 'Tis good. Go to the gate; somebody knocks. 60
                                    [*Lucius obeys*
Since Cassius first did whet me against Cæsar
I have not slept.
Between the acting of a dreadful thing
And the first motion all the interim is
Like a phantasma or a hideous dream:
The Genius and the mortal instruments
Are then in council, and the state of man
Like to a little kingdom suffers then
The nature of an insurrection.

Lucius returns

Lucius. Sir, 'tis your brother Cassius at the door,   70
Who doth desire to see you.

Brutus.   Is he alone?

Lucius. No, sir, there are mo with him.

Brutus.   Do you know them?

Lucius. No, sir, their hats are plucked about their ears,
And half their faces buried in their cloaks,
That by no means I may discover them
By any mark of favour.

Brutus.   Let 'em enter.   [*Lucius goes*
They are the faction. O conspiracy,
Sham'st thou to show thy dang'rous brow by night,
When evils are most free? O, then, by day

80 Where wilt thou find a cavern dark enough
To mask thy monstrous visage? Seek none, conspiracy;
Hide it in smiles and affability:
†For if thou path, thy native semblance on,
Not Erebus itself were dim enough
To hide thee from prevention.

Enter the conspirators, CASSIUS, CASCA, DECIUS,
CINNA, METELLUS, and TREBONIUS

Cassius. I think we are too bold upon your rest:
Good morrow, Brutus, do we trouble you?

Brutus. I have been up this hour, awake all night.
Know I these men that come along with you?

90 *Cassius.* Yes, every man of them; and no man here
But honours you; and every one doth wish
You had but that opinion of yourself
Which every noble Roman bears of you.
This is Trebonius.

Brutus.   He is welcome hither.

Cassius. This, Decius Brutus.

Brutus.   He is welcome too.

Cassius. This, Casca; this, Cinna; and this,
     Metellus Cimber.

Brutus. They are all welcome.
What watchful cares do interpose themselves
Betwixt your eyes and night?
  Cassius. Shall I entreat a word?   *[they whisper* 100
  Decius. Here lies the east: doth not the day break here?
  Casca. No.
  Cinna. O, pardon, sir, it doth, and yon grey lines
That fret the clouds are messengers of day.
  Casca. You shall confess that you are both deceived.
Here, as I point my sword, the sun arises;
Which is a great way growing on the south,
Weighing the youthful season of the year.
Some two months hence up higher toward the north
He first presents his fire, and the high east   110
Stands as the Capitol, directly here.
  Brutus. Give me your hands all over, one by one.
  Cassius. And let us swear our resolution.
  Brutus. †No, not an oath: if not the face of men,
The sufferance of our souls, the time's abuse—
If these be motives weak, break off betimes,
And every man hence to his idle bed;
So let high-sighted tyranny range on
Till each man drop by lottery. But if these,
As I am sure they do, bear fire enough   120
To kindle cowards and to steel with valour
The melting spirits of women, then; countrymen,
What need we any spur but our own cause
To prick us to redress? what other bond
Than secret Romans that have spoke the word,
And will not palter? and what other oath
Than honesty to honesty engaged
That this shall be or we will fall for it?
Swear priests and cowards and men cautelous,
Old feeble carrions and such suffering souls   130

That welcome wrongs; unto bad causes swear
Such creatures as men doubt: but do not stain
The even virtue of our enterprise,
Nor th'insuppressive mettle of our spirits,
To think that or our cause or our performance
Did need an oath; when every drop of blood
That every Roman bears, and nobly bears,
Is guilty of a several bastardy
If he do break the smallest particle
140 Of any promise that hath passed from him.
    Cassius. But what of Cicero? shall we sound him?
I think he will stand very strong with us.
    Casca. Let us not leave him out.
    Cinna.   No, by no means.
    Metellus. O, let us have him, for his silver hairs
Will purchase us a good opinion
And buy men's voices to commend our deeds:
It shall be said his judgement ruled our hands;
Our youths and wildness shall no whit appear,
But all be buried in his gravity.
150 *Brutus.* O, name him not: let us not break
        with him,
For he will never follow anything
That other men begin.
    Cassius.   Then leave him out.
    Casca. Indeed he is not fit.
    Decius. Shall no man else be touched but only Cæsar?
    Cassius. Decius, well urged: I think it is not meet
Mark Antony, so well beloved of Cæsar,
Should outlive Cæsar: we shall find of him
A shrewd contriver; and you know his means,
If he improve them, may well stretch so far
160 As to annoy us all: which to prevent,
Let Antony and Cæsar fall together.

Brutus. Our course will seem too bloody,
     Caius Cassius,
To cut the head off and then hack the limbs,
Like wrath in death and envy afterwards;
For Antony is but a limb of Cæsar:
Let us be sacrificers, but not butchers, Caius.
We all stand up against the spirit of Cæsar,
And in the spirit of men there is no blood:
O, that we then could come by Cæsar's spirit,
And not dismember Cæsar! But, alas,   170
Cæsar must bleed for it! And, gentle friends,
Let's kill him boldly, but not wrathfully;
Let's carve him as a dish fit for the gods,
Not hew him as a carcass fit for hounds:
And let our hearts, as subtle masters do,
Stir up their servants to an act of rage
And after seem to chide 'em. This shall make
Our purpose necessary and not envious:
Which so appearing to the common eyes,
We shall be called purgers, not murderers.   180
And for Mark Antony, think not of him;
For he can do no more than Cæsar's arm
When Cæsar's head is off.

   Cassius.   Yet I fear him,
For in the ingrafted love he bears to Cæsar—

   Brutus. Alas, good Cassius, do not think of him:
If he love Cæsar, all that he can do
Is to himself, take thought and die for Cæsar:
And that were much he should, for he is given
To sports, to wildness and much company.

   Trebonius. There is no fear in him; let him not die; 190
For he will live and laugh at this hereafter.

                              [*clock strikes*

   Brutus. Peace! count the clock.

Cassius. The clock hath stricken three.

Trebonius. 'Tis time to part.

Cassius. But it is doubtful yet
Whether Cæsar will come forth to-day or no;
For he is superstitious grown of late,
Quite from the main opinion he held once
Of fantasy, of dreams and ceremonies:
It may be these apparent prodigies,
The unaccustomed terror of this night,
200 And the persuasion of his augurers
May hold him from the Capitol to-day.

Decius. Never fear that: if he be so resolved,
I can o'ersway him; for he loves to hear
That unicorns may be betrayed with trees
And bears with glasses, elephants with holes,
Lions with toils and men with flatterers:
But when I tell him he hates flatterers,
He says he does, being then most flatteréd.
Let me work;
210 For I can give his humour the true bent,
And I will bring him to the Capitol.

Cassius. Nay, we will all of us be there to fetch him.

Brutus. By the eighth hour: is that the uttermost?

Cinna. Be that the uttermost, and fail not then.

Metellus. Caius Ligarius doth bear Cæsar hard,
Who rated him for speaking well of Pompey:
I wonder none of you have thought of him.

Brutus. Now, good Metellus, go along by him:
He loves me well, and I have given him reasons;
220 Send him but hither, and I'll fashion him.

Cassius. The morning comes upon's: we'll leave
you, Brutus:
And, friends, disperse yourselves: but all remember
What you have said and show yourselves true Romans.

Brutus. Good gentlemen, look fresh and merrily;
Let not our looks put on our purposes;
But bear it as our Roman actors do,
With untired spirits and formal constancy:
And so, good morrow to you every one.

[all but Brutus depart

Boy! Lucius! Fast asleep! It is no matter;
Enjoy the honey-heavy dew of slumber: 230
Thou hast no figures nor no fantasies,
Which busy care draws in the brains of men;
Therefore thou sleep'st so sound.

PORTIA *comes from the house*

Portia.   Brutus, my lord!
Brutus. Portia, what mean you? wherefore rise
   you now?
It is not for your health thus to commit
Your weak condition to the raw cold morning.
Portia. Nor for yours neither. You've
   ungently, Brutus,
Stole from my bed: and yesternight at supper
You suddenly arose and walked about,
Musing and sighing, with your arms across; 240
And when I asked you what the matter was,
You stared upon me with ungentle looks:
I urged you further; then you scratched your head
And too impatiently stamped with your foot:
Yet I insisted, yet you answered not,
But with an angry wafture of your hand
Gave sign for me to leave you: so I did,
Fearing to strengthen that impatience
Which seemed too much enkindled, and withal
Hoping it was but an effect of humour, 250
Which sometime hath his hour with every man.

It will not let you eat, nor talk, nor sleep,
And, could it work so much upon your shape
As it hath much prevailed on your condition,
I should not know you Brutus. Dear my lord,
Make me acquainted with your cause of grief.
   Brutus. I am not well in health, and that is all.
   Portia. Brutus is wise, and, were he not in health,
He would embrace the means to come by it.
260 *Brutus.* Why, so I do: good Portia, go to bed.
   Portia. Is Brutus sick, and is it physical
To walk unbracéd and suck up the humours
Of the dank morning? What, is Brutus sick,
And will he steal out of his wholesome bed,
To dare the vile contagion of the night
And tempt the rheumy and unpurgéd air
To add unto his sickness? No, my Brutus;
You have some sick offence within your mind,
Which by the right and virtue of my place
270 I ought to know of: [*kneels*] and, upon my knees,
I charm you, by my once commended beauty,
By all your vows of love and that great vow
Which did incorporate and make us one,
That you unfold to me, your self, your half,
Why you are heavy—and what men to-night
Have had resort to you; for here have been
Some six or seven, who did hide their faces
Even from darkness.
   Brutus.   Kneel not, gentle Portia.
   Portia. I should not need, if you were gentle Brutus.
280 Within the bond of marriage, tell me, Brutus,
Is it excepted I should know no secrets
That appertain to you? Am I your self
But, as it were, in sort or limitation,
To keep with you at meals, comfort your bed,

And talk to you sometimes? Dwell I but in the suburbs
Of your good pleasure? If it be no more,
Portia is Brutus' harlot, not his wife.

  Brutus. You are my true and honourable wife,
As dear to me as are the ruddy drops
That visit my sad heart.   290

  Portia. If this were true, then should I know
      this secret.
I grant I am a woman, but withal
A woman that Lord Brutus took to wife:
I grant I am a woman, but withal
A woman well reputed, Cato's daughter.
Think you I am no stronger than my sex,
Being so fathered and so husbanded?
Tell me your counsels, I will not disclose 'em:
I have made strong proof of my constancy,
Giving myself a voluntary wound   300
Here in the thigh: can I bear that with patience
And not my husband's secrets?

  Brutus.   O ye gods,
Render me worthy of this noble wife!   [*knocking*
Hark, hark! one knocks: Portia, go in awhile;
And by and by thy bosom shall partake
The secrets of my heart:
All my engagements I will construe to thee,
All the charactery of my sad brows.
Leave me with haste. [*she goes*] Lucius, who's
      that knocks?

        Lucius comes forth followed by Ligarius,
                his head muffled

  Lucius. Here is a sick man that would speak with you. 310
  Brutus. Caius Ligarius, that Metellus spake of.
Boy, stand aside. Caius Ligarius! how?

      J.C. – 5

Ligarius. Vouchsafe good-morrow from a
    feeble tongue.
Brutus. O, what a time have you chose out,
    brave Caius,
To wear a kerchief! Would you were not sick!
  Ligarius. I am not sick, if Brutus have in hand
Any exploit worthy the name of honour.
  Brutus. Such an exploit have I in hand, Ligarius,
Had you a healthful ear to hear of it.
320 *Ligarius.* By all the gods that Romans bow before,
I here discard my sickness! [*casts the kerchief off*]
    Soul of Rome!
Brave son, derived from honourable loins!
Thou, like an exorcist, hast conjured up
My mortifiéd spirit. Now bid me run,
And I will strive with things impossible,
Yea, get the better of them. What's to do?
  Brutus. A piece of work that will make sick
    men whole.
  Ligarius. But are not some whole that we must
    make sick?
  Brutus. That must we also. What it is, my Caius,
330 I shall unfold to thee, as we are going
To whom it must be done.
  Ligarius.   Set on your foot,
And with a heart new-fired I follow you,
To do I know not what: but it sufficeth
That Brutus leads me on.
  Brutus.   Follow me then.
                  [*they leave the orchard*

[2. 2.]   *Cæsar's house*

Thunder and lightning. Enter JULIUS CÆSAR,
in his night-gown

Cæsar. Nor heaven nor earth have been at
    peace to-night:
Thrice hath Calphurnia in her sleep cried out,
'Help, ho! they murder Cæsar!' [*calls*]
    Who's within?

A servant appears

Servant. My lord?
Cæsar. Go bid the priests do present sacrifice,
And bring me their opinions of success.
Servant. I will, my lord.   [*goes*

Enter CALPHURNIA

Calphurnia. What mean you, Cæsar? think you to
    walk forth?
You shall not stir out of your house to-day.
Cæsar. Cæsar shall forth: the things that   10
    threatened me
Ne'er looked but on my back; when they shall see
The face of Cæsar, they are vanishéd.
Calphurnia. Cæsar, I never stood on ceremonies,
Yet now they fright me. There is one within,
Besides the things that we have heard and seen,
Recounts most horrid sights seen by the watch.
A lioness hath whelpéd in the streets;
And graves have yawned and yielded up their dead;
Fierce fiery warriors fought upon the clouds,
In ranks and squadrons and right form of war,   20
Which drizzled blood upon the Capitol;

The noise of battle hurtled in the air,
Horses did neigh and dying men did groan,
And ghosts did shriek and squeal about the streets.
O Cæsar! these things are beyond all use,
And I do fear them.

   Cæsar.   What can be avoided
Whose end is purposed by the mighty gods?
Yet Cæsar shall go forth; for these predictions
Are to the world in general as to Cæsar.

30 *Calphurnia.* When beggars die, there are no
        comets seen;
The heavens themselves blaze forth the death of princes.

   Cæsar. Cowards die many times before their deaths;
The valiant never taste of death but once.
Of all the wonders that I yet have heard,
It seems to me most strange that men should fear,
Seeing that death, a necessary end,
Will come when it will come.

The servant returns

                        What say the augurers?

   Servant. They would not have you to stir forth to-day.
Plucking the entrails of an offering forth,
40 They could not find a heart within the beast.

   Cæsar. The gods do this in shame of cowardice:
Cæsar should be a beast without a heart
If he should stay at home to-day for fear.
No, Cæsar shall not: Danger knows full well
That Cæsar is more dangerous than he:
We are two lions littered in one day,
And I the elder and more terrible:
And Cæsar shall go forth.

   Calphurnia.   Alas, my lord,
Your wisdom is consumed in confidence.

Do not go forth to-day: call it my fear   50
That keeps you in the house and not your own.
We'll send Mark Antony to the Senate House,
And he shall say you are not well to-day:
Let me, upon my knee, prevail in this.   [*she kneels*
  Cæsar. Mark Antony shall say I am not well,
And, for thy humour, I will stay at home.

Enter DECIUS

Here's Decius Brutus, he shall tell them so.
  Decius. Cæsar, all hail! good morrow, worthy Cæsar:
I come to fetch you to the Senate House.
  Cæsar. And you are come in very happy time,   60
To bear my greeting to the senators
And tell them that I will not come to-day:
Cannot, is false, and that I dare not, falser:
I will not come to-day: tell them so, Decius.
  Calphurnia. Say he is sick.
  Cæsar.   Shall Cæsar send a lie?
Have I in conquest stretched mine arm so far,
To be afeard to tell graybeards the truth?
Decius, go tell them Cæsar will not come.
  Decius. Most mighty Cæsar, let me know some cause,
Lest I be laughed at when I tell them so.   70
  Cæsar. The cause is in my will: I will not come;
That is enough to satisfy the senate.
But, for your private satisfaction,
Because I love you, I will let you know.
Calphurnia here, my wife, stays me at home:
She dreamt to-night she saw my statua,
Which like a fountain with an hundred spouts
Did run pure blood, and many lusty Romans
Came smiling and did bathe their hands in it:
And these does she apply for warnings and portents   80

And evils imminent; and on her knee
Hath begged that I will stay at home to-day.
  Decius. This dream is all amiss interpreted;
It was a vision fair and fortunate:
Your statue spouting blood in many pipes,
In which so many smiling Romans bathed,
Signifies that from you great Rome shall suck
Reviving blood, and that great men shall press
For tinctures, stains, relics, and cognizance.
90 This by Calphurnia's dream is signified.
  Cæsar. And this way have you well expounded it.
  Decius. I have, when you have heard what I can say:
And know it now: the senate have concluded
To give this day a crown to mighty Cæsar.
If you shall send them word you will not come,
Their minds may change. Besides, it were a mock
Apt to be rendered, for some one to say
'Break up the senate till another time,
When Cæsar's wife shall meet with better dreams.'
100 If Cæsar hide himself, shall they not whisper
'Lo, Cæsar is afraid'?
Pardon me, Cæsar, for my dear dear love
To your proceeding bids me tell you this,
And reason to my love is liable.
  Cæsar. How foolish do your fears seem
        now, Calphurnia!
I am ashaméd I did yield to them.
Give me my robe, for I will go.

Enter PUBLIUS, BRUTUS, LIGARIUS, METELLUS,
  CASCA, TREBONIUS, *and* CINNA

And look where Publius is come to fetch me.
  Publius. Good morrow, Cæsar.
  Cæsar.   Welcome, Publius.

What, Brutus, are you stirred so early too?   110
Good morrow, Casca. Caius Ligarius,
Cæsar was ne'er so much your enemy
As that same ague which hath made you lean.
What is't o'clock?
  Brutus.   Cæsar, 'tis strucken eight.
  Cæsar. I thank you for your pains and courtesy.

Enter ANTONY

See! Antony, that revels long a-nights,
Is notwithstanding up. Good morrow, Antony.
  Antony. So to most noble Cæsar.
  Cæsar [*to Calphurnia*].   Bid them
    prepare within: [*she goes*
I am to blame to be thus waited for.
Now, Cinna: now, Metellus: what, Trebonius!   120
I have an hour's talk in store for you;
Remember that you call on me to-day:
Be near me, that I may remember you.
  Trebonius. Cæsar, I will. [*aside*] And so near will
    I be,
That your best friends shall wish I had been further.
  Cæsar. Good friends, go in and taste some wine
    with me;
And we like friends will straightway go together.
  (*Brutus.* That every like is not the same, O Cæsar,
The heart of Brutus earns to think upon!   [*they go*

[2. 3.]   *A street near the Capitol, before
       the house of Brutus*

Enter ARTEMIDORUS, *reading a paper*

  Artemidorus. 'Cæsar, beware of Brutus; take heed of
Cassius; come not near Casca; have an eye to Cinna;

trust not Trebonius; mark well Metellus Cimber:
Decius Brutus loves thee not: thou hast wronged Caius
Ligarius. There is but one mind in all these men, and
it is bent against Cæsar. If thou beest not immortal,
look about you: security gives way to conspiracy. The
mighty gods defend thee!

Thy lover, ARTEMIDORUS.'

10 Here will I stand till Cæsar pass along,
And as a suitor will I give him this.
My heart laments that virtue cannot live
Out of the teeth of emulation.
If thou read this, O Cæsar, thou mayst live;
If not, the Fates with traitors do contrive.

[he stands aside

[2. 4.]   PORTIA *and* LUCIUS *come from the house*

   Portia. I prithee, boy, run to the Senate House;
Stay not to answer me, but get thee gone.
Why dost thou stay?
   Lucius.   To know my errand, madam.
   Portius. I would have had thee there and here again,
Ere I can tell thee what thou shouldst do there.
O constancy, be strong upon my side!
Set a huge mountain 'tween my heart and tongue!
I have a man's mind, but a woman's might.
How hard it is for women to keep counsel!
Art thou here yet?
10 *Lucius.*   Madam, what should I do?
Run to the Capitol, and nothing else?
And so return to you, and nothing else?
   Portia. Yes, bring me word, boy, if thy lord look well,
For he went sickly forth: and take good note
What Cæsar doth, what suitors press to him.
Hark, boy! what noise is that?

Lucius. I hear none, madam.

Portia.   Prithee, listen well:
I heard a bustling rumour like a fray,
And the wind brings it from the Capitol.

Lucius. Sooth, madam, I hear nothing.

Enter the Soothsayer

Portia.   Come hither, fellow: 20
Which way hast thou been?

Soothsayer.   At mine own house, good lady.

Portia. What is't o'clock?

Soothsayer.   About the ninth hour, lady.

Portia. Is Cæsar yet gone to the Capitol?

Soothsayer. Madam, not yet: I go to take my stand,
To see him pass on to the Capitol.

Portia. Thou hast some suit to Cæsar, hast thou not?

Soothsayer. That I have, lady: if it will please Cæsar
To be so good to Cæsar as to hear me,
I shall beseech him to befriend himself.

Portia. Why, know'st thou any harm's intended   30
     towards him?

Soothsayer. None that I know will be, much that I fear
     may chance.
Good morrow to you. Here the street is narrow:
The throng that follows Cæsar at the heels,
Of senators, of prætors, common suitors,
Will crowd a feeble man almost to death:
I'll get me to a place more void and there
Speak to great Cæsar as he comes along. [*he passes on*

Portia. I must go in....Ay me, how weak a thing
The heart of woman is! O Brutus,
The heavens speed thee in thine enterprise!   40
Sure, the boy heard me. Brutus hath a suit
That Cæsar will not grant. O, I grow faint.

Run, Lucius, and commend me to my lord;
Say I am merry: come to me again,
And bring me word what he doth say to thee.

       [Lucius goes forward: she turns home

[3. 1.] *Before the Senate House; Senators in session
seen through open doors, with an empty chair of gold at
the head of their table; without, a statue of Pompey
beside one of the doors*

A crowd of people stand waiting; among them ARTEMI-
DORUS *and the Soothsayer. Flourish. Enter* CÆSAR,
BRUTUS, CASSIUS, CASCA, DECIUS, METELLUS,
TREBONIUS, CINNA, ANTONY, LEPIDUS, POPILIUS,
PUBLIUS, *and others*

 Cæsar [*to the Soothsayer*]. The ides of March are
  come.
 Soothsayer. Ay, Cæsar; but not gone.
 Artemidorus. Hail, Cæsar! read this schedule.
 Decius. Trebonius doth desire you to o'er-read,
At your best leisure, this his humble suit.
 Artemidorus. O Cæsar, read mine first; for mine's
  a suit
That touches Cæsar nearer: read it, great Cæsar.
 Cæsar. What touches us ourself shall be last served.
 Artemidorus. Delay not, Cæsar, read it instantly.
 Cæsar. What, is the fellow mad?
10 *Publius* [*thrusts Artemidorus aside*]. Sirrah, give place.
 Cassius. What, urge you your petitions in the street?
Come to the Capitol.

  CÆSAR *enters the Senate House, the rest following;
   the Senators rise as he takes his seat*

 Popilius. I wish your enterprise to-day may thrive.

Cassius. What enterprise, Popilius?

Popilius.   Fare you well.

    [*advances to Cæsar, and they speak together*

(*Brutus.* What said Popilius Lena?

(*Cassius.* He wished to-day our enterprise
    might thrive.

I fear our purpose is discovberéd.

    (*Brutus.* Look, how he makes to Cæsar: mark him.

    (*Cassius.*   Casca,

Be sudden, for we fear prevention.

Brutus, what shall be done? If this be known,   20

Cassius or Cæsar never shall turn back,

For I will slay myself.

    (*Brutus.*   Cassius, be constant:

Popilius Lena speaks not of our purposes;

For, look, he smiles, and Cæsar doth not change.

    (*Cassius.* Trebonius knows his time; for, look
      you, Brutus,

He draws Mark Antony out of the way.

      [*Antony and Trebonius depart, laughing together*

(*Decius.* Where is Metellus Cimber? Let him go,

And presently prefer his suit to Cæsar.

    (*Brutus.* He is addressed: press near and second him.

    (*Cinna.* Casca, you are the first that rears your hand. 30

Cæsar. Are we all ready?

*The conspirators draw near and stand about Cæsar's
chair, Casca a little to the side*

                What is now amiss

That Cæsar and his senate must redress?

  Metellus [*kneels*]. Most high, most mighty, and most
    puissant Cæsar,

Metellus Cimber throws before thy seat

An humble heart—

Cæsar. I must prevent thee, Cimber.
These couchings and these lowly courtesies
Might fire the blood of ordinary men,
And turn pre-ordinance and first decree
Into the law of children. Be not fond,
40 To think that Cæsar bears such rebel blood
That will be thawed from the true quality
With that which melteth fools, I mean, sweet words,
Low-crookéd curtsies and base spaniel-fawning.
Thy brother by decree is banishéd:
If thou dost bend and pray and fawn for him,
I spurn thee like a cur out of my way.
†Know, Cæsar doth not wrong, nor without cause
Will he be satisfied.

Metellus. Is there no voice more worthy than my own,
50 To sound more sweetly in great Cæsar's ear
For the repealing of my banished brother?

Brutus. I kiss thy hand, but not in flattery, Cæsar;
Desiring thee that Publius Cimber may
Have an immediate freedom of repeal.

Cæsar. What, Brutus!

Cassius [*makes profound obeisance*]. Pardon, Cæsar;
Cæsar, pardon:
As low as to thy foot doth Cassius fall,
To beg enfranchisement for Publius Cimber.

Cæsar. I could be well moved, if I were as you;
If I could pray to move, prayers would move me:
60 But I am constant as the northern star,
Of whose true-fixed and resting quality
There is no fellow in the firmament.
The skies are painted with unnumbered sparks;
They are all fire and every one doth shine;
But there's but one in all doth hold his place:
So in the world; 'tis furnished well with men,

And men are flesh and blood, and apprehensive;
Yet in the number I do know but one
That unassailable holds on his rank,
Unshaked of motion: and that I am he,   70
Let me a little show it, even in this:
That I was constant Cimber should be banished,
And constant do remain to keep him so.

Cinna. O Cæsar—
Cæsar.   Hence! wilt thou lift up Olympus?
Decius. Great Cæsar—
Cæsar.   Doth not Brutus bootless kneel?
Casca. Speak, hands, for me!

[strikes him from behind

*Cæsar rises, and struggles to escape; the conspirators
close in upon him near Pompey's statue, and hack
eagerly at him; he stands awhile at bay, until, seeing
Brutus about to strike also, he covers his face*

Cæsar. Et tu, Brute? Then fall, Cæsar!   *[dies*
Cinna. Liberty! freedom! Tyranny is dead!
Run hence, proclaim, cry it about the streets.
Cassius. Some to the common pulpits, and cry out   80
'Liberty, freedom and enfranchisement!'
Brutus. People, and senators, be not affrighted;
Fly not; stand still: ambition's debt is paid.
Casca. Go to the pulpit, Brutus.
Decius. And Cassius too.
Brutus. Where's Publius?
Cinna. Here, quite confounded with this mutiny.
Metellus. Stand fast together, lest some friend of Cæsar's
Should chance—
Brutus. Talk not of standing. Publius, good cheer;   90
There is no harm intended to your person,
Nor to no Roman else: so tell them, Publius.

Cassius. And leave us, Publius, lest that the people
Rushing on us should do your age some mischief.
Brutus. Do so: and let no man abide this deed
But wè the doers.

TREBONIUS *returns alone*

Cassius. Where is Antony?
Trebonius.   Fled to his house amazed:
Men, wives and children stare, cry out and run
As it were doomsday.
Brutus.   Fates, we will know your pleasures:
100 That we shall die, we know; 'tis but the time,
And drawing days out, that men stand upon.
Casca. Why, he that cuts off twenty years of life
Cuts off so many years of fearing death.
Brutus. Grant that, and then is death a benefit:
So are we Cæsar's friends, that have abridged
His time of fearing death. Stoop, Romans, stoop,
And let us bathe our hands in Cæsar's blood
Up to the elbows, and besmear our swords:
Then walk we forth, even to the market-place,
110 And waving our red weapons o'er our heads,
Let's all cry 'Peace, freedom and liberty!'
Cassius. Stoop then, and wash. [*they obey*] How
      many ages hence
Shall this our lofty scene be acted over
In states unborn and accents yet unknown!
Brutus. How many times shall Cæsar bleed in sport,
That now on Pompey's basis lies along
No worthier than the dust!
Cassius.   So oft as that shall be,
So often shall the knot of us be called
The men that gave their country liberty.
Decius. What, shall we forth?
120 *Cassius.*   Ay, every man away:

Brutus shall lead, and we will grace his heels
With the most boldest and best hearts of Rome.

A servant enters and kneels to Brutus

Brutus. Soft! who comes here? A friend of Antony's.
Servant. Thus, Brutus, did my master bid me kneel;
Thus did Mark Antony bid me fall down;
And, being prostrate, thus he bade me say:
Brutus is noble, wise, valiant and honest;
Cæsar was mighty, bold, royal and loving:
Say I love Brutus and I honour him;
Say I feared Cæsar, honoured him and loved him.   130
If Brutus will vouchsafe that Antony
May safely come to him and be resolved
How Cæsar hath deserved to lie in death,
Mark Antony shall not love Cæsar dead
So well as Brutus living, but will follow
The fortunes and affairs of noble Brutus
Thorough the hazards of this untrod state
With all true faith. So says my master Antony.
Brutus. Thy master is a wise and valiant Roman;
I never thought him worse.   140
Tell him, so please him come unto this place,
He shall be satisfied; and, by my honour,
Depart untouched.
Servant.   I'll fetch him presently.   [*goes*
Brutus. I know that we shall have him well to friend.
Cassius. I wish we may: but yet have I a mind
That fears him much, and my misgiving still
Falls shrewdly to the purpose.

Enter ANTONY, meeting the servant at the door, who nods

Brutus. But here comes Antony. Welcome,
     Mark Antony.

Antony makes direct to the body and kneels before it

Antony. O mighty Cæsar! dost thou lie so low?
150 Are all thy conquests, glories, triumphs, spoils,
Shrunk to this little measure? Fare thee well. [*he rises*
I know not, gentlemen, what you intend,
Who else must be let blood, who else is rank:
If I myself, there is no hour so fit
As Cæsar's death hour, nor no instrument
Of half that worth as those your swords, made rich
With the most noble blood of all this world.
I do beseech ye, if you bear me hard,
Now, whilst your purpled hands do reek and smoke,
160 Fulfil your pleasure. Live a thousand years,
I shall not find myself so apt to die:
No place will please me so, no mean of death,
As here by Cæsar, and by you cut off,
The choice and master spirits of this age.
  Brutus. O Antony, beg not your death of us.
Though now we must appear bloody and cruel,
As, by our hands and this our present act,
You see we do; yet see you but our hands
And this the bleeding business they have done:
170 Our hearts you see not; they are pitiful;
And pity to the general wrong of Rome—
As fire drives out fire, so pity pity—
Hath done this deed on Cæsar. For your part,
To you our swords have leaden points, Mark Antony:
†Our arms in strength of malice, and our hearts
Of brothers' temper, do receive you in
With all kind love, good thoughts and reverence.
  Cassius. Your voice shall be as strong as any man's
In the disposing of new dignities.
180 *Brutus.* Only be patient till we have appeased
The multitude, beside themselves with fear,
And then we will deliver you the cause

Why I, that did love Cæsar when I struck him,
Have thus proceeded.

Antony.　　　　　　　　I doubt not of your wisdom.
Let each man render me his bloody hand:
First, Marcus Brutus, will I shake with you;
Next, Caius Cassius, do I take your hand;
Now, Decius Brutus, yours; now yours, Metellus;
Yours, Cinna; and, my valiant Casca, yours;
Though last, not least in love, yours, good Trebonius. 190
Gentlemen all...alas, what shall I say?
My credit now stands on such slippery ground,
That one of two bad ways you must conceit me,
Either a coward or a flatterer.
That I did love thee, Cæsar, O, 'tis true:
If then thy spirit look upon us now,
Shall it not grieve thee dearer than thy death,
To see thy Antony making his peace,
Shaking the bloody fingers of thy foes,
Most noble! in the presence of thy corse?　　　　　200
Had I as many eyes as thou hast wounds,
Weeping as fast as they stream forth thy blood,
It would become me better than to close
In terms of friendship with thine enemies.
Pardon me, Julius! Here wast thou bayed, brave hart,
Here didst thou fall, and here thy hunters stand,
Signed in thy spoil and crimsoned in thy lethe.
O world, thou wast the forest to this hart;
And this, indeed, O world, the heart of thee.
How like a deer strucken by many princes　　　　210
Dost thou here lie!

Cassius. Mark Antony—
Antony.　　　　　　　　Pardon me, Caius Cassius:
The enemies of Cæsar shall say this;
Then, in a friend, it is cold modesty.

Cassius. I blame you not for praising Cæsar so,
But what compact mean you to have with us?
Will you be pricked in number of our friends,
Or shall we on, and not depend on you?

Antony. Therefore I took your hands, but was indeed
220 Swayed from the point by looking down on Cæsar.
Friends am I with you all and love you all,
Upon this hope that you shall give me reasons
Why and wherein Cæsar was dangerous.

Brutus. Or else were this a savage spectacle:
Our reasons are so full of good regard
That were you, Antony, the son of Cæsar,
You should be satisfied.

Antony.   That's all I seek,
And am moreover suitor that I may
Produce his body to the market-place,
230 And in the pulpit as becomes a friend
Speak in the order of his funeral.

Brutus. You shall, Mark Antony.

(*Cassius.*   Brutus, a word with you.
You know not what you do: do not consent
That Antony speak in his funeral:
Know you how much the people may be moved
By that which he will utter?

(*Brutus.*   By your pardon:
I will myself into the pulpit first,
And show the reason of our Cæsar's death:
What Antony shall speak, I will protest
240 He speaks by leave and by permission,
And that we are contented Cæsar shall
Have all true rites and lawful ceremonies.
It shall advantage more than do us wrong.

(*Cassius.* I know not what may fall; I like it not.

Brutus. Mark Antony, here, take you Cæsar's body.
You shall not in your funeral speech blame us,

But speak all good you can devise of Cæsar;
And say you do 't by our permission;
Else shall you not have any hand at all
About his funeral. And you shall speak   250
In the same pulpit whereto I am going,
After my speech is ended.

  Antony.   Be it so;
I do desire no more.

  Brutus. Prepare the body then, and follow us.

                                             [they go

Antony kneels again by the body

  Antony. O, pardon me, thou bleeding piece of earth,
That I am meek and gentle with these butchers!
Thou art the ruins of the noblest man
That ever livéd in the tide of times.
Woe to the hands that shed this costly blood!
Over thy wounds now do I prophesy   260
(Which like dumb mouths do ope their ruby lips
To beg the voice and utterance of my tongue),
A curse shall light upon the limbs of men;
Domestic fury and fierce civil strife
Shall cumber all the parts of Italy;
Blood and destruction shall be so in use,
And dreadful objects so familiar,
That mothers shall but smile when they behold
Their infants quartered with the hands of war;
All pity choked with custom of fell deeds: 270
And Cæsar's spirit ranging for revenge,
With Até by his side come hot from hell,
Shall in these confines with a monarch's voice
Cry 'Havoc,' and let slip the dogs of war;
That this foul deed shall smell above the earth
With carrion men, groaning for burial.

Enter a servant

You serve Octavius Cæsar, do you not?
  Servant. I do, Mark Antony.
  Antony. Cæsar did write for him to come to Rome.
280 *Servant.* He did receive his letters and is coming,
And bid me say to you by word of mouth—
O Cæsar!   *[seeing the body*
  Antony. Thy heart is big; get thee apart and weep:
Passion I see is catching, for mine eyes,
Seeing those beads of sorrow stand in thine,
Began to water. Is thy master coming?
  Servant. He lies to-night within seven leagues of Rome.
  Antony. Post back with speed, and tell him what
      hath chanced:
Here is a mourning Rome, a dangerous Rome,
290 No Rome of safety for Octavius yet;
Hie hence, and tell him so. Yet stay awhile;
Thou shalt not back till I have borne this corse
Into the market-place: there shall I try,
In my oration, how the people take
The cruel issue of these bloody men;
According to the which, thou shalt discourse
To young Octavius of the state of things.
Lend me your hand.   *[they bear away the body*

[3. 2.]   *The Forum; with a pulpit to one side*

Enter BRUTUS *and* CASSIUS, *and a throng
of plebeians*

  Plebeians. We will be satisfied; let us be satisfied.
  Brutus. Then follow me, and give me audience, friends.
Cassius, go you into the other street,
And part the numbers.

Those that will hear me speak, let 'em stay here;
Those that will follow Cassius, go with him;
And public reasons shall be renderéd
Of Cæsar's death.

  1 *Plebeian.*   I will hear Brutus speak.
  2 *Plebeian.* I will hear Cassius; and compare
    their reasons,
When severally we hear them renderéd.   10

        [*Cassius departs with some of the plebeians.*
                 Brutus goes up into the pulpit

  3 *Plebeian.* The noble Brutus is ascended: silence!
  Brutus. Be patient till the last.

Romans, countrymen, and lovers! hear me for my
cause, and be silent, that you may hear: believe me for
mine honour, and have respect to mine honour, that
you may believe: censure me in your wisdom, and
awake your senses, that you may the better judge.
If there be any in this assembly, any dear friend of
Cæsar's, to him I say that Brutus' love to Cæsar was
no less than his. If then that friend demand why Brutus 20
rose against Cæsar, this is my answer: not that I loved
Cæsar less, but that I loved Rome more. Had you rather
Cæsar were living, and die all slaves, than that Cæsar
were dead, to live all free men? As Cæsar loved me,
I weep for him; as he was fortunate, I rejoice at it;
as he was valiant, I honour him; but as he was ambitious,
I slew him. There is tears for his love; joy for his fortune;
honour for his valour; and death for his ambition. Who
is here so base that would be a bondman? If any, speak;
for him have I offended. Who is here so rude that would 30
not be a Roman? If any, speak; for him have I offended.
Who is here so vile that will not love his country?
If any, speak; for him have I offended. I pause for
a reply.

All. None, Brutus, none.

Brutus. Then none have I offended. I have done no
more to Cæsar than you shall do to Brutus. The question
of his death is enrolled in the Capitol; his glory not
extenuated, wherein he was worthy, nor his offences
40 enforced, for which he suffered death.

Antony enters in mourning, with bearers carrying
Cæsar's body in an open coffin on a bier

Here comes his body, mourned by Mark Antony, who,
though he had no hand in his death, shall receive the
benefit of his dying, a place in the commonwealth; as
which of you shall not? With this I depart—that, as
I slew my best lover for the good of Rome, I have the
same dagger for myself, when it shall please my country
to need my death.

All. Live, Brutus! live, live!

1 *Plebeian.* Bring him with triumph home unto
his house.

50 2 *Plebeian.* Give him a statue with his ancestors.

3 *Plebeian.* Let him be Cæsar.

4 *Plebeian.*   Cæsar's better parts
Shall be crowned in Brutus.

1 *Plebeian.* We'll bring him to his house with shouts
and clamours.

Brutus. My countrymen—

2 *Plebeian.*   Peace! silence! Brutus speaks.

1 *Plebeian.* Peace, ho!

Brutus. Good countrymen, let me depart alone,
And, for my sake, stay here with Antony:
Do grace to Cæsar's corpse, and grace his speech
Tending to Cæsar's glories, which Mark Antony
60 By our permission is allowed to make.
I do entreat you, not a man depart,

Save I alone, till Antony have spoke.   [*he goes*

   1 *Plebeian*. Stay, ho! and let us hear Mark Antony.

   3 *Plebeian*. Let him go up into the public chair;

We'll hear him. Noble Antony, go up.

   Antony. For Brutus' sake, I am beholding to you.

                                  [*goes into the pulpit*

   4 *Plebeian*. What does he say of Brutus?

   3 *Plebeian*.   He says, for Brutus' sake,

He finds himself beholding to us all.

   4 *Plebeian*. 'Twere best he speak no harm of

       Brutus here.

   1 *Plebeian*. This Cæsar was a tyrant.

   3 *Plebeian*.   Nay, that's certain: 70

We are blest that Rome is rid of him.

   2 *Plebeian*. Peace! let us hear what Antony can say.

   Antony. You gentle Romans—

   All.   Peace, ho! let us hear him.

   Antony. Friends, Romans, countrymen, lend me

       your ears;

I come to bury Cæsar, not to praise him;

The evil that men do lives after them,

The good is oft interréd with their bones,

So let it be with Cæsar....The noble Brutus

Hath told you Cæsar was ambitious:

If it were so, it was a grievous fault,   80

And grievously hath Cæsar answered it....

Here, under leave of Brutus and the rest,

(For Brutus is an honourable man;

So are they all; all honourable men)

Come I to speak in Cæsar's funeral....

He was my friend, faithful and just to me:

But Brutus says he was ambitious;

And Brutus is an honourable man....

He hath brought many captives home to Rome,

90 Whose ransoms did the general coffers fill:
Did this in Cæsar seem ambitious?
When that the poor have cried, Cæsar hath wept:
Ambition should be made of sterner stuff:
Yet Brutus says he was ambitious;
And Brutus is an honourable man.
You all did see that on the Lupercal
I thrice presented him a kingly crown,
Which he did thrice refuse: was this ambition?
Yet Brutus says he was ambitious;
100 And, sure, he is an honourable man.
I speak not to disprove what Brutus spoke,
But here I am to speak what I do know.
You all did love him once, not without cause:
What cause withholds you then to mourn for him?
O judgement! thou art fled to brutish beasts,
And men have lost their reason....Bear with me;
My heart is in the coffin there with Cæsar,
And I must pause till it come back to me.   [*he weep*

  1 *Plebeian.* Methinks there is much reason in
    his sayings.
110 2 *Plebeian.* If thou consider rightly of the matter,
Cæsar has had great wrong.
  3 *Plebeian.*   Has he, masters?
I fear there will a worse come in his place.
  4 *Plebeian.* Marked ye his words? He would no
    take the crown;
Therefore 'tis certain he was not ambitious.
  1 *Plebeian.* If it be found so, some will dear abide i
  2 *Plebeian.* Poor soul! his eyes are red as fire
    with weeping.
  3 *Plebeian.* There's not a nobler man in Rome
    than Antony.
  4 *Plebeian.* Now mark him, he begins again to spea

Antony. But yesterday the word of Cæsar might
Have stood against the world: now lies he there, 120
And none so poor to do him reverence.
O masters, if I were disposed to stir
Your hearts and minds to mutiny and rage,
I should do Brutus wrong and Cassius wrong,
Who, you all know, are honourable men:
I will not do them wrong; I rather choose
To wrong the dead, to wrong myself and you,
Than I will wrong such honourable men.
But here's a parchment with the seal of Cæsar;
I found it in his closet; 'tis his will: 130
Let but the commons hear this testament—
Which, pardon me, I do not mean to read—
And they would go and kiss dead Cæsar's wounds,
And dip their napkins in his sacred blood,
Yea, beg a hair of him for memory,
And, dying, mention it within their wills,
Bequeathing it as a rich legacy
Unto their issue.

4 *Plebeian.* We'll hear the will: read it, Mark Antony.

All. The will, the will! we will hear Cæsar's will. 140

Antony. Have patience, gentle friends, I must not
        read it;
It is not meet you know how Cæsar loved you.
You are not wood, you are not stones, but men;
And, being men, hearing the will of Cæsar,
It will inflame you, it will make you mad:
'Tis good you know not that you are his heirs;
For if you should, O, what would come of it!

4 *Plebeian.* Read the will; we'll hear it, Antony;
You shall read us the will, Cæsar's will.

Antony. Will you be patient? will you stay awhile? 150
I have o'ershot myself to tell you of it:

I fear I wrong the honourable men
Whose daggers have stabbed Cæsar; I do fear it.

4 *Plebeian.* They were traitors: honourable men!

All. The will! the testament!

2 *Plebeian.* They were villains, murderers: the will!
read the will!

Antony. You will compel me then to read the will?
Then make a ring about the corpse of Cæsar,
160 And let me show you him that made the will.
Shall I descend? and will you give me leave?

All. Come down.

2 *Plebeian.* Descend.   [*Antony comes down*

3 *Plebeian.* You shall have leave.

4 *Plebeian.* A ring; stand round.

1 *Plebeian.* Stand from the hearse, stand from
   the body.

2 *Plebeian.* Room for Antony, most noble Antony.

Antony. Nay, press not so upon me; stand far off.

All. Stand back. Room! Bear back.

170 *Antony.* If you have tears, prepare to shed them now.
You all do know this mantle: I remember
The first time ever Cæsar put it on;
'Twas on a summer's evening, in his tent,
That day he overcame the Nervii:
Look, in this place ran Cassius' dagger through:
See what a rent the envious Casca made:
Through this the well-belovéd Brutus stabbed;
And as he plucked his curséd steel away,
Mark how the blood of Cæsar followed it,
180 As rushing out of doors, to be resolved
If Brutus so unkindly knocked, or no:
For Brutus, as you know, was Cæsar's angel:
Judge, O you gods, how dearly Cæsar loved him!
This was the most unkindest cut of all;

For when the noble Cæsar saw him stab,
Ingratitude, more strong than traitors' arms,
Quite vanquished him: then burst his mighty heart;
And, in his mantle muffling up his face,
Even at the base of Pompey's statua
(Which all the while ran blood), great Cæsar fell.   190
O, what a fall was there, my countrymen!
Then I, and you, and all of us fell down,
Whilst bloody Treason flourished over us.
O, now you weep, and I perceive you feel
The dint of pity: these are gracious drops.
Kind souls, what weep you when you but behold
Our Cæsar's vesture wounded? Look you here,
Here is himself, marred, as you see, with traitors.

                                       [he plucks off the mantle

  1 *Plebeian.* O piteous spectacle!
  2 *Plebeian.* O noble Cæsar!   200
  3 *Plebeian.* O woful day!
  4 *Plebeian.* O traitors, villains!
  1 *Plebeian.* O most bloody sight!
  2 *Plebeian.* We will be revenged.
  All. Revenge! About! Seek! Burn! Fire! Kill! Slay!
Let not a traitor live!
  Antony. Stay, countrymen.
  1 *Plebeian.* Peace there! hear the noble Antony.
  2 *Plebeian.* We'll hear him, we'll follow him, we'll die
with him.   210
  Antony. Good friends, sweet friends, let me not stir
    you up
To such a sudden flood of mutiny:
They that have done this deed are honourable.
What private griefs they have, alas, I know not,
That made them do it: they are wise and honourable,
And will, no doubt, with reasons answer you.

I come not, friends, to steal away your hearts:
I am no orator, as Brutus is;
But, as you know me all, a plain blunt man,
220 That love my friend; and that they know full well
That gave me public leave to speak of him:
For I have neither wit, nor words, nor worth,
Action, nor utterance, nor the power of speech
To stir men's blood: I only speak right on;
I tell you that which you yourselves do know;
Show you sweet Cæsar's wounds, poor poor
  dumb mouths,
And bid them speak for me: but were I Brutus,
And Brutus Antony, there were an Antony
Would ruffle up your spirits, and put a tongue
230 In every wound of Cæsar, that should move
The stones of Rome to rise and mutiny.
 All. We'll mutiny.
 1 *Plebeian.* We'll burn the house of Brutus.
 3 *Plebeian.* Away, then! come, seek the conspirators.
 Antony. Yet hear me, countrymen; yet hear me speak.
 All. Peace, ho! Hear Antony! Most noble Antony!
 Antony. Why, friends, you go to do you know not
  what:
Wherein hath Cæsar thus deserved your loves?
Alas, you know not; I must tell you then:
240 You have forgot the will I told you of.
 All. Most true: the will! Let's stay and hear the will.
 Antony. Here is the will, and under Cæsar's seal.
To every Roman citizen he gives,
To every several man, seventy five drachmas.
 2 *Plebeian.* Most noble Cæsar! we'll revenge his death.
 3 *Plebeian.* O royal Cæsar!
 Antony. Hear me with patience.
 All. Peace, ho!
 Antony. Moreover, he hath left you all his walks,

His private arbours and new-planted orchards,   250
On this side Tiber; he hath left them you,
And to your heirs for ever; common pleasures,
To walk abroad and recreate yourselves.
Here was a Cæsar! when comes such another?
  1 *Plebeian.* Never, never. Come, away, away!
We'll burn his body in the holy place,
And with the brands fire the traitors' houses.
Take up the body.
  2 *Plebeian.* Go fetch fire.
  3 *Plebeian.* Pluck down benches.   260
  4 *Plebeian.* Pluck down forms, windows, anything.
                            [*they rush forth; the bearers
                                  follow with the body*
  Antony. Now let it work. Mischief, thou art afoot,
Take thou what course thou wilt.

                Octavius's servant enters the Forum

                            How now, fellow!
  Servant. Sir, Octavius is already come to Rome.
  Antony. Where is he?
  Servant. He and Lepidus are at Cæsar's house.
  Antony. And thither will I straight to visit him:
He comes upon a wish. Fortune is merry,
And in this mood will give us anything.
  Servant. I heard him say, Brutus and Cassius   270
Are rid like madmen through the gates of Rome.
  Antony. Belike they had some notice of the people,
How I had moved them. Bring me to Octavius.
                                            [*they go*

[3. 3.]   *Enter* CINNA *the poet, with plebeians
          carrying clubs stealing behind him*

  Cinna. I dreamt to-night that I did feast with Cæsar,
And things unluckily charge my fantasy:

I have no will to wander forth of doors,
Yet something leads me forth.

Plebeians surround him

1 *Plebeian.* What is your name?
2 *Plebeian.* Whither are you going?
3 *Plebeian.* Where do you dwell?
4 *Plebeian.* Are you a married man or a bachelor?
2 *Plebeian.* Answer every man directly.
10 1 *Plebeian.* Ay, and briefly.
4 *Plebeian.* Ay, and wisely.
3 *Plebeian.* Ay, and truly, you were best.
Cinna. What is my name? Whither am I going?
Where do I dwell? Am I a married man or a bachelor?
Then, to answer every man directly and briefly, wisely
and truly: wisely I say, I am a bachelor.

2 *Plebeian.* That's as much as to say, they are fools
that marry: you'll bear me a bang for that, I fear.
Proceed; directly.
20 *Cinna.* Directly, I am going to Cæsar's funeral.
1 *Plebeian.* As a friend or an enemy?
Cinna. As a friend.
2 *Plebeian.* That matter is answered directly.
4 *Plebeian.* For your dwelling, briefly.
Cinna. Briefly, I dwell by the Capitol.
3 *Plebeian.* Your name, sir, truly.
Cinna. Truly, my name is Cinna.
1 *Plebeian.* Tear him to pieces, he's a conspirator.
Cinna. I am Cinna the poet, I am Cinna the poet.
30 4 *Plebeian.* Tear him for his bad verses, tear him for
his bad verses.
Cinna. I am not Cinna the conspirator.
4 *Plebeian.* It is no matter, his name's Cinna; pluck
but his name out of his heart, and turn him going.

3 *Plebeian*. Tear him, tear him! [*they set upon him*]
Come, brands, ho! fire-brands: to Brutus', to Cassius',
burn all: some to Decius' house, and some to Casca's;
some to Ligarius': away, go! [*they rush forth dragging
the mangled body of Cinna after them*

[4. 1.] *A room in Antony's house*

ANTONY, OCTAVIUS, and LEPIDUS, seated at a table

Antony. These many then shall die; their names
  are pricked.
Octavius. Your brother too must die; consent
  you, Lepidus?
Lepidus. I do consent—
Octavius.   Prick him down, Antony.
Lepidus. Upon condition Publius shall not live,
Who is your sister's son, Mark Antony.
Antony. He shall not live; look, with a spot
  I damn him.
But, Lepidus, go you to Cæsar's house;
Fetch the will hither, and we shall determine
How to cut off some charge in legacies.
Lepidus. What, shall I find you here?   10
Octavius. Or here, or at the Capitol. [*Lepidus goes*
Antony. This is a slight unmeritable man,
Meet to be sent on errands: is it fit,
The three-fold world divided, he should stand
One of the three to share it?
Octavius.   So you thought him,
And took his voice who should be pricked to die
In our black sentence and proscription.
Antony. Octavius, I have seen more days than you:
And though we lay these honours on this man,

20 To ease ourselves of divers sland'rous loads,
He shall but bear them as the ass bears gold,
To groan and sweat under the business,
Either led or driven, as we point the way;
And having brought our treasure where we will,
Then take we down his load and turn him off,
Like to the empty ass, to shake his ears
And graze in commons.

 Octavius.   You may do your will:
But he's a tried and valiant soldier.

 Antony. So is my horse, Octavius, and for that
30 I do appoint him store of provender:
It is a creature that I teach to fight,
To wind, to stop, to run directly on,
His corporal motion governed by my spirit.
And in some taste is Lepidus but so;
He must be taught, and trained, and bid go forth;
A barren-spirited fellow; one that feeds
On objects, arts, and imitations
Which, out of use and staled by other men,
Begin his fashion: do not talk of him
40 But as a property. And now, Octavius,
Listen great things: Brutus and Cassius
Are levying powers: we must straight make head:
Therefore let our alliance be combined,
†Our best friends made, our means stretched;
And let us presently go sit in council,
How covert matters may be best disclosed,
And open perils surest answeréd.

 Octavius. Let us do so: for we are at the stake,
And bayed about with many enemies;
50 And some that smile have in their hearts, I fear,
Millions of mischiefs.   [*they go*

[4. 2.]   *Before Brutus's tent in the camp*
near Sardis

Drum. LUCILIUS marches up at the head of troops;
PINDARUS, the bondman of Cassius, with them. BRUTUS
comes from the tent with LUCIUS in attendance

Brutus. Stand, ho!

Lucilius. Give the word, ho! and stand!

Brutus. What now, Lucilius! is Cassius near?

Lucilius. He is at hand, and Pindarus is come
To do you salutation from his master.

Brutus. He greets me well. Your master, Pindarus,
In his own change, or by ill officers,
Hath given me some worthy cause to wish
Things done undone: but if he be at hand,
I shall be satisfied.

Pindarus.   I do not doubt   10
But that my noble master will appear
Such as he is, full of regard and honour.

Brutus. He is not doubted. A word, Lucilius;
How he received you, let me be resolved.

Lucilius. With courtesy and with respect enough,
But not with such familiar instances,
Nor with such free and friendly conference,
As he hath used of old.

Brutus.   Thou hast described
A hot friend cooling: ever note, Lucilius,
When love begins to sicken and decay,   20
It useth an enforcéd ceremony.
There are no tricks in plain and simple faith:
But hollow men, like horses hot at hand,
Make gallant show and promise of their mettle,
But when they should endure the bloody spur,

They fall their crests and like deceitful jades
Sink in the trial. Comes his army on?
   Lucilius. They mean this night in Sardis to
     be quartered;
The greater part, the horse in general,
Are come with Cassius.   *[drums heard*
30 *Brutus.*   Hark, he is arrived:
March gently on to meet him.

    CASSIUS approaches with TITINIUS and his powers

   Cassius. Stand, ho!
   Brutus. Stand, ho! Speak the word along.
   1 *Officer.* Stand!
   2 *Officer.* Stand!
   3 *Officer.* Stand!
   Cassius. Most noble brother, you have done
     me wrong.
   Brutus. Judge me, you gods; wrong I mine enemies?
And, if not so, how should I wrong a brother?
40 *Cassius.* Brutus, this sober form of yours hides wrongs,
And when you do them—
   Brutus.   Cassius, be content,
Speak your griefs softly, I do know you well.
Before the eyes of both our armies here,
Which should perceive nothing but love from us,
Let us not wrangle. Bid them move away;
Then in my tent, Cassius, enlarge your griefs,
And I will give you audience.
   Cassius.   Pindarus,
Bid our commanders lead their charges off
A little from this ground.
50 *Brutus.* †Lucius, do you the like, and let no man
Come to our tent till we have done our conference.
Lucilius and Titinius guard our door.

[4. 3.]   *The armies march away; BRUTUS and CASSIUS enter the tent; LUCILIUS and TITINIUS stand guard without*

Cassius. That you have wronged me doth appear
    in this:
You have condemned and noted Lucius Pella
For taking bribes here of the Sardians;
Wherein my letters, praying on his side,
Because I knew the man, was slighted off.
  Brutus. You wronged yourself to write in such a case.
  Cassius. In such a time as this it is not meet
That every nice offence should bear his comment.
  Brutus. Let me tell you, Cassius, you yourself
Are much condemned to have an itching palm,   10
To sell and mart your offices for gold
To undeservers.
  Cassius.   I an itching palm!
You know that you are Brutus that speaks this,.
Or, by the gods, this speech were else your last.
  Brutus. The name of Cassius honours this corruption,
And chastisement doth therefore hide his head.
  Cassius. Chastisement!
  Brutus. Remember March, the ides of
     March remember!
Did not great Julius bleed for justice' sake?
What villain touched his body, that did stab,   20
And not for justice? What, shall one of us,
That struck the foremost man of all this world
But for supporting robbers, shall we now
Contaminate our fingers with base bribes,
And sell the mighty space of our large honours
For so much trash as may be graspéd thus?
I had rather be a dog, and bay the moon,

Than such a Roman.

 Cassius.   †Brutus, bay not me,
I'll not endure it: you forget yourself,
30 To hedge me in; I am a soldier, I,
Older in practice, abler than yourself
To make conditions.

 Brutus.   Go to; you are not, Cassïus.

 Cassius. I am.

 Brutus. I say you are not.

 Cassius. Urge me no more, I shall forget myself;
Have mind upon your health; tempt me no farther.

 Brutus. Away, slight man!

 Cassius. Is't possible?

 Brutus.   Hear me, for I will speak.
Must I give way and room to your rash choler?
40 Shall I be frighted when a madman stares?

 Cassius. O ye gods, ye gods! must I endure all this?

 Brutus. All this! ay, more: fret till your proud
   heart break;
Go show your slaves how choleric you are,
And make your bondmen tremble. Must I budge?
Must I observe you? must I stand and crouch
Under your testy humour? By the gods,
You shall digest the venom of your spleen,
Though it do split you; for, from this day forth,
I'll use you for my mirth, yea, for my laughter,
When you are waspish.

50 *Cassius.*   Is it come to this?

 Brutus. You say you are a better soldier:
Let it appear so; make your vaunting true,
And it shall please me well: for mine own part,
†I shall be glad to learn of noble men.

 Cassius. You wrong me every way; you wrong
   me, Brutus;

I said, an elder soldier, not a better:
Did I say, better?
  Brutus.   If you did, I care not.
  Cassius. When Cæsar lived, he durst not thus have
    moved me.
  Brutus. Peace, peace! you durst not so have
    tempted him.
  Cassius. I durst not?   60
  Brutus. No.
  Cassius. What, durst not tempt him?
  Brutus.   For your life you durst not.
  Cassius. Do not presume too much upon my love,
I may do that I shall be sorry for.
  Brutus. You have done that you should be sorry for.
There is no terror, Cassius, in your threats;
For I am armed so strong in honesty
That they pass by me as the idle wind
Which I respect not. I did send to you
For certain sums of gold, which you denied me: 70
For I can raise no money by vile means:
By heaven, I had rather coin my heart,
And drop my blood for drachmas, than to wring
From the hard hands of peasants their vile trash
By any indirection. I did send
To you for gold to pay my legions,
Which you denied me: was that done like Cassius?
Should I have answered Caius Cassius so?
When Marcus Brutus grows so covetous,
To lock such rascal counters from his friends,   80
Be ready, gods, with all your thunderbolts,
Dash him to pieces!
  Cassius.   I denied you not.
  Brutus. You did.
  Cassius.   I did not: he was but a fool

That brought my answer back. Brutus hath rived
   my heart:
A friend should bear his friend's infirmities,
But Brutus makes mine greater than they are.
  Brutus. I do not, till you practise them on me.
  Cassius. You love me not.
  Brutus.   I do not like your faults.
  Cassius. A friendly eye could never see such faults.
90 *Brutus.* A flatterer's would not, though they do appear
As huge as high Olympus.
   Cassius. Come, Antony, and young Octavius, come,
Revenge yourselves alone on Cassius,
For Cassius is aweary of the world;
Hated by one he loves; braved by his brother;
Checked like a bondman; all his faults observed,
Set in a note-book, learned and conned by rote,
To cast into my teeth. O, I could weep
My spirit from mine eyes! There is my dagger,
100 And here my naked breast; within, a heart
Dearer than Pluto's mine, richer than gold:
If that thou be'st a Roman, take it forth;
I, that denied thee gold, will give my heart:
Strike, as thou didst at Cæsar; for I know,
When thou didst hate him worst, thou lovedst him better
Than ever thou lovedst Cassius.
  Brutus.   Sheathe your dagger:
Be angry when you will, it shall have scope;
Do what you will, dishonour shall be humour.
O Cassius, you are yokéd with a lamb,
110 That carries anger as the flint bears fire,
Who, much enforcéd, shows a hasty spark
And straight is cold again.
  Cassius.   Hath Cassius lived
To be but 'mirth' and 'laughter' to his Brutus,

When grief and blood ill-tempered vexeth him?
Brutus. When I spoke that, I was ill-tempered too.
Cassius. Do you confess so much? Give me your hand.
Brutus. And my heart too.
Cassius.   O Brutus!
Brutus.   What's the matter?
Cassius. Have not you love enough to bear with me,
When that rash humour which my mother gave me
Makes me forgetful?
Brutus.   Yes, Cassius, and from henceforth, 120
When you are over-earnest with your Brutus,
He'll think your mother chides, and leave you so.
A Voice without. Let me go in to see the generals;
There is some grudge between 'em; 'tis not meet
They be alone.
Lucilius. [*without*] You shall not come to them.
Voice without. Nothing but death shall stay me.

Enter a poet, followed by LUCILIUS, TITINIUS,
and LUCIUS

Cassius. How now! what's the matter?
Poet. For shame, you generals! what do you mean?
Love and be friends, as two such men should be;
For I have seen more years, I'm sure, than ye.   130
Cassius. Ha, ha! how vilely doth this cynic rhyme!
Brutus. Get you hence, sirrah; saucy fellow, hence!
Cassius. Bear with him, Brutus; 'tis his fashion.
Brutus. I'll know his humour when he knows his
     time:
What should the wars do with these jigging fools?
Companion, hence!
Cassius.   Away, away, be gone!
                           [*they drive him out*
Brutus. Lucilius and Titinius, bid the commanders

Prepare to lodge their companies to-night.

Cassius. And come yourselves, and bring Messala
    with you

Immediately to us.   [*Lucilius and Titinius depart*

140 *Brutus.*   Lucius, a bowl of wine!

            [*Lucius goes to an inner chamber of the tent*

Cassius. I did not think you could have been so
    angry.

Brutus. O Cassius, I am sick of many griefs.

Cassius. Of your philosophy you make no use,

If you give place to accidental evils.

Brutus. No man bears sorrow better: Portia is dead.

Cassius. Ha! Portia!

Brutus. She is dead.

Cassius. How scaped I killing when I crossed you so?

O insupportable and touching loss!

Upon what sickness?

150 *Brutus.*   Impatient of my absence,

And grief that young Octavius with Mark Antony

Have made themselves so strong: for with her death

That tidings came: with this she fell distract,

And, her attendants absent, swallowed fire.

Cassius. And died so?

Brutus.   Even so.

Cassius.   O ye immortal gods!

Lucius brings wine and tapers

Brutus. Speak no more of her. Give me a bowl
    of wine.

In this I bury all unkindness, Cassius.   [*drinks*

Cassius. My heart is thirsty for that noble pledge.

Fill, Lucius, till the wine o'erswell the cup;

160 I cannot drink too much of Brutus' love.

             [*drinks; Lucius goes*

Enter TITINIUS, with MESSALA

Brutus. Come in, Titinius! Welcome, good Messala.
Now sit we close about this taper here,
And call in question our necessities.

Cassius. Portia, art thou gone?

Brutus.   No more, I pray you.
Messala, I have here receivéd letters,
That young Octavius and Mark Antony
Come down upon us with a mighty power,
Bending their expedition toward Philippi.

Messala. Myself have letters of the selfsame tenour.

Brutus. With what addition?   170

Messala. That by proscription and bills of outlawry
Octavius, Antony, and Lepidus
Have put to death an hundred senators.

Brutus. Therein our letters do not well agree;
Mine speak of seventy senators that died
By their proscriptions, Cicero being one.

Cassius. Cicero one!

Messala.   Cicero is dead,
And by that order of proscription.
[Had you your letters from your wife, my lord?   ]

Brutus. No, Messala.   180

Messala. Nor nothing in your letters writ of her?

Brutus. Nothing, Messala.

Messala.   That, methinks, is strange.

Brutus. Why ask you? hear you aught of her in yours?

Messala. No, my lord.

Brutus. Now, as you are a Roman, tell me true.

Messala. Then like a Roman bear the truth I tell:
For certain she is dead, and by strange manner.

Brutus. Why, farewell, Portia. We must die, Messala:
With meditating that she must die once

190 I have the patience to endure it now.
  Messala. Even so great men great losses should endure.
  Cassius. I have as much of this in art as you,
[But yet my nature could not bear it so.   ]
  Brutus. Well, to our work alive. What do you think
Of marching to Philippi presently?
  Cassius. I do not think it good.
  Brutus.   Your reason?
  Cassius.   This it is:
'Tis better that the enemy seek us:
So shall he waste his means, weary his soldiers,
Doing himself offence; whilst we lying still
200 Are full of rest, defence and nimbleness.
  Brutus. Good reasons must of force give place to
    better.
The people 'twixt Philippi and this ground
Do stand but in a forced affection,
For they have grudged us contribution:
The enemy, marching along by them,
By them shall make a fuller number up,
Come on refreshed, new-added and encouraged;
From which advantage shall we cut him off
If at Philippi we do face him there,
These people at our back.
210 *Cassius.*   Hear me, good brother.
  Brutus. Under your pardon. You must note beside
That we have tried the utmost of our friends,
Our legions are brim-full, our cause is ripe:
The enemy increaseth every day;
We, at the height, are ready to decline.
There is a tide in the affairs of men
Which taken at the flood leads on to fortune;
Omitted, all the voyage of their life
Is bound in shallows and in miseries.

On such a full sea are we now afloat,   220
And we must take the current when it serves,
Or lose our ventures.
 Cassius.   Then, with your will, go on;
We'll along ourselves and meet them at Philippi.
 Brutus. The deep of night is crept upon our talk,
And nature must obey necessity;
Which we will niggard with a little rest.
There is no more to say?
 Cassius.   No more. Good night:
Early to-morrow will we rise and hence.
 Brutus. Lucius! [*Lucius re-enters*] My gown. [*Lucius
  goes*] Farewell, good Messala:
Good night, Titinius: noble, noble Cassius,   230
Good night, and good repose.
 Cassius.   O my dear brother!
This was an ill beginning of the night:
Never come such division 'tween our souls!
Let it not, Brutus.
 Brutus.   Everything is well.
 Cassius. Good night, my lord.
 Brutus.   Good night, good brother.
 Titinius, Messala. Good night, Lord Brutus.
 Brutus.   Farewell, every one.
          [*they go out*

   Re-enter LUCIUS, with the gown

Give me the gown. Where is thy instrument?
 Lucius. Here in the tent.
 Brutus.   What, thou speak'st drowsily?
Poor knave, I blame thee not; thou art o'erwatched.
Call Claudius and some other of my men;   240
I'll have them sleep on cushions in my tent.
 Lucius. Varro and Claudius!

VARRO and CLAUDIUS enter

Varro. Calls my lord?

Brutus. I pray you, sirs, lie in my tent and sleep;
It may be I shall raise you by and by
On business to my brother Cassius.

Varro. So please you, we will stand and watch
     your pleasure.

Brutus. I will not have it so: lie down, good sirs;
It may be I shall otherwise bethink me.

250 Look, Lucius, here's the book I sought for so;
I put it in the pocket of my gown.

                  [*Varro and Claudius lie down*

Lucius. I was sure your lordship did not give it me.

Brutus. Bear with me, good boy, I am much forgetful.
Canst thou hold up thy heavy eyes awhile,
And touch thy instrument a strain or two?

Lucius. Ay, my lord, an't please you.

Brutus.   It does, my boy:
I trouble thee too much, but thou art willing.

Lucius. It is my duty, sir.

Brutus. I should not urge thy duty past thy might;

260 I know young bloods look for a time of rest.

Lucius. I have slept, my lord, already.

Brutus. It was well done; and thou shalt sleep again;
I will not hold thee long: if I do live,
I will be good to thee.   [*music and a song*
This is a sleepy tune. O murd'rous slumber,
Layest thou thy leaden mace upon my boy,
That plays thee music? Gentle knave, good night;
I will not do thee so much wrong to wake thee:
If thou dost nod, thou break'st thy instrument;

270 I'll take it from thee; and, good boy, good night.

                  [*he gently disengages the lute*

Let me see, let me see; is not the leaf turned down
Where I left reading? Here it is, I think.   *[he sits*

Enter the Ghost of Cæsar

How ill this taper burns! Ha! who comes here?
I think it is the weakness of mine eyes
That shapes this monstrous apparition.
It comes upon me. Art thou any thing?
Art thou some god, some angel, or some devil,
That mak'st my blood cold, and my hair to stare?
Speak to me what thou art.
  Ghost. Thy evil spirit, Brutus.
  Brutus.   Why com'st thou?   280
  Ghost. To tell thee thou shalt see me at Philippi.
  Brutus. Well; then I shall see thee again?
  Ghost. Ay, at Philippi.
  Brutus. Why, I will see thee at Philippi then.
                    [the Ghost disappears
Now I have taken heart thou vanishest.
Ill spirit, I would hold more talk with thee.
Boy, Lucius! Varro! Claudius! Sirs, awake!
Claudius!
  Lucius. The strings, my lord, are false.
  Brutus. He thinks he still is at his instrument.   290
Lucius, awake!
  Lucius. My lord?
  Brutus. Didst thou dream, Lucius, that thou so
    criedst out?
  Lucius. My lord, I do not know that I did cry.
  Brutus. Yes, that thou didst: didst thou see any thing?
  Lucius. Nothing, my lord.
  Brutus. Sleep again, Lucius. Sirrah Claudius!
[*to Varro*] Fellow thou, awake!
  Varro. My lord?

300 *Claudius.* My lord?
     Brutus. Why did you so cry out, sirs, in your sleep?
     Varro, Claudius. Did we, my lord?
     Brutus.   Ay: saw you any thing?
     Varro. No, my lord, I saw nothing.
     Claudius.   Nor I, my lord.
     Brutus. Go and commend me to my brother Cassius;
Bid him set on his powers betimes before,
And we will follow.
     Varro, Claudius.   It shall be done, my lord.

                                                [they go

     [5. 1.]   *The plains of Philippi; to one side*
                        rocks and a hill

          Enter OCTAVIUS, ANTONY, *and their army*

     Octavius. Now, Antony, our hopes are answeréd:
You said the enemy would not come down,
But keep the hills and upper regions;
It proves not so: their battles are at hand;
They mean to warn us at Philippi here,
Answering before we do demand of them.
     Antony. Tut, I am in their bosoms, and I know
Wherefore they do it: they could be content
To visit other places; and come down
10 With fearful bravery, thinking by this face
To fasten in our thoughts that they have courage;
But 'tis not so.

               A messenger comes up

     Messenger.   Prepare you, generals:
The enemy comes on in gallant show;
Their bloody sign of battle is hung out,

And something to be done immediately.

Antony. Octavius, lead your battle softly on,
Upon the left hand of the even field.

Octavius. Upon the right hand I; keep thou the
left.

Antony. Why do you cross me in this exigent?

Octavius. I do not cross you; but I will do so.　20

> *Drum. Enter* BRUTUS, CASSIUS, *and their army;*
> LUCILIUS, TITINIUS, MESSALA, *and others*

Brutus. They stand, and would have parley.

Cassius. Stand fast, Titinius: we must out and talk.

Octavius. Mark Antony, shall we give sign of battle?

Antony. No, Cæsar, we will answer on their charge.
Make forth; the generals would have some words.

Octavius. Stir not until the signal.

Brutus. Words before blows: is it so, countrymen?

Octavius. Not that we love words better, as you do.

Brutus. Good words are better than bad
strokes, Octavius.

Antony. In your bad strokes, Brutus, you give　30
good words:
Witness the hole you made in Cæsar's heart,
Crying 'Long live! hail, Cæsar!'

Cassius.　　　　　　　　　　　　Antony,
The posture of your blows are yet unknown;
But for your words, they rob the Hybla bees,
And leave them honeyless.

Antony.　　　　　　　　　Not stingless too?

Brutus. O, yes, and soundless too;
For you have stol'n their buzzing, Antony,
And very wisely threat before you sting.

Antony. Villains, you did not so, when your vile daggers
Hacked one another in the sides of Cæsar:　40

You showed your teeth like apes, and fawned
    like hounds,
And bowed like bondmen, kissing Cæsar's feet;
Whilst damnéd Casca, like a cur, behind
Struck Cæsar on the neck. O you flatterers!
  Cassius. Flatterers! Now, Brutus, thank yourself:
This tongue had not offended so to-day,
If Cassius might have ruled.
    Octavius. Come, come, the cause: if arguing make
    us sweat,
The proof of it will turn to redder drops.
50 Look;
I draw a sword against conspirators;
When think you that the sword goes up again?
Never, till Cæsar's three and thirty wounds
Be well avenged, or till another Cæsar
Have added slaughter to the sword of traitors.
  Brutus. Cæsar, thou canst not die by traitors' hands,
Unless thou bring'st them with thee.
    Octavius.   So I hope;
I was not born to die on Brutus' sword.
  Brutus. O, if thou wert the noblest of thy strain,
60 Young man, thou couldst not die more honourable.
  Cassius. A peevish schoolboy, worthless of
    such honour,
Joined with a masker and a reveller!
  Antony. Old Cassius still!
  Octavius.   Come, Antony; away!
Defiance, traitors, hurl we in your teeth;
If you dare fight to-day, come to the field:
If not, when you have stomachs.
        [*Octavius, Antony, and their army march away*
  Cassius. Why, now, blow wind, swell billow and
    swim bark!

The storm is up, and all is on the hazard.

  Brutus. Ho, Lucilius! hark, a word with you.

  Lucilius.   *[standing forth]* My lord?
                                     [they talk apart

  Cassius. Messala!

  Messala. *[standing forth]* What says my general?

  Cassius.   Messala, 70

This is my birth-day; as this very day

Was Cassius born. Give me thy hand, Messala:

Be thou my witness that, against my will,

(As Pompey was) am I compelled to set

Upon one battle all our liberties.

You know that I held Epicurus strong,

And his opinion: now I change my mind,

And partly credit things that do presage.

Coming from Sardis, on our former ensign

Two mighty eagles fell, and there they perched,   80

Gorging and feeding from our soldiers' hands;

Who to Philippi here consorted us:

This morning are they fled away and gone,

And in their steads do ravens, crows, and kites

Fly o'er our heads and downward look on us,

As we were sickly prey: their shadows seem

A canopy most fatal, under which

Our army lies, ready to give up the ghost.

  Messala. Believe not so.

  Cassius.   I but believe it partly,

For I am fresh of spirit and resolved   90

To meet all perils very constantly.

  Brutus. Even so, Lucilius.   *[he turns to Cassius*

  Cassius.   Now, most noble Brutus,

The gods to-day stand friendly, that we may,

Lovers in peace, lead on our days to age!

But, since the affairs of men rest still incertain,

Let's reason with the worst that may befall.
If we do lose this battle, then is this
The very last time we shall speak together:
What are you then determinéd to do?

100 *Brutus.* Even by the rule of that philosophy
By which I did blame Cato for the death
Which he did give himself, I know not how
But I do find it cowardly and vile,
For fear of what might fall, so to prevent
The time of life; arming myself with patience
To stay the providence of some high powers
That govern us below.

    Cassius.   Then, if we lose this battle,
You are contented to be led in triumph
Thorough the streets of Rome?

110 *Brutus.* No, Cassius, no! think not, thou noble Roman,
That ever Brutus will go bound to Rome;
He bears too great a mind. But this same day
Must end that work the ides of March begun;
And whether we shall meet again I know not.
Therefore our everlasting farewell take.
For ever, and for ever, farewell, Cassius!
If we do meet again, why, we shall smile;
If not, why then this parting was well made.

    Cassius. For ever and for ever farewell, Brutus!
120 If we do meet again, we'll smile indeed;
If not, 'tis true this parting was well made.

    Brutus. Why then, lead on. O, that a man might know
The end of this day's business ere it come!
But it sufficeth that the day will end,
And then the end is known. Come, ho! away!

[5. 2.]   *They march forward with their army. After
a while the noise of battle is heard, at first afar off, then
drawing near.* BRUTUS *comes in sight with* MESSALA

Brutus. Ride, ride, Messala, ride, and give these bills
Unto the legions on the other side:
Let them set on at once; for I perceive
But cold demeanour in Octavius' wing,
And sudden push gives them the overthrow.
Ride, ride, Messala: let them all come down.
                                    [*they hurry forth*

[5. 3.]   *Distant alarums as of battle raging to and
fro.* CASSIUS *appears from another quarter, angry and
troubled, grasping a standard in his hand, and after him*
TITINIUS

Cassius. O, look, Titinius, look, the villains fly!
Myself have to mine own turned enemy:
This ensign here of mine was turning back;
I slew the coward, and did take it from him.
Titinius. O Cassius, Brutus gave the word too early;
Who, having some advantage on Octavius,
Took it too eagerly: his soldiers fell to spoil,
Whilst we by Antony are all enclosed.

PINDARUS *hurries up*

Pindarus. Fly further off, my lord, fly further off;
Mark Antony is in your tents, my lord: 10
Fly, therefore, noble Cassius, fly far off.

CASSIUS *plants the standard in the ground*

Cassius. This hill is far enough. Look, look, Titinius;
Are those my tents where I perceive the fire?
Titinius. They are, my lord.

Cassius.   Titinius, if thou lovest me,
Mount thou my horse and hide thy spurs in him,
Till he have brought thee up to yonder troops
And here again; that I may rest assured
Whether yond troops are friend or enemy.
  Titinius. I will be here again, even with a thought.
                                              [*he goes*

20 *Cassius.* Go, Pindarus, get higher on that hill;
My sight was ever thick; regard Titinius,
And tell me what thou not'st about the field.
                                       [*Pindarus ascends*
This day I breathéd first! time is come round,
And where I did begin, there shall I end;
My life is run his compass. Sirrah, what news?
  Pindarus [*above*]. O my lord!
  Cassius. What news?
  Pindarus [*above*]. Titinius is encloséd round about
With horsemen that make to him on the spur;
30 Yet he spurs on. Now they are almost on him.
Now, Titinius! Now some light. O, he lights too.
He's ta'en. [*a shout*] And, hark! they shout for joy.
  Cassius. Come down, behold no more.
O, coward that I am, to live so long,
To see my best friend ta'en before my face!

          Pindarus descends

Come hither, sirrah:
In Parthia did I take thee prisoner;
And then I swore thee, saving of thy life,
That whatsoever I did bid thee do,
40 Thou shouldst attempt it. Come now, keep thine oath!
Now be a freeman, and with this good sword
That ran through Cæsar's bowels search this bosom.
Stand not to answer: here, take thou the hilts,

And when my face is covered, as 'tis now,
Guide thou the sword. [*Pindarus thrusts him through*]
    Cæsar, thou art revenged,
Even with the sword that killed thee.   [*dies*
  Pindarus. So, I am free, yet would not so have been,
Durst I have done my will. O Cassius!
Far from this country Pindarus shall run,
Where never Roman shall take note of him.   50
                       [*he steals away*

    TITINIUS returns with MESSALA

  Messala. It is but change, Titinius; for Octavius
Is overthrown by noble Brutus' power,
As Cassius' legions are by Antony.
  Titinius. These tidings will well comfort Cassius.
  Messala. Where did you leave him?
  Titinius.   All disconsolate,
With Pindarus his bondman, on this hill.
  Messala. Is not that he that lies upon the ground?
  Titinius. He lies not like the living. O my heart!
  Messala. Is not that he?
  Titinius.   No, this was he, Messala,
But Cassius is no more. O setting sun,   60
As in thy red rays thou dost sink to night,
So in his red blood Cassius' day is set,
The sun of Rome is set! Our day is gone;
Clouds, dews and dangers come; our deeds are done!
Mistrust of my success hath done this deed.
  Messala. Mistrust of good success hath done this deed.
O hateful error, melancholy's child,
Why dost thou show to the apt thoughts of men
The things that are not? O error, soon conceived,
Thou never com'st unto a happy birth,   70
But kill'st the mother that engend'red thee!

Titinius. What, Pindarus! where art thou, Pindarus?
Messala. Seek him, Titinius, whilst I go to meet
The noble Brutus, thrusting this report
Into his ears: I may say 'thrusting' it,
For piercing steel and darts envenoméd
Shall be as welcome to the ears of Brutus
As tidings of this sight.

 Titinius.   Hie you, Messala,
And I will seek for Pindarus the while. [*Messala goes*
80 Why didst thou send me forth, brave Cassius?
Did I not meet thy friends? and did not they
Put on my brows this wreath of victory,
And bid me give it thee? Didst thou not hear
  their shouts?
Alas, thou hast misconstrued everything!
But, hold thee, take this garland on thy brow;
Thy Brutus bid me give it thee, and I
Will do his bidding. Brutus, come apace,
And see how I regarded Caius Cassius.
By your leave, gods: this is a Roman's part:
90 Come, Cassius' sword, and find Titinius' heart.
            [*kills himself*

*A brief pause; the noise of battle dies away; then re-
enter* MESSALA, *with* BRUTUS, *young* CATO, LUCILIUS,
LABEO, FLAVIUS, *and others*

Brutus. Where, where, Messala, doth his body lie?
Messala. Lo, yonder, and Titinius mourning it.
Brutus. Titinius' face is upward.
Cato.   He is slain.
Brutus. O Julius Cæsar, thou art mighty yet!
Thy spirit walks abroad, and turns our swords
In our own proper entrails.

Cato.   Brave Titinius!
Look, whe'r he have not crowned dead Cassius!
  Brutus. Are yet two Romans living such as these?
The last of all the Romans, fare thee well!
It is impossible that ever Rome   100
Should breed thy fellow. Friends, I owe mo tears
To this dead man than you shall see me pay.
I shall find time, Cassius, I shall find time.
Come therefore, and to Thasos send his body:
His funerals shall not be in our camp,
Lest it discomfort us. Lucilius, come,
And come, young Cato: let us to the field.
Labeo and Flavius, set our battles on.
'Tis three o'clock; and, Romans, yet ere night
We shall try fortune in a second fight.   110
          [they pass on, soldiers bearing off the bodies

[5. 4.]   *The battle resumes and the sound of fighting
draws near. Presently re-enter* BRUTUS, MESSALA, *young*
CATO, LUCILIUS, *and their army, yielding ground to
the opposing force*

  Brutus. Yet, countrymen! O, yet hold up your heads!
       [he charges, followed out by Messala, and others
  Cato. What bastard doth not? Who will go with me?
I will proclaim my name about the field.
I am the son of Marcus Cato, ho!
A foe to tyrants, and my country's friend;
I am the son of Marcus Cato, ho!
  †*Lucilius* [*joins him*]. And I am Brutus, Marcus
     Brutus, I;
Brutus, my country's friend; know me for Brutus!
        [they charge in turn; young Cato is slain
O young and noble Cato, art thou down?

10 Why, now thou diest as bravely as Titinius,
And mayst be honoured, being Cato's son.

He encounters two of the enemy and is borne down

1 *Soldier*. Yield, or thou diest.
Lucilius.   Only I yield to die:
There is so much that thou wilt kill me straight:
Kill Brutus, and be honoured in his death.
1 *Soldier*. We must not: a noble prisoner.
2 *Soldier*. Room, ho! Tell Antony, Brutus is ta'en.
1 *Soldier*. I'll tell the news. Here comes the general.

Enter Antony

Brutus is ta'en, Brutus is ta'en, my lord.
Antony. Where is he?
20 *Lucilius*. Safe, Antony; Brutus is safe enough:
I dare assure thee that no enemy
Shall ever take alive the noble Brutus:
The gods defend him from so great a shame!
When you do find him, or alive or dead,
He will be found like Brutus, like himself.
Antony. This is not Brutus, friend, but, I assure you,
A prize no less in worth: keep this man safe,
Give him all kindness: I had rather have
Such men my friends than enemies. Go on,
30 And see whe'r Brutus be alive or dead,
And bring us word unto Octavius' tent
How everything is chanced.   [*they pass on; the noise
                                   of battle dies away again*

[5.5.]   *Enter Brutus, Dardanius, Clitus,
         Strato, and Volumnius*

Brutus. Come, poor remains of friends, rest on
    this rock.
Clitus. Statilius showed the torch-light, but, my lord,

He came not back: he is or ta'en or slain.
  Brutus. Sit thee down, Clitus: slaying is the word;
It is a deed in fashion. Hark thee, Clitus.　　[*whispers*
  Clitus. What, I, my lord? No, not for all
    the world.
  Brutus. Peace then, no words.
  Clitus.　　　　　　　　　I'll rather kill myself.
  Brutus. Hark thee, Dardanius.　　　　　[*whispers*
  Dardanius.　　　　　Shall I do such a deed?
  Clitus. O Dardanius!
  Dardanius. O Clitus!　　　　　　　　　　　10
  Clitus. What ill request did Brutus make to thee?
  Dardanius. To kill him, Clitus. Look, he meditates.
  Clitus. Now is that noble vessel full of grief,
That it runs over even at his eyes.
  Brutus. Come hither, good Volumnius; list a word.
  Volumnius. What says my lord?
  Brutus.　　　　　　　　　Why, this, Volumnius:
The ghost of Cæsar hath appeared to me
Two several times by night: at Sardis once,
And this last night here in Philippi fields:
I know my hour is come.
  Volumnius.　　　　　Not so, my lord.　　　　20
  Brutus. Nay, I am sure it is, Volumnius.
Thou seest the world, Volumnius, how it goes;
Our enemies have beat us to the pit:
　　　　　　　　　　　[*fighting heard at a distance*
It is more worthy to leap in ourselves
Than tarry till they push us. Good Volumnius,
Thou know'st that we two went to school together:
Even for that our love of old, I prithee,
Hold thou my sword-hilts, whilst I run on it.
  Volumnius. That's not an office for a friend, my lord.
　　　　　　　　　　[*the sound draws near once more*

30 *Clitus.* Fly, fly, my lord, there is no tarrying here.
      Brutus. Farewell to you; and you; and
            you, Volumnius.   [*taking each by the hand*
      Strato, thou hast been all this while asleep;
      Farewell to thee too, Strato. Countrymen,
      My heart doth joy that yet in all my life
      I found no man but he was true to me.
      I shall have glory by this losing day,
      More than Octavius and Mark Antony
      By this vile conquest shall attain unto.
      So, fare you well at once; for Brutus' tongue
40 Hath almost ended his life's history:
      Night hangs upon mine eyes; my bones would rest,
      That have but laboured to attain this hour.
                [*loud alarum and cries of* 'Fly, fly, fly!' *heard*
      Clitus. Fly, my lord, fly.
      Brutus.   Hence! I will follow
                [*Clitus, Dardanius, and Volumnius escape*
      I prithee, Strato, stay thou by thy lord:
      Thou art a fellow of a good respect;
      Thy life hath had some smatch of honour in it:
      Hold then my sword, and turn away thy face,
      While I do run upon it. Wilt thou, Strato?
      Strato. Give me your hand first: fare you well,
            my lord.
50 *Brutus.* Farewell, good Strato. [*runs on his sword*]
            Cæsar, now be still:
      I killed not thee with half so good a will.   [*dies*

*Enter the army of Antony, pursuing the remnant of
Brutus' forces, and later sounding the 'retreat'. Then
enter* OCTAVIUS *and* ANTONY, *with* MESSALA, LUCILIUS,
as prisoners

  Octavius. What man is that?

Messala. My master's man. Strato, where is
　　thy master?

　Strato. Free from the bondage you are in, Messala:
The conquerors can but make a fire of him;
For Brutus only overcame himself,
And no man else hath honour by his death.

　Lucilius. So Brutus should be found. I thank
　　thee, Brutus,
That thou hast proved Lucilius' saying true.

　Octavius. All that served Brutus, I will entertain them. 60
Fellow, wilt thou bestow thy time with me?

　Strato. Ay, if Messala will prefer me to you.

　Octavius. Do so, good Messala.

　Messala. How died my master, Strato?

　Strato. I held the sword, and he did run on it.

　Messala. Octavius, then take him to follow thee,
That did the latest service to my master.

　Antony. This was the noblest Roman of them all:
All the conspirators save only he
Did that they did in envy of great Cæsar; 70
He only, in a general honest thought
And common good to all, made one of them.
His life was gentle, and the elements
So mixed in him that Nature might stand up
And say to all the world 'This was a man!'

　Octavius. According to his virtue let us use him,
With all respect and rites of burial.
Within my tent his bones to-night shall lie,
Most like a soldier, ordered honourably.
So call the field to rest, and let's away, 80
To part the glories of this happy day.

They march on, the while some take up the body of Brutus

THE COPY FOR
JULIUS CÆSAR, 1623

The Folio *Julius Cæsar*, our only substantive text, was pronounced by the Cambridge editors to be 'more correctly printed than any other play', and even 'perhaps printed from the original manuscript of the author'. We now realize that what is in question is the tidiness of the copy rather than the competence of the printers, and that such tidiness almost certainly denotes transcription of some kind, probably from the prompt-book.[1] Indications of transcription are the absence of those Shakespearian spellings which crop up in other texts, the comparatively correct lineation of the verse[2] and distribution of speeches, and a punctuation which is generally adequate and creates relatively few problems for an editor.[3] The chief features suggesting prompt-book origin are certain stage directions connected with 'noises off' (thunder and the 'alarums' of battle) which seem to have been prompter's notes added in the margin, since they sometimes duplicate directions in the centre of the page.[4] The S.D. with which 4. 2 opens cannot, again, be derived from Shakespeare's MS.

[1] See my Introduction to *Julius Cæsar* ('Folio facsimiles', 1929), and W. W. Greg, *The Editorial Problem in Shakespeare* (1942), p. 143.

[2] There are, as usual in F. texts, a number of lines the lineation of which has been regularized by editors, but nearly all these cases can, I think, be attributed to the compositor, who was forced, or found it convenient, to depart from the arrangement in his copy in order to conform to the F. double-column.

[3] See below, p. 100.

[4] See notes below at 2. 1. 334; 4. 2. 30; 5. 2 S.D. (head); 5. 3. 90; 5. 4 S.D. (head); 5. 5. 23 S.D.

Yet though pretty confident that we have to reckon with prompt-book influence, I think the actual copy was a transcript from the prompt-book rather than that document itself. In this edition of Shakespeare I have not so far encountered any clear evidence of printing from the prompt-book direct. Indeed, it seems unlikely that the players would have risked the loss of their 'allowed books' by sending them to press. In any case, despite the confidence of Aldis Wright, I cannot avoid the suspicion of corruption here and there in the present text by a copyist, of all agents the most difficult to detect or bring to book. An editor can do little more than register his suspicions and pass on. Here then, apart from trivial or obvious misprints, is a list of F. readings either accepted as corrupt by all or suspected of corruption by myself, together with more or less plausible emendations of various editors.

1. 2. 72	Laughter	laugher (Rowe)	lover
	155	Walkes	walls (Rowe)	[(Hudson)
1. 3. 129	Is fauors, like	In favour's like (Johnson)	
2. 1. 40	first	ides (Theobald)	
	83	path	put (Coleridge)	
	114	face	faith (Mason)	
2. 2. 46	We heare	We are (Upton)	
3. 1. 39	lane	law (Johnson)	
	175	malice	amity (Singer)	
	263	limbes	lives (Johnson)	
3. 2. 222	writ	wit (F 2)	
4. 3. 28	baite	bay (Theobald)	
	54	noble	able (Singer)	

Furthermore, *Julius Cæsar* is famous as the only Shakespearian text which was almost certainly altered in deference to literary criticism, and this alteration must, I am pretty sure, have been made expressly for the 1623 edition. In F. 3. 1. 47–8 runs thus:

> Know Cæsar doth not wrong, nor without cause
> Will he be satisfied.

That this is not what Shakespeare originally wrote is to be inferred from the following observation in Ben Jonson's *Discoveries*:

Many times he fell into those things could not escape laughter: as when he said in the person of Cæsar, one speaking to him 'Cæsar, thou dost me wrong', he replied, 'Cæsar did never wrong but with just cause', and such like; which were ridiculous.[1]

Discoveries was not printed until after Jonson's death, but he was putting the collection together about 1626 or a little later,[2] and that he had this passage from *Julius Cæsar* much in mind about that time is shown by the fun he made of it in the Induction to *The Staple of News* produced by 'His Majesty's Servants' in 1626. Such jesting is, moreover, strong evidence that *Julius Cæsar* had itself been recently seen on the same stage by Jonson's audience. And yet by 1626 the First Folio had been before the public for three years. It seems therefore reasonable to suppose (i) that the offending line was still in the prompt-book in 1626, and (ii) that, nevertheless, the scribe responsible for the Folio text was already aware of Jonson's criticism in 1622 or 1623, and either altered it himself or asked Jonson to do so.[3] Some have even supposed that Jonson himself was charged with preparing the text for the press. The presence of solecisms, such as the Italian forms occasionally given to some of the Latin names,[4] renders this highly improbable. On the other hand, the names

[1] *Ben Jonson*, ed. Herford and Simpson, VIII, 584.

[2] *Ibid.* I, 104.

[3] For a fuller statement of this argument see my article on 'Ben Jonson and *Julius Cæsar*' in *Shakespeare Survey*, II (1949).

[4] See notes 1. 2. 3, 4; 1. 2. 190; 1. 3. 37; 3. 1. 276; 4. 3. 240, 242, etc.

are in general so much more correct than those found in other Roman plays that the scribe responsible may conceivably have submitted a list of the characters to Jonson or some other scholar before making his transcript, in which case the spasmodic occurrence of forms like 'Antonio', which we find also in *Antony and Cleopatra*, are readily explained as careless oversight.[1]

It remains to note one or two indications of change in the text made for reasons other than literary or scholarly 'correctness'. Sir Edmund Chambers observes that the play 'is a very short one' and contains 'a few abrupt short lines which may be evidence of cuts'.[2] He finds, too, with most critics 'a trace of revision', though 'not necessarily more than an afterthought at the time of composition', in the two references to Portia's death in 4. 3.[3] Another afterthought may, I think, be seen in the appearance of Publius in place of Cassius in 2. 2. Cassius at 2. 1. 212 declares he will help to 'bring' Cæsar 'to the Capitol'. His absence in 2. 2 has been variously explained—as arising from scruples of honesty (Hunter),[4] as due to 'caution' rather than 'conscience' (Granville-Barker).[5] But Shakespeare gives no hint of any shrinking or change of mind. Indeed, the substitution of Publius escapes notice on the stage. What we have here in fact is a piece of theatrical legerdemain. Though not at Cæsar's house (2. 2), Cassius *is* on the Capitol (3. 1) with Cæsar and the others who had

[1] *Julius Cæsar* is peculiar in the spelling of this name without an *h*, and this may perhaps be attributed to the scribe.

[2] *William Shakespeare*, I, 397. Hart (*R.E.S.* VIII, 21) reckons that it contains 2450 lines and is the shortest but seven in the canon.

[3] See my note 4. 3. 179–93.

[4] P. cxxxviii. See above p. vii, note 1.

[5] *Prefaces to Shakespeare* (1st ser.), p. 65.

fetched him; he 'brings him' after all, though he did
not 'fetch him'. And a reverse game of bo-peep is
played by Ligarius, who goes to Cæsar's house to 'fetch'
him, yet is not with him in 3. 1 and never reappears.
The explanation is that Ligarius and Cassius were played
by the same actor, and therefore could not appear
together.

The text followed scene by scene shows how it came
about. At 2. 1. 228 the 'lean and hungry' Cassius
departs from Brutus's house. After 80 lines of dialogue,
chiefly with Portia, a knock at the door as she goes out
brings in Ligarius, a sick man with kerchiefed head,
whom, we learn in 2. 2. 113, 'ague hath made lean'.
The temptation to give this 'lean' part to the actor of
'lean' Cassius would be strong, if not irresistible, seeing
that the 80 lines between Cassius's exit and Ligarius's
entry afforded plenty of time for a change in make-up.
In the text the only alterations needed were in 2. 2,
where Cassius has but three words to say (line 109)
while Cæsar addresses two and a half lines (111–13)
to Ligarius. Substitute Publius for Cassius as the
character greeting and greeted by Cæsar in line 109, and
since the names are metrical equivalents no further
change would be required. As for the inconsistency of
Publius's role (a conspirator here and an aged panic-
stricken senator in 3. 1. 86–94), the audience might be
relied upon to overlook it. Yet clearly these little shifts
spring from changes of intention more likely to have
been the prompter's than afterthoughts of Shakespeare's,
though it is noticeable that he finds the name 'Publius'
useful at other points; v. notes 3. 1. 53; 4. 1. 4.

Coleridge similarly suggested that 'for want of actors
the part of some other conspirator was thrown into
Casca's'.[1] Certainly the character of Casca is a bundle

[1] *Coleridge's Shakesperian Criticism*, ed. T. M. Raysor, 1, 15.

contradictions. The humorous cynic, speaking prose
in 1. 2, becomes in 1. 3 a man quivering with superstitious fears, speaking verse. Dowden regards this as
an illustration of a 'higher art' than that of the ordinary
dramatist's consistency.[1] But 'if it were so', remarks
Granville-Barker,[2] 'the thing would still be very clumsily
done', adding—'it is doubtful whether he [the actor]
can make this "piece of higher art" very evident to an
audience'. And there are further inconsistencies. The
obsequious Casca at the beginning of 1. 2[3] consorts
oddly with the contemptuous narrator in ll. 215–95.
Again Brutus's description of him as 'blunt' and
Cassius's reference to 'tardy form', both apparently
used in contrast with 'quick mettle' (1. 2. 296–300),
square ill with Casca's very 'quick' account of the offer
and refusal of the crown. Again, the charge of being
'dull' and wanting the 'sparks of life that should be in a
Roman' (1. 3. 57) is as inapplicable to such a reporter
as could well be imagined. Finally, his impassioned
eulogy of Brutus (1. 3. 157 ff.) adds a finishing touch
of incongruity.[4] Is the explanation the doubling of parts
by one actor to meet stage necessities? Or is it, this time,
Shakespearian revision? If 1. 2. 215–95 were a piece of
re-writing or a later addition, most of these inconsistencies would be explained; and, though they set him
a problem the actor would have found compensation
in the increased interest and vitality of the character.

[1] *Shakespeare's Mind and Art*, p. 292.
[2] *Op. cit.* 83–4.   [3] See note 1. 2. 1.
[4] For related anomalies see head-note 1. 3.

NOTES

All significant departures from F. are recorded; the name of the text or edition in which the accepted reading first appeared being placed in brackets. Line-numeration for references to plays not yet issued in this edition is that found in Bartlett's *Concordance* and the *Globe Shakespeare*.

F. stands for the First Folio (1623); G. for Glossary; O.E.D. for *The Oxford English Dictionary*; S.D. for stage-direction; Sh. for Shakespeare and Shakespearian; Plut. for Plutarch's *Parallel Lives of Greeks and Romans* (c. A.D. 100); Sk. for *Sh.'s Plut.*, ed. W. W. Skeat, 1892. Quotations from North's translation of Plutarch are modernized in spelling and punctuation as in Sk., to whom page references are given for readers' convenience; but Sk. reprints 4th ed. of 1612, and in wording our quotations follow text of North in *Tudor Translations* (vols. XI and XII) ed. W. E. Henley, 1896, which reprints 1st ed., 1579.

The following is a list of the books cited with abridged titles: Amyot=*Vies des Hommes Illustres, Grecs et Romains*, transl. of Plut. by Jacques Amyot, 1559; Apperson=*English Proverbs and Proverbial Phrases* by G. L. Apperson, 1929; Appian=Appian's *Civil Wars* (Loeb *Classical Texts*); Barker=*Prefaces to Sh.* 1st Series, by H. Granville-Barker, 1927; C. A. H. =*Cambridge Ancient History*, vol. IX, 1932, vol. X, 1934; Camb.=*Cambridge Shakespeare*, ed. by W. Aldis Wright, 2nd ed. 1887; Chambers, *Wm. Sh.*, =*Wm. Sh.; Facts and Problems*, by E. K. Chambers, 1930; Cap.=ed. by Edward Capell, 1768; Clar.=*Clarendon Press* ed. by W. Aldis Wright, 1884; Coleridge=*Coleridge's Sh. Criticism*, ed. T. M. Raysor, 1930; Daniel=*Time-analysis of Sh.'s plays* by P. A. Daniel (New Sh. Soc.

Trans. 1877–9); *E.M.O.* = *Everyman Out of His Humour* by Ben Jonson; Franz = *Die Sprache Shakespeares* (4th ed.) by W. Franz, 1939; Furness = ed. in *Variorum Sh.* by H. H. Furness, 1913; Heath = *Revisal of Sh.'s Text* by B. Heath, 1768 (cited from Furness); Herford = *Eversley Sh.* ed. by C. H. Herford, 1901; Hunter = ed. by Mark Hunter (*College Classics Series*, ed. F. W. Kellett, Madras, 1900); J. = ed. by Samuel Johnson, 1765; Jonson = *Ben Jonson*, ed. Herford and Simpson, 1925– ; K. = ed. by G. L. Kittredge, 1939; Linthicum = *Costume in the Drama of Sh.* by M. C. Linthicum, 1936; MacCallum = *Sh.'s Roman Plays* by M. W. MacCallum, 1910; Madden = *The Diary of Master William Silence* by D. H. Madden, 1907; Mal. = *Variorum* ed. by Edward Malone and J. Boswell, 1821; Mason = *Comments on...Sh.'s Plays*, by J. M. Mason, 1788 (cited from Furness); Moulton = *Sh. as a Dramatic Artist*, by R. G. Moulton, 1901; *MSH.* = *The MS. of Sh.'s 'Hamlet'* by J. Dover Wilson, 1934; Nashe = *Works of Thomas Nashe*, ed. R. B. McKerrow, 1904; Noble = *Sh.'s Biblical Knowledge* by Richmond Noble, 1935; North = *Plutarch's Lives of the Noble Grecians and Romans, Englished by Sir Thomas North*, 1579; Palmer = *The Political Chars. of Sh.'s Plays*, by John Palmer, 1945; Raleigh = *Shakespeare* by Walter Raleigh (*Engl. Men of Letters*), 1926; Schmidt = *Sh.-Lexicon*, by A. Schmidt (3rd ed.), 1902; Simpson = *Sh.'s Punctuation* by Percy Simpson, 1911; Skillan = ed. in French's Acting Edition by George Skillan; Steev. = ed. by George Steevens, 1773; Sprague = *Sh. and the Actors* by A. C. Sprague, 1944; Syme = *The Roman Revolution* by Ronald Syme, 1939; V. = Pitt Press ed. by A. W. Verity.

Names of the Characters. List first given imperfectly by Rowe, later more fully by Theob. *Marullus* (> *Plut.*) is spelt 'Murellus' in F. *Publius* and *Lucius* (Brut.'s servant) are invented by Sh.; the rest come from Plut. In one case also Sh. takes from North a form divergent from the correct Lat. (found in Amyot) viz. *Decius Brutus* (for 'Decimus Brutus'); but he or F. printer changed North's (and Amyot's) 'Porcia', 'Laena' (Lat. Laenas), and 'Dardanus' to 'Portia', 'Lena', and 'Dardanius', while F. prints 'Antonio' for 'Antonius' four times, 'Octavio' twice, and on one occasion 'Labio' and 'Flauio'. For *Labeo* and *Flavius* (Brut.'s man), v. notes on 5. 3. 90 S.D., 108; for *Calphurnia* (Lat. Calpurnia) v. that on 1. 2. 1–11.

Acts and Scenes. F. contains Act divisions, but, after announcing 1. 1 as '*Actus Primus. Scæna Prima*', gives no subsequent scene divisions. These were introduced by edd. from Rowe onwards, but many of them interrupt the action where no real break in it or change of place occurs (v. head-notes, S.D. 1. 2, 2. 4, 3. 3, 4. 3, 5. 1).

Punctuation. Reasonably good on the whole, though not strikingly interesting. There are some fourteen cases where it appears to be definitely incorrect (see notes 1. 1. 24, 37–9; 1. 2. 166, 252; 1. 3.125, 129; 2. 1. 15, 330–1; 2. 4. 27–8; 3. 1. 284; 5. 1. 9–10, 102, 104–5; 5. 5. 33), which is not a large number comparatively.

Stage-directions. See p. 92. Only those in F. which require special comment have been recorded.

I. I.

PLUTARCH. Cæs. has just returned from his victorious but bloody campaign against the sons of Pompey and is about to celebrate a triumph, which 'did as much offend the Romans, and more, than anything that ever he had done before; because he had not overcome captains that were strangers, nor barbarous kings, but...the sons of the noblest man in Rome, whom fortune had overthrown'. (*Cæsar*,

Sk. 91.) But 'Cæsar's flatterers...beside many other ex-
ceeding and unspeakable honours they daily devised for
him, in the night-time they put diadems upon the heads of
his images, supposing thereby to allure the common people
to call him King instead of Dictator'. (*Brutus*, Sk. 112.)
'Those the two tribunes, Flavius and Marullus, went and
pulled down, and furthermore, meeting with them that
first saluted Cæsar as King, they committed them to prison.
The people followed them rejoicing at it, and called them
Brutes, because of Brutus, who had in the time driven
the kings out of Rome.' (*Cæsar*, Sk. 96.) Actually, Cæs.
celebrated the triumph over Pompey's sons in Oct. 45 B.C.,
while the date of the Lupercalia is 15 Feb. 44 B.C., and Plut.
deals with the two events quite separately. Sh. combines
them for dramatic purposes, and makes the tribunes partisans
of Pompey, for which Plut. gives no warrant; cf. note l. 64.

The Tribunes are disgruntled representatives of the
defeated Pompeians, not (as in *Coriolanus*) champions
of the people, to whom they here speak scornfully. The
scene, like other first scenes in Sh., introduces us to the
'underlying forces' of the play, viz. (i) the fickleness of
the Roman populace, (ii) the inevitability of 'Cæsarism'
as the solution of Rome's political problem. It shows us
the people as

thoroughly monarchical in sentiment. They have not the
smallest desire to be 'free' in the conspirators' sense. Thus,
even before we hear of the conspiracy, we see that such a
thing is bound to prove futile. (Hunter.)

Note Sh.'s skilful use of references to Pompey in this
and later scenes.

　　S.D. Locality (Cap.) Entry (F.) After 'commoners'
F. reads 'ouer the Stage', which Cap. interprets 'driving
them' (cf. l. 74).

　　3–6. *mechanical...profession...trade...carpenter*
see G. and *M.N.D.* 3. 2. 9.

　　4. *without the sign* Variously explained by edd. But

'the sign' is simply the leather apron; 'you ought not' Flav.'s insolence.

6. *Why, sir,* etc. F. heads the commoners' speeches in this scene *Car.* and *Cobl.* I follow Cap. and Camb. as more convenient in a text for readers.

10–11. *in respect...cobbler* He quibbles: 'I don't make shoes like a master-craftsman, I only mend them.' In Plut.'s *Brutus* (Sk. 113) Cass. speaks contemptuously of 'cobblers, tapsters or suchlike base mechanical people'.

13. *directly* i.e. without quibbling; cf. G. and 3. 3. 9.

16. *soles* (Knight, Camb.) F. 'foules'. Cf. *Merch.* 5. 1. 91.

17. *What trade, thou* etc. F. assigns to 'Flav.' But as Cap. notes, 'the immediate reply' and 'the reply to that reply' prove 'Mar.' to be the speaker; see note l. 60.

19–20. *out* = (*a*) angry, (*b*) out at heels.

21. *mean'st thou* The tribunes speak verse elsewhere; omit 'thou' and this line is also verse, as Steevens and Coleridge note.

26–7. *women's matters* Perhaps 'trades' omitted before 'women's'; perhaps equivocal; cf. *Ham.* 3. 2. 114 (note).

27. *withal I* (F.). Cf. *Mod. Lang. Rev.* Ap. 1953, p. 178 [1955].

28. *recover* (F.) Pope, Camb. etc. 're-cover'. v. G.

29–30. *As proper...neat's leather* Prov. = as fine (English-) men as ever walked. Patriotic people wore neat's leather instead of Spanish leather in order to encourage home industry (Linthicum, 239). *gone* v. G.

36 ff. *Wherefore rejoice?* etc. The poet Campbell thought these lines

among the most magnificent in the English language. They roll over my mind's ear like the loudest notes of a cathedral organ.

The speech and its effect upon the crowd prepare us

for Ant.'s greater speech in 3. 2. In Plut. the people are hostile to Cæsar and republican in sympathy (see head-note and Introd. p. xvii).

36–7. *home?...Rome* Not a rhyme; 'Rome' pron. 'room'; cf. 1. 2. 156 (note).

41–3. *Pompey? Many...oft | Have...windows*, (Rowe) F. 'Pompey many...oft? | Haue...Win-dowes?'

41–6. *Many a time...streets of Rome* Prob. suggested by the extraordinary scenes in London on the departure of Essex for Ireland (v. my Introd. to *Henry V*, p. ix). Plut. says nothing of popular enthusiasm at Pompey's triumph, Sept. 61 B.C., and Hunter notes that 'windows and chimney-tops suit the architecture of old London better than that of ancient Rome'.

55. *Pompey's blood* i.e. his sons, Gnaeus and Sextus, whom Cæsar had just defeated at Munda.

58. *intermit* i.e. stay the angel of death. Cf. Nashe (ed. McKerrow, II. 164. 30) 'beseeching with God to intermit his furie'.

60. *Go, go*, etc. 'Flav. adopts a much more conciliatory tone' than Mar. 'This confirms Cap.'s correction in l. 17.' (Hunter.)

62–4. *weep...shores of all*. See p. lii of my Introd. to *Titus*.

64. S.D. For 'melts' see next note. Shame at being convicted of ingratitude moves them here, as pity does in 3. 2.

65. *whe'r* F. 'where'=whether.

their basest mettle=their very base spirit. N.B. 'the basest metal', alchemically, was lead, which melts rapidly, as the crowd melted before the fire of the tribunes' indignation.

68–9. *images...ceremonies* v. G. 'ceremony' (i), and cf. 'trophies' (l. 73), 'scarfs' (1. 2. 286). Plut. (see head-note) speaks of 'diadems' on Cæs.'s 'images'.

Sh., wishing to connect the affair with the celebration of Cæs.'s triumph, decks the statues like images in church on saints' days. Cf. *1 Hen. IV*, 4. 1. 100.

71. *Lupercal* 15 Feb. See head-note (end) for Sh.'s hist. foreshortening. Cf. G. and note 1. 2. 8.

76–9. *These growing feathers...fearfulness*. Cæs. is pictured as a growing hawk, which, once become a long-winged falcon 'towering in her pride of place' (*Macb.* 2. 4. 14), would make all smaller birds 'couch down in fear' (*Hen. V*, 4. 2. 36), but might be rendered harm-less through 'the loss of a principal feather' from her wing. Cf. Madden, pp. 139–40, 151, 154–5; *Rich. II*, 2. 1. 292; *Son.* 78. 6; *Tit.* 4. 4. 84–7; *Lucr.* 506–7. Note also Dante, *Inf.* iv, 123, 'Cæsar with the falcon eye'.

1. 2.

PLUTARCH. (i) *The Lupercalia*. 'That day...divers noblemen's sons, young men (and some of them magistrates) ...run naked through the city, striking in sport them they meet in their way with leather thongs, hair and all on, to make them give place. And many noblewomen and gentle-women also...stand in their way and do put forth their hands to be stricken with the ferula, persuading themselves... being barren that it will make them to conceive with child. Cæsar sat to behold that sport upon the pulpit for orations, in a chair of gold, apparelled in triumphing manner. Antonius, who was consul at that time, was one of them that ran this holy course.' (*Cæsar*, Sk. 95–6.) Plut. gives no hint of any procession ('Cæsar sat to behold'); says nothing of Calpurnia here, or anywhere of her sterility; and, though referring to the legal heirs named in Cæsar's will (Sk. 98, 230), lays no stress on Cæsar's lack of a legitimate son.

(ii) *The soothsayer*. 'A certain soothsayer...had given Cæsar warning long time afore to take heed of the day of the Ides of March...for on that day he should be in great danger. That day being come, Cæsar going unto the Senate-house, and speaking merrily to the soothsayer, told him "The Ides of March be come": "so be they," softly answered the soothsayer, "but yet are they not past".' (*Cæsar*, Sk. 98.) This is merely cited as one of the 'strange and wonderful signs' before Cæsar's death (v. head-note 1. 3); by duplicating the encounter and attaching the first to his Lupercal procession, Sh. more than doubles the dramatic force of the incident.

(iii) *The dialogue* (ll. 25–177), introducing the two chief characters, defining their attitudes towards Cæs., and showing Cass. attempting to attach Brut. to the Liberators' cause. Derived in the main from the first seven paragraphs of *Brutus* (Sk. 105–12). Salient passages are: 'Marcus Brutus came of that Junius Brutus, for whom the ancient Romans made his statue of brass to be set up in the Capitol, with the images of the kings, holding a naked sword in his hand; because he had valiantly put down the Tarquins from their kingdom of Rome' (105). 'This Marcus Brutus...framed his manners of life by the rules of virtue and study of philosophy, and having employed his wit, which was gentle and constant, in attempting of great things, methinks he was rightly made and framed unto virtue' (105–6). 'Being moved with reason and discretion [he] did always incline to that which was good and honest....For by flattering of him a man could never obtain anything at his hands, nor make him to do that which was unjust' (109). 'I am persuaded that Brutus might indeed have come to have been the chiefest man of Rome, if he could have contented himself for a time to have been next unto Cæsar, and to have suffered his glory and authority, which he had gotten by his great victories, to consume with time. But Cassius, being a choleric man, and hating Cæsar privately more than he did the tyranny openly, he incensed Brutus against him. It is also reported that Brutus could evil away with [=ill put up with] the tyranny, and that Cassius hated the tyrant: making many complaints for the injuries he had done him. ...And this was the cause (as some do report) that made Cassius conspire against Cæsar. But this holdeth no water: for Cassius even from his cradle, could not abide any manner of tyrants.' He then relates how the boy Cass., incensed with a braggart at school, 'gave him two good wirts [blows] on the ear', and concludes: 'Such was Cassius' hot stirring nature' (111–12).

Plut. describes the winning over of Brut. thus: 'Now when Cassius felt his friends, and did stir them up against Cæsar: they all agreed and promised to take part with him, so Brutus were the chief of their conspiracy. For they told him...that by his only presence the fact [=deed] were holy and just.... Therefore Cassius, considering this matter with himself, did first of all speak to Brutus...[and] asked him if he were determined to be in the Senate-house the first day of the month of March, because he heard say that Cæsar's friends should move the council that day that Cæsar should be called King by the Senate. Brutus answered him, he would not be there. "But if we be sent for", said Cassius, "how then?" "For myself then", said Brutus, "I mean not to hold my peace, but to withstand it, and rather die than lose my liberty." Cassius being bold, and taking hold of this word: "Why", quoth he, "what Roman is he alive that will suffer thee to die for the liberty? What? Knowest thou not that thou art Brutus?...The noblest and best citizens...be thou well assured...specially require (as a due debt unto them) the taking away of the tyranny, being fully bent to suffer any extremity for thy sake, so that thou wilt show thyself to be the man thou art taken for, and that they hope thou art." Thereupon he kissed Brutus and embraced him: and so each taking leave of other, they went both to speak with their friends about it.' (Sk. 112–13.) See also note ll. 32–4. From this Sh. departs widely, while taking hints here and there; e.g. the opening question is much the same in both accounts; in both Cass. appeals to Brutus' high reputation with those 'of the best respect in Rome', and reminds him of his ancestor; finally in both Brut. reveals his determination to withstand tyranny. On the other hand, though Sh.'s Cass. begins like Plut.'s, he goes off into a long impeachment of Cæs.'s personal courage which directly contradicts everything the biographer says about Cæs. elsewhere (v. Introd. p. xxviii).

(iv) *Cæsar suspects Brutus and Cassius* (ll. 190–214). 'Cæsar also had Cassius in great jealousy [suspicion], and suspected him much: whereupon he said on a time to his friends, "What will Cassius do, think ye? I like not his pale looks". Another time when Cæsar's friends complained unto him of Antonius and Dolabella, that they pretended [plotted] some mischief towards him: he answered them again, "As for those fat men and smooth-combed heads", quoth he, "I never reckon of them; but those pale-visaged and carrion-lean people, I fear them most," meaning Brutus and Cassius.' (*Cæsar*, Sk. 97.)

(v) *Antony offers Cæsar a crown* (ll. 215–74). Plut. gives two closely similar accounts: *Cæsar* (Sk. 96) and *Antonius* (Sk. 163–4). Sh. seems to have followed the second, which runs: 'Antonius, being one among the rest that was to run, leaving the ancient ceremonies...ran to the tribune where Cæsar was set, and carried a laurel crown in his hand, having a royal band or diadem wreathed about it, which in old time was the ancient mark and token of a king. When he was come to Cæsar, he made his fellow-runners with him lift him up, and so he did put his laurel crown upon his head, signifying thereby that he had deserved to be king. But Cæsar, making as though he refused it, turned away his head. The people were so rejoiced at it, that they all clapped their hands for joy. Antonius again did put it on his head; Cæsar again refused it; and thus they were striving off and on a great while together. As oft as Antonius did put this laurel crown unto him, a few of his followers rejoiced at it: and as oft as Cæsar refused it, all the people together clapped their hands.... Cæsar, in a rage, arose out of his seat, and plucking down the collar of his gown from his neck he showed it naked, bidding any man strike off his head that would. [In *Cæsar* (Sk. 95) this last incident is referred to another occasion and related in words that come closer to Sh.'s: 'thereupon also Cæsar rising departed home to his house, and tearing open his doublet-collar, making his neck bare, he cried aloud to his friends, "that his throat was ready to offer to any man that would come and cut it"'.] This laurel crown was afterwards put upon the head of one of Cæsar's statues or images, the which one of the tribunes plucked off.... Howbeit, Cæsar did turn them out of their offices for it.'

(vi) *Cassius' soliloquy* (ll. 309–23). Hints for this were
taken from *Brutus* (Sk. 110–11): 'For if he had listed, he
[Brutus] might have been one of Cæsar's chiefest friends
and of greatest authority and credit about him. Howbeit,
Cassius' friends did dissuade him from it...and prayed
him to beware of Cæsar's sweet enticements, and to fly his
tyrannical favours: the which they said Cæsar gave him, not
to honour his virtue, but to weaken his constant mind,
framing it to the bent of his bow.'

S.D. F.+'in...music' (Rowe; cf. l. 16)+'reclining
...litter' (v. Introd. p. xxix, n. 2)+'a great...among
them' (Camb.). For some reason all edd. except K.
omit 'after...Flavius'. The tribunes provide a background of contempt. For 'Decius' see 'Characters',
p. 100. Cap. and edd. unnecess. begin a fresh sc. here.

1–11. *Calphurnia...out* Cf. Introd. p. xxix. N.B.
'our elders say' shows Cæs. 'half ashamed' of his belief
in this 'old-wives' tale' (see Palmer, p. 37 and cf.
below, note 2. 1. 195–7), while 'leave no ceremony
out' shows the belief is serious.

The sp. 'Calphurnia' (Lat. Calpurnia) also occurs
in *Cæsar's Revenge*, v. Introd. p. xxvi.

1. S.D. from Cap. *Peace, ho!* etc. Cf. l. 14.
Contrast Casca's attitude later; and see pp. 96–7.

3. *Antonius'* (Pope) F. 'Antonio's'.

4. *Antonius* (Pope) F. 'Antonio'. V. pp. 94–5, 100.

6–9. *Forget...curse* See head-note *Plutarch* (i).

8. *this holy chase* 'this holy course' (Plut.); v. G.
'chase'.

11. S.D. From Cap. (Camb. reads 'Flourish').

17. *Cæsar...hear* By this use of the 3rd pers.
Cæs. 'collaborates, as it were, in his own deification'
(Palmer, p. 37). See also Ayres, *P.M.L.A.* xxv, 183–227.

18. *Beware...March* 'In Plut. [v. supra] the
warning is more precise; here the vague sense of un-
defined peril inspires greater awe' (V.).

19. *A soothsayer...March* In making this Brut.'s first speech Sh. is deliberately ominous.

24. *He is...pass* Also ominous, and theatrically very effective.

S.D. 'Sennet' (v. G.) from F., which continues 'Exeunt. Manet Brut. & Caff.'

28–9. *gamesome...quick spirit* Contemptuous; 'quick' is a pregnant quibble, referring to Ant.'s speed in running, lively disposition, and prompt compliance (v. ll. 9–10); 'gamesome' also=(*a*) fond of sport, (*b*) merry. The whole speech breathes disgust at the sc. just witnessed.

33–4. *I have not...to have* Plut. speaks of a coolness between Brut. and Cass. arising out of competition for a praetorship, which Cæs. granted to Brut.; 'the first cause of Cass.'s malice against Cæs.' (*Brutus*, Sk. 110–11). Sh. adopts the coolness, assigns it to a deeper cause, and uses it to introduce a theme later enlarged upon (4. 3).

37. *veiled my look* turned from you. Did Sh. intend 'vailed' = cast down?

40. *passions...difference* 'conflicting emotions' (Clar.).

46. *poor Brutus...at war* A leading theme of the play. Cf. notes on 2. 1. 63–9.

52–8. *No...shadow* Mal. cites Sir John Davies, *Nosce Teipsum*, 1599, st. 48:

> Mine eyes, which view all objects, nigh and far,
> Look not into this little world of mine,
> *Nor see my face*, wherein they fixéd are.

Cf. also sts. 23 and 27; even more to the point. Sh. develops the thought further in *Troil.* 3. 3. 96–111.

58. *your shadow* i.e. yourself as others see you.

59. *Where* v. G. *respect* v. G.

60. *Except immortal Cæsar* i.e. who, being im-

mortal, is of course of 'best respect', above all men. Cass.'s first word of Cæs. is bitterly sarcastic.

62. *his eyes* i.e. the speaker's.

66. *Therefore, good Brutus* He ignores Brut.'s question.

69–70. *discover to yourself* etc. Yet all he actually does is to stress Cæs.'s unworthiness, and Brut.'s public duty. But, as Hunter well notes, both men 'are moving to the same end, the murder of Cæs., but...each is wrapt up in himself', and neither attends to the other. Thereby Sh. skilfully contrives that each reveals himself to the audience.

71. *jealous on* suspicious of.

72. *laughter* (F.) Rowe and edd. 'laugher' (= jester). Some explain F. as = laughing-stock (cf. 4. 3. 49). But the context has solely to do with (pretended) loving, and 'lover' (conj. Herr, *ap.* Furness, and Hudson) would fit exactly; i.e. 'everyone's friend', Cass. would imply, 'is no one's friend'. Perhaps 'loffer' in the copy (fr. 'loff', obs. form of both 'love' and 'laugh') was misinterpreted.

77. *profess myself* make professions of friendship; cf. *Wint.* 1. 2. 456.

78. S.D. From F. 'All through the conversation between Brut. and Cass. the shouting of the mob reminds us [or rather 'forewarns us'; J.D.W.] of the sc....going on in the Capitol' (Moulton, p. 190).

86–7. *Set honour...indifferently* Much discussed. I take 'in one eye' = on the one hand, and 'indifferently' = with indifference. Warburton conj. 'death' for 'both', upon which Coleridge (1, 14) commented:

I prefer the old reading. There are three things here, the public good, the individual Brut.'s honour, and his death. The two latter so balanced each other that he could decide for the first by equipoise. Nay. (the thought *growing*), honour had more weight than death. That Cassius understood it as Warburton is the beauty of Cassius as contrasted with Brutus.

And J. has much the same explanation. I paraphrase: 'I would sacrifice both life and reputation for the good of Rome, though God knows I value my personal integrity more than life itself.' Thus Sh. prepares us for the death of Brut. in 5. 5.

92. *honour...story* But the 'general good', not 'honour', had been the subject of Brut.'s. Cf. Coleridge's comment above. Cass. identifies his own honour with the public good, and by 'honour' he means standing or status in Rome, as he now explains.

95–6. *I had as lief...myself* Cf. head-note *Plutarch* (iii).

99–128. *Endure the winter's cold...sick girl* See Introd. p. xxviii.

109. *hearts of controversy* 'hearts eager for combat' (Schmidt) with the stream (or for our match).

112–14. *as Aeneas...bear* Cf. *Aeneid*, II, 721 ff. and *2 Hen. VI*, 5. 2. 62.

122. *coward lips...fly* Cæs.'s pale lips call up the image of a cowardly soldier deserting his colours, the more pertinent 'that the cowardice of a *soldier* is the subject of the narrative' (Whiter, *Commentary on Sh.* 1774, p. 107; *ap.* Furness).

125–6. *that bade...books* Suggested by Plut., who speaks (Sk. p. 44) of the brilliance of Cæs.'s eloquence rivalling that of Cicero himself.

127. *Titinius* See 4. 2 and 5. 3.

129. *temper* See G. and Introd. p. xxviii.

135. *man* The word shows that Cass. is growing more excited, rather than 'more familiar' (Clar.) or more impatient 'that Brut. is so little moved' (Hunter).

136. *Colossus* v. G.

139. *some time* (F 3) F. 'ſometime'.

140–1. *not in our stars...ourselves* The stars, potent

as they are, cannot compel, for the human will remains free. Cf. *Rom.* 5. 3. 111–12, and Sherrington, *Man on his Nature* (1940), p. 53.

142–3. *what...name* Cf. *Rom.* 2. 2. 38–49.

146–7. *conjure...a spirit* Ironical. 'As soon as' = as little as. Spirits could only be raised in the name of a god. Cf. Greene, *Friar Bacon*, l. 289. Cass., as l. 148 shows, is thinking again of Cæs. the 'god' (ll. 116, 121).

154. *say, till now*, F. 'say (till now)'.

155. *walls* (Rowe) F. 'Walkes'. A corruption prob. due to the influence of 'talked' (l. 154). Sh. himself would not have been guilty of 'such a disagreeable assonance', while 'the word "encompassed"...points to "the walls" as the true reading.' (Clar.)

156. *Rome...and room enough* Cf. *K. John*, 3. 1. 180 (note). Sh. rhymes 'Rome' with 'doom' and 'groom' (*Lucr.* 715, 1614).

159. *a Brutus once* See head-note (iii). Mod. historians regard M. Brutus's descent from Junius Brutus as mythical. But both M. Brutus and his contemporaries believed it.

160. *eternal* v. G.

162. *That...jealous* Brut. only now replies to Cass.'s words at ll. 71 ff. Has he been lost in thought meanwhile, or are ll. 79–161 a later addition on the part of Sh.? For 'jealous' v. G.

166. *not, so with...you*, (Theo.) F. 'not ſo (with ...you)'.

172–5. *Brutus...us* Clar. notes the cold calm of this and cites 4. 3. 111–2, and *Troil.* 3. 3. 257.

176–7. *I am glad...Brutus* 'Cass. is disappointed that Brut. has been apparently so little moved by his passionate appeal.' (Hunter.)

177. S.D. I retain F. position; Dyce, Camb. etc. transfer to l. 181. N.B. There is no music this time; Cæs. is angry.

179. *sleeve* Contrast l. 215; togas had no sleeves. Cf. note, l. 266.

183–8. *The angry spot* etc. A picture of an oriental court when its master is displeased.

185–8. *Cicero...senator* 'From Sh.'s own imagination' (Clar.); but shrewd, cf. note 2. 1. 150–2.

188. *senator* (Walker) F. 'senators'. With 'some' the plur. awkward.

190. *Antonius* (Rowe etc.) F. 'Antonio'. See notes ll. 3, 4.

192–5. *Let me...dangerous* See head-note (iv).

199. *my name* a being called Cæsar; cf. l. 212.

204. *hears no music* Cf. *Merch.* 5. 1. 83–5. A Platonic doctrine going back to Pythagoras. Brutus, with a harmonious temperament (see 5. 5. 73–5 and note), loves music.

211–12. *I rather...Cæsar* This sounds particularly ridiculous with Cass.'s stories of his pusillanimity fresh in our minds. Cf. Introd. p. xxviii.

213. *this ear is deaf* The infirmity, invented by Sh., is significantly introduced to us immediately after Cæs. has referred to himself as almost divine. It shows, too, that Cæs. like Cass. 'hears no music'.

221. *a crown offered* See head-note (v). Plut.'s 'laurel crown' is a less solid affair than Sh.'s Tudor coronet.

245. *hooted* (J.) F. 'howted'. Cf. *L.L.L.* 4. 2. 61. The word expresses Casc.'s contempt for the mob, and not their disapproval of Cæs.'s action; cf. next note.

246–7. *sweaty...breath* cf. *Cor.* 4. 6. 129–32.

night-caps 'exclusively masculine wear...sometimes worn by old men in the street, but a 'day-worn night-cap' usually indicated...ill-health'. (Linthicum, 227.)

249–52. *swooned...swoon* (Rowe) F. 'ſwoonded... ſwound'. Another addition by Sh., as is 'foamed at mouth' (l. 253), thus presenting the unpleasant side of the 'falling-sickness' or epilepsy, several times mentioned by Plut., though not in connexion with the Lupercalia.

252. *But, soft...swoon?* 'Ironical' (K.). Cf. ll. 97–131.

255. *like: he* (Camb.) F. 'like he'.

266. *plucked...doublet* See head-note (v). The 'doublet' comes from North; it is 'robe' in Amyot, and in Plut. ἱμάτιον. For other references to costume see notes l. 179 above; 1.1.7; 2.1.73. The usual assumption that Romans wore Eliz. costume on Sh.'s stage is dubious. The extant sketch of a scene from *Titus Andronicus*, dated 1595 (v. frontispiece to my ed. and *Shakespeare Survey*, 1, pp. 17–22) shows quasi-classical dress; and Ben Jonson's knowledge would prob. prevent a 'doublet' being worn in 1599. Sh. uses the word because North did, and in 'unbracéd' (1.3.48; 2.1.262) prob. implies it again. Sylvester, *Du Bartas his Divine Weeks*, 1605 (Second Week, 'Handicrafts') dresses Adam himself in hat and doublet.

267. *of any occupation* (*a*) 'of action' (Grant White), (*b*) 'of any trade' (Herford), (*c*) 'one of the plebeians to whom he offered his throat' (J.).

269. *so he fell* A reference to the falling-sickness in Plut., immediately after the passage from *Cæsar* cited in head-note (v), prob. accounts for Sh. giving Cæs. a fit at this moment (cf. note ll. 249–52); an unfortunate moment for an aspirant to the crown, claiming divine honours.

275. *stabbed their mothers* Prob. equivocal; cf. *2 Hen. IV*, 2.1.13 (note and G.).

277. *away?* (Theob.) F. 'away.'

280. *Greek* Plut. (*Cicero*, 'Tudor Trans.' v, 317) relates that when Cicero first came to Rome

he was not greatly esteemed; for they commonly called him the Græcian, and scholar, which are two words the which

the artificers (and such base mechanical people at Rome)
have ever ready at their tongues' end.

The point here is that Cic. made some caustic remark
which he thought it discreet to veil in a classical tongue
(but which a few highbrow friends of his understood
and smiled at).

286. *Marullus and Flavius* etc. See head-note to 1. 1
and 1. 2 (end of v).

291. *dine* Dinner was a midday meal in Sh.'s day.

296. *blunt* v. G. and note l. 301 below.

297. *quick mettle* sharp enough. Cf. G. 'mettle',
and notes 1. 1. 65; 1. 2. 309–23.

300. *tardy form* affectation of stupidity.

301. *sauce...wit* Cf. G. 'sauce' and *Lear*, 2. 2.
101–3. But there is some contradiction here which
may be due to revision, v. 'Note on Copy', pp. 96–7.

302. *digest* (F 3) F. 'difgeſt'. An obs. sp.

308. *world* state of affairs; cf. 5. 5. 22.

309–23. *Well, Brutus...endure* Cass.'s first soliloquy, like Brut.'s (2. 1. 10–34), is unhappily subject to
debate. J., Cap., Furness, Hunter take 'he' (l. 315)
as Cæs., in which case ll. 309–16 express the fear,
inspired by Brut.'s tepid reception of his appeal (v. ll.
176–7 note), that Cæs. is corrupting his 'honourable
metal' by humouring him. Most critics, however, think
'he' is Brut., in which case 'the whole speech is occupied
with the speaker's success in cajoling Brut. and with
plans for cajoling him and shaping him still further'
(Hudson). See also Palmer (p. 5), who interprets the
speech as the cynical reflections of a 'realist' politician.
I agree with J. etc. for two reasons: (i) that it obviously
derives, as Hunter notes, from a passage in Plut. (see
head-note vi) in which the friends of Cass. warn Brut.
against Cæs.'s 'sweet enticements' and 'tyrannical
favours', and (ii) that I cannot believe Sh. meant Cass.
to be a 'cynic' at any time, though he is more of a

'realist' than Brut. Read '*Caesar*' for '*Cassius*' (l. 315),
as Mr A. F. Giles suggests to me, and all is plain,
while 'Caes.' might easily be mistaken for 'Cass.' in
MS. Cf. notes 3. 1. 31; 4. 2. 50–2.

309–11. *noble...disposed* Alchem. imagery (cf.
note 1. 1. 65). The 'noble' metal, gold, could not be
'wrought from that it is disposed'.

314. *bear me hard*, v. G. 'bear' and cf. 2. 1. 215;
3. 1. 158, together with *R. III*, 2. 1. 57 'hardly borne'.

1. 3.

PLUTARCH. 'Certainly destiny may easier be foreseen
than avoided considering the strange and wonderful signs
that were said to be seen before Cæsar's death.' He then
names 'fires in the element [=sky]', 'spirits running up and
down in the night', 'solitary birds to be seen at noon-
days sitting in the great market-place', 'divers men...going
up and down in fire', and 'a slave of the soldiers that did
cast a marvellous burning flame out of his hand, in so much
as they that saw it thought he had been burnt, but when the
fire was out it was found he had no hurt'. (*Cæsar*, Sk. 97.)
Sh. adds the escaped lion and the panic-stricken women.

P. A. Daniel posits the interval of a month, 15 Feb.
(Lupercalia) to 15 March (Ides of March), between
scenes 2 and 3, and notes that 2. 1. 61–5 implies 'a long
period of mental agony' and 2. 1. 49–50 a similar
period, while 1. 3 and 2. 1 belong to the same night.
On the other hand, 'brought you Cæsar home?' (l. 1)
is clearly meant to suggest 'home' from the Lupercalia,
i.e. a few hours only after 1. 2. In a word, we are dealing
with 'double time' (see Introd. p. vii, n. 1). Yet that will
not explain all, e.g. (i) the striking difference between
Casca in 1. 2 and Casca in 1. 3 (see 'Note on Copy',
p. 97); (ii) the fact that Cass., who asks Casca to dinner
at 1. 2. 289–93, obviously to enlist his support, has
forgotten all about this in 1. 3 when he actually succeeds

in doing so; (iii) his very cautious approach to Casca here after the latter has professed himself ready to cut Cæs.'s throat at 1. 2. 267–9; (iv) why he should not mention Brut. among 'the noblest-minded Romans' (1. 3. 122) when they had all three been so recently talking together about Cæs. and the offer of the crown; or (v) why Casca, contemptuous about Cicero at 1. 2. 279 ff., should be effusive with him in 1. 3 (see 'Note on Copy' pp. 96–7).

S.D. F. 'Thunder and Lightning. Enter Caska and Cicero'. Rowe and Capell supply the rest.

1–40. *Good even...Cicero* Cf. the omen-scene (2. 4) in *Macb.*; but this is before, that after, the assassination of a prince.

3. *sway* O.E.D. and edd. gloss 'motion of a rotating or revolving body', and cite Chaucer, *Man of Lawe's Tale*, l. 296, etc. But that refers to the firmament with its 'diurnal swegh', this to the earth, which to Sh. and his contemps. was the only fixed thing in the universe, though its surface might quake in times of portent. Thus 'sway' must here=realm, rule, as usual in Sh. (cf. *1 Hen. IV*, 3. 1. 16).

5–28. *I have seen...shrieking* For these prodigies and those at 2. 2. 17 ff. (v. note), cf. Nashe's description of the prodigies that 'overhung the element' before the Fall of Jerusalem (ed. McKerrow, II, 60–2) and Marlowe, *Lucan*, bk. I, 554–82.

6. *rived the knotty oaks* Cf. *Temp.* 1. 2. 295.

7–8. *Th'ambitious...clouds* Cf. *Temp.* 1. 2. 2–4; *2 Hen. IV*, 3. 1. 23–4.

14. *more* 'else' (Craik). Politely contemptuous. A gale and a few meteors!—can't you tell me of anything really striking?

15. *you know...sight* 'A graphic touch' added by Sh. (Clar.).

21. *glazed* (F., Hunter). Rowe and most edd.

'glared'. O.E.D. supports 'glazed' (v. G.), still found
in Devon and Cornwall (dial.). Yet 'glared' is more
emphatic; and it would be easy for a z to stray into the
compositor's r-box.

22–3. *drawn...heap* huddled into a crowd.

26. *the bird of night* Lat. 'noctua', the screech-
owl; cf. *Macb.* 2. 2. 4.

29–30. *say...natural* As the Epicureans might,
and as Cicero implies in the next speech. Cf. *All's
Well* 2. 3. 1–6.

32. *climate...point upon* Astrol. terms, v. G.; for
'climate' cf. Browne, *Religio Medici*, II, §1, 'I was
born in the eighth climate, but seem for to be framed
and constellated unto all'.

33. *strange-disposed time* extraordinary weather.

34. *after their fashion* each in his own way.

35. *Clean from* clean contrary to. *purpose* =
meaning.

37. *Antonius* (Pope) F. 'Antonio' cf. pp. 95, 100.

39–40. *this disturbed...in* i.e. this is not a night
to be out in.

41. *Who's there?* Cf. *Ham.* 1. 1. 1. Such questions
darkened Sh.'s stage for his audience.

46–52. *For my part...of it.* At 5. 1. 76–8 (v. note)
Cass. professes himself an Epicurean who did not
'credit things that do presage'.

48. *unbraced* Cf. 2. 1. 262, *Ham.* 2. 1. 75 and note
1. 2. 266.

49–50. *thunder-stone...lightning* Cf. *Cymb.* 4. 2.
270–1; *Lear* 4. 7. 33–5; and G. 'cross'.

54. *part* v. G.

56. *astonish* v. G.

57–9. *You are dull...use not* This contradicts 1. 2.
296–300, but agrees with 'blunt' (1. 2. 296). See
'Note on Copy', p. 97.

60. *put on fear* Cf. *Ado*, 4. 1. 144 'attired in won-

der', *Macb.* 1. 7. 35–6, 2. 3. 133 and *Lucr.* 1601. For *cast* v. G.

63. *ghosts* Cf. Plut. (Sk. p. 97) 'spirits running up and down in the night'.

64. *Why...kind* Poss. a line is lost after this.

65. *Why...calculate* (F.) Mitford, Camb. and most edd. read 'men fool' (vb.), for 'men, fools'. But the meaning of F. is plain: so obvious and so numerous are the portents that any dotard, fool or infant can interpret them; v. G. 'calculate'.

67. *preforméd faculties* original qualities or virtues.

68. *monstrous* abnormal. *shall* 'will certainly' (K.).

69. *infused...spirits* imparted these qualities.

75. *the lion...Capitol* Not necessarily the same as at l. 20 (before Cass. entered). References to the lions in the royal menagerie at the Tower were frequent at this period; cf. *Gent.* 2. 1. 26 (note).

77. *prodigious* v. G.   78. *eruptions* v. G.

79. *'Tis...Cassius?* In this childish questioner we seem to have a 'blunt' Casca.

83. *governed* Cf. *Merch.* 4. 1. 133–4.

84. *Our yoke and sufferance* the patience with which we put up with this slavery.

85–8. *the senators...Italy* This proposal, prob. the deciding cause of Cæs.'s death (v. *C.A.H.* IX, 737–8), is mentioned casually three times in different connexions by Plut. (Sk. 94–5, 99, 112). Sh. borrows from the second of these, where Dec. Brut., persuading Cæs. to go to the Senate, declared they 'were ready...to proclaim him *King* of all the provinces of the empire of Rome *out of Italy* and that *he should wear his crown in all other places both by sea and land*'. Historically the pretext was that Cæs. was about to set out for Parthia to avenge the overthrow and death of Crassus, and that acc. to the Sibylline books Parthia could only be over thrown by an army led by a king (Sk. 94–5).

90. *Cassius...Cassius* Furness notes the 'curious resemblance' with Kyd's *Cornelia*, 4. 1. 147–50:

> But know, while Cassius hath one drop of blood
> To feed this worthless body that you see,
> What reck I death to do so many good?
> In spite of Cæsar, Cassius will be free.

Cf. Introd. pp. xxv–xxvi.

101–2. *bondman...cancel* Cf. G., *Macb.* 3. 2. 49, Apperson, p. 140, and *1 Hen. IV*, 3. 2. 157—'the end of life cancels all bands'.

106. *hinds* v. G.   108. *trash* v. G.

114. *My answer...made* 'I shall be called to account...for seditious words' (J.).

118. *factious...griefs* v. G.   123. *undergo* v. G.

125. *know, by this they* (Rowe) F. 'know by this, they'.

126. *Pompey's porch* v. G. Scene of Cæs.'s death in Plut. (Sk. 116). Sh., transferring that event to the Capitol, makes the porch a rendezvous for the conspirators. Cf. note l. 147.

128. *complexion...element* v. G.; cf. *Ric. II*, 3. 2. 194.

129. *In favour's like* (J.) F. 'Is Fauors, like'.

130. *bloody-fiery* (Walker, Hunter) F. 'bloodie, fierie'. The double 'most' and the earlier description of the 'complexion' virtually prove the hyphen.

131. *close* aside, out of sight.

132. *by his gait* Cf. note l. 41, and 'Who's that?' (l. 134).

143. *praetor's chair* See note l. 145.

144. *may but find it* alone can find it.

145. *set...with wax* Cf. Plut. (Sk. 112) quoted in 2. 1 head-note (ii). The affixing of scrolls to monuments was an Eliz. practice; cf. *Ado*, 5. 3. 9, *Hen. V*, 1. 2. 234.

147. *Repair...porch* Clearly the conspirators assemble at the 'porch' before calling upon Brut. Yet

ll. 154–5, 162–4, suggest that Cass. and Casca go to
Brut. first.

157–60. *O, he...worthiness* How unlike the Casca
of 1. 2 again!

158–60. *And that...worthiness* Much as the
Archb.'s support 'turns insurrection to religion' in
2 Hen. IV (1. 1. 201). But cf. Plut. (Sk. 112): 'by his
only presence the fact were holy and just'.

159. *like...alchemy* Cf. *Son.* 114, and *K. John*,
3. 1. 77.

2. 1.

PLUTARCH. (i) *Brutus' soliloquy* (ll. 10–34). Suggestions
for this prob. come from *Cæsar* (Sk. 45), in which Plut.
notes that Cæs.'s 'enemies suffered him to run on, till by
little and little he was grown to be of great strength and
power', and 'when they had thus given him the bridle to
grow to this greatness...they could not then pull him back,
though indeed in sight it would turn one day to the destruction of the whole state and commonwealth of Rome'.

(ii) '*Brutus, thou sleep'st*' (ll. 46–58). 'His friends....by
many bills also did openly call and procure him to do that
he did. For under the image of his ancestor Junius Brutus
(that drave the Kings out of Rome) they wrote: "O that it
pleased the gods thou wert now alive, Brutus!" And again,
"that thou wert here among us now!" His tribunal or
chair, where he gave audience during the time he was
Praetor, was full of such bills: "Brutus, thou art asleep, and
art not Brutus indeed."' (*Brutus*, Sk. 112.) Cf. 'they
durst not come to him themselves...but in the night did
cast sundry papers into the Praetor's seat' etc. (*Cæsar*,
Sk. 97).

(iii) '*I have not slept*' (ll. 4, 61–9; cf. 1. 2. 46, 'poor
Brutus with himself at war'). Plut. notes the sleeplessness,
but assigns it to mere anxiety for the success of the enterprise
(see below §v).

(iv) *The conspirators' meeting* (ll. 70–228) Sh.'s invention.
But see *Brutus* (Sk. 113–14). Cass. and Brut. after their
talk (see 1. 2 head-note iii) 'began to feel all their acquaint-

ance whom they trusted, and laid their heads together, consulting upon it, and did not only pick out their friends but all those also whom they thought stout enough to attempt any desperate matter and that were not afraid to lose their lives. For this cause they durst not acquaint Cicero with their conspiracy, although he was a man whom they loved dearly and trusted best: for they were afraid that he being a coward by nature, and age also having increased his fear, he would quite turn and alter all their purpose and quench the heat of their enterprise.' The highly important point of the sparing of Antony Sh. took from *Brutus* (Sk. 119, see below note ll. 156–91) and from *Antonius* (Sk. 164), in which Plut., first noting that 'Brutus and Cassius...fell into a consort with their trustiest friends to execute their enterprise, but yet stood doubtful whether they should make Antonius privy to it or not', continues: 'after that they consulted whether they should kill Antonius with Cæsar. But Brutus would in no wise consent to it, saying that venturing on such an enterprise as that for the maintenance of law and justice, it ought to be clear of all villainy.' And in *Brutus* he writes of 'the wonderful faith and secrecy of the conspirators' [marginal heading] that 'having never taken oaths together, nor taken or given any caution or assurance, nor binding themselves one to another by any religious oaths, they all kept the matter so secret to themselves, and could so cunningly handle it, that notwithstanding the gods did reveal it by manifest signs and tokens from above and by predictions of sacrifices, yet all this would not be believed'. (Sk. 114.)

(v) *The Portia episode* (ll. 233–309). The source passage, which runs straight on from that just quoted, is followed very closely by Sh., though as ever with significant changes. 'Now Brutus, who knew very well that for his sake all the noblest, valiantest, and most courageous men of Rome did venture their lives, weighing with himself the greatness of the danger: when he was out of his house, he did so frame and fashion his countenance and looks that no man could discern he had anything to trouble his mind. But when night came that he was in his own house, then he was clean changed: for either care did wake him against his will when he would have slept, or else oftentimes of himself he fell into such deep thoughts of this enterprise, casting in his mind all the dangers that might happen: that his wife, lying by him, found that there was some marvellous great matter that troubled his mind, not being wont to be in that taking, and that he could not well determine with himself.

'His wife Porcia (as we have told you before) was the daughter of Cato, whom Brutus married being his cousin, not a maiden, but a young widow after the death of her first husband Bibulus, by whom she had also a young son called Bibulus, who afterwards wrote a book of the acts and gests of Brutus, extant at this present day. This young lady, being excellently well seen in philosophy, loving her husband well, and being of a noble courage as she was also wise: because she would not ask her husband what he ailed before she had made some proof by her self: she took a little razor, such as barbers occupy to pare men's nails, and, causing all her maids and women to go out of her chamber, gave herself a great gash withal in her thigh, that she was straight all of a gore blood: and incontinently after a vehement fever took her, by reason of the pain of her wound. Then perceiving her husband was marvellously out of quiet, and that he could take no rest, even in her greatest pain of all she spake in this sort unto him: "I being, O Brutus", said she, "the daughter of Cato, was married unto thee; not to be thy bed-fellow and companion in bed and at board only, like a harlot, but to be partaker also with thee of thy good and evil fortune. Now for thyself, I can find no cause of fault in thee touching our match: but for my part, how may I show my duty towards thee and how much I would do for thy sake, if I cannot constantly bear a secret mischance or grief with thee, which requireth secrecy and fidelity? I confess that a woman's wit commonly is too weak to keep a secret safely: and yet, Brutus, good education and the company of virtuous men have some power to reform the defect of nature. And for myself, I have this benefit moreover that I am the daughter of Cato, and wife of Brutus. This notwithstanding, I did not trust to any of these things before, until that now I have found by experience that no pain or grief whatsoever can overcome me." With those words she showed him her wound on her thigh, and told him what she had done to prove herself. Brutus was amazed to hear what she said unto him, and lifting up his hands to heaven, he besought the gods to give him the grace he might bring his enterprise to so good pass, that he might be found a husband worthy of so noble a wife as Porcia: so he then did comfort her the best he could.'

(vi) *Caius Ligarius* (ll. 310–34). Cf. *Brutus* (Sk.113): 'Now amongst Pompey's friends, there was one called Caius Ligarius, who had been accused unto Cæsar for taking part with Pompey, and Cæsar discharged him. But Ligarius thanked not Cæsar so much for his discharge, as he was offended with him for that he was brought in danger by his tyrannical power; and therefore in his heart he was always his mortal enemy, and was besides very familiar with Brutus, who went to see him being sick in his bed, and said unto him: "O Ligarius, in what a time art thou sick!" Ligarius rising up in his bed, and taking him by the right hand, said unto him: "Brutus," said he, "if thou hast any great enterprise in hand worthy of thyself, I am whole."'

S.D. F. 'Enter Brutus in his Orchard'. See G. 'orchard'.

2–3. *I cannot...day* Raleigh (p. 122) notes

The whole sc. is heavy with the sense of night and the darkness of conspiracy. Yet the effect is produced by nothing but the spoken words and the gestures of the players.

Cf. ll. 2–7, 39, 44–5, 77–81, 101–11, 191–2, 221, 229–33, 235–7, 261–7, 277–8 for Sh.'s constant preoccupation with this effect.

10–34. *It must be by his death* etc. Cf. Introd. pp. xxx–xxxi and 2.1 head-note (i). For the monosyllabic opening sentence, stating the theme, cf. Hamlet's 'To be or not to be', and Macbeth's 'If it were done when 'tis done', etc.

11. *no personal cause* i.e. my own motives are disinterested. *spurn at* v. G., perhaps used with Acts ix, 5 in mind, as at *Lucr.* 1026.

12. *general—he* F. 'generall. He'. My change assumes a comma in Sh.'s MS. and gives 'But I know a public cause to spurn at him, viz. his desire for the crown', which lends a point and sequence previously absent. See G. 'general'.

he would be crowned Spoken, I think, in tones of extreme repugnance, repeated with even greater force in 'Crown him!—that!' (l. 15).

13. *there's the question* And the point of the whole soliloquy.

14. *the bright day...the adder* Cf. the 'serpent's egg' etc. (ll. 32–4). Similarly More (Add. III of *Sir Thomas More*; see 3. 2. 12–18, in *The Sh. Apocrypha*, or p. 79, Mal. Soc. repr.) speaks of the temptations of power as of 'serpent's nature', bids himself 'Fear their gay skins with thoughts of their sharp state', and observes 'sure these things | Not physicked by respect might turn our blood | To much corruption.' The attitudes of the two speakers are different; their subject, treatment and imagery are almost identical.

15. *him!—that!* (Delius) F. 'him that,' Rowe 'him— that—' Camb. 'him?— that;—'. Clar. (= Camb.) takes 'that' as meaning 'do that'; I take it as an exclamation of horror or disgust; cf. note l. 12 (end).

18–19. *Th'abuse...power* Cf. G. 'remorse' and *Vindication of Natural Society* (*Works of Burke*, 'World's Class.', I, 25–6):

Many of the greatest tyrants on the records of history have begun their reigns in the fairest manner. But the truth is this unnatural power corrupts both the heart and the understanding.

20–1. *his affections...reason* his desires have influenced his judgement.

proof experience.

22. *lowliness* A reference to Cæs.'s bid for popularity; cf. Plut. (Sk. 45) 'the people loved him

marvellously because of the courteous manner he had to speak to every man.' Cf. also Bolingbroke's 'courtship of the common people' (*Ric. II*, 1. 4. 24—34).

ambition's ladder Cf. 'base degrees' l. 26 and *Troil.* 1. 3. 102.

27. *so Cæsar may* i.e. Brut. admits as only a possibility what Cass. has declared (1. 2. 116, 121, 161) is already a fact. And when Coleridge (1. 16) asks

Had he not passed the Rubicon? Entered Rome as a conqueror? Placed his Gauls in the Senate?

his own words, 'Sh. has not brought these things forward', answer him.

28—30. *prevent...quarrel...colour...Fashion* See G.

31. *these...extremities* such and such acts of tyranny.

33. *as his kind* 'like the rest of his species' (Mason).

37. *This paper* Cf. 1. 3. 144—5 and 2. 1 head-note (ii).

40. *ides* (Theob.) F. 'firſt'. Theob. conj. 'that *Ides* in the MS. was written jᵃ and thus confused by the compositors with the old symbol for 1st'. That the error is not Sh.'s is proved by l. 59.

53. *ancestors* Dyce plausibly conj. 'ancestor'; cf. notes 1. 2. 159; 3. 2. 51.

59. *fifteen* Warb. and other precisians read 'fourteen' because Luc. speaks only at dawn on the 15th; but the boy naturally includes the day already reached.

S.D. F. 'Knocke within'.

60. S.D. After Theob. F. omits.

61—9. *Since Cassius first* etc. suggests a considerable interval. See also 2. 1 head-note (iii).

63—9. *Between the acting* etc. Clar. notes:

The best comment on these lines is Sh.'s own description of the conduct of Macbeth from the time of his interview with the witches to the murder of Duncan.

66. *The Genius...instruments* Here 'Genius' may
=*daimon* or 'good angel', but is more prob. the
'reasonable Soul' (cf. the Athanasian Creed) of the old
psychology (derived from Aristotle), the celestial and
only immortal part of man's mind, while its 'instruments' or agents are the passions, affections, etc., always
ready to rise in rebellion against their sovereign. Cf.
l. 176 below, and Th. Wright, *Passions of the Minde*
(1601), pp. 12–16. K. explains 'mortal instruments'
as 'the means of carrying out the deadly purpose'. But
how can these be 'in council'?

67. *Are...in council* i.e. deliberate together.

67–9. *the state...insurrection* As at 1.2.86–7
(v. note) the thought 'grows'; deliberation (v. last note)
leads to disagreement and so to insurrection.

man (F2) F. 'a man'.

68. *Like to a little kingdom* Cf. Spencer, *Sh and
the Nature of Man*, 1943, p. 17:

Nothing is more striking in serious sixteenth century lit.
than the universal use of analogy: the cosmos is explained
by the body and the body is explained by the state; all three
hierarchies are parallel—as they had been for centuries.

Cf. Menenius on the Belly and the Members, *Cor.*
1.1.99 ff.

70. *your brother* 'Cass. had married Junia, Brut.'s
sister' (Sk. p. 110). Sh.'s first intimation of this fact.

73. *their hats...ears* Sh., knowing nothing of
Roman headgear, 'dressed his Romans in the slouch
hats of his own time' (Clar.). Pope, who could not
bring himself to give 'hats' to Romans, left the word
blank. See note 1.2.266.

77–81. *O conspiracy...visage?* Brut. 'feels intensely
the moral repugnance that a fine nature must feel to the
dreadful deed' (Hen. Sidgwick, *Misc. Essays*, p. 98);
cf. ll. 63–5 above. But both passages also give vent to

the abhorrence of an Eliz. audience for conspiracy in general.

82. *Hide...affability* Cf. note ll. 224–5 below.

83. *path, thy* (F2) F. 'path thy' Q. 1691, etc. 'hath thy'. See G. 'path'; but this suggests walking *openly*, and so goes ill with l. 84. Coleridge (1, 16) conj. 'put', which is attractive and agrees with 2. 1. 225, 'Let not our looks *put on our purposes*'.

85. S.D. From F. For *Decius* see 'Characters', p. 100.

86–228. *I think we are...to you everyone* See 2. 1 head-note (iv).

98. *watchful* v. G.

100. S.D. From F. Thus Sh. dispenses with the speech of explanation, unneeded by the audience.

101–111. *Here lies the east...directly here* And thus he keeps his audience in play while Brut. and Cass. 'whisper'. The brief digression, which serves for a lighting effect (cf. headnote and note *Ham*. 1. 1. 166–7), also raises a curious point in astronomy. Casca is perfectly correct acc. to the Julian calendar invented in his own day and acc. to the reformed Gregorian calendar introduced into Catholic Europe in 1582. But acc. to the unreformed Julian calendar, still used in Sh.'s England and by then ten days in error, the sun rose north of east on 15 March. Was Casca astronomically exact by accident or was Sh. being historically exact to the facts of 44 B.C.? All I know is that but for help from Prof. Greaves, Astronomer Royal of Scotland, this note would have been sadly inexact.

103–4. *grey lines...fret the clouds* Cf. Keats, *Autumn*, 1. 25, 'While barréd clouds bloom the soft-dying day', and v. G. 'fret' and *Ham*. 2. 2. 305, 'this majestical roof fretted with golden fire'.

107. *a great...on* encroaching far upon.

113. *let us swear* The first of three proposals Cass. makes in this sc.; Brut. negatives them all. Cf. ll. 141–52,

155–66. 'Throughout the play Brut. is represented as opinionated and intolerant of advice' (K.). Cf. note l. 185.

114. *No, not an oath* Plut. (Sk. 114) remarks 'the wonderful faith and secrecy of the conspirators' although they had 'never taken oaths together'. (See head-note iv.) Sh. seizes upon this for use in his portrait of Brut.

face Almost certainly a corruption of 'faith' (Mason, conj. *ap*. Camb.), Plut.'s word (see above); 'face' has been interpreted 'sorrowful looks' (Theob.), 're-proachful looks' (Heath), 'troubled looks' (Clar.), 'appealing looks' (Hunter), and 'looks of esteem for the conspirators' (J.)—in fact anything the critic fancies.

115. *abuse—* (Theob.) F. 'abuſe;'. The semicolon 'marks a sudden pause, or a break in the construction' (Simpson, p. 60).

117. *idle* A transferred epithet; cf. mod. 'sick-bed

118. *high-sighted...range on* A metaphor from falconry (Clar.). Tyranny is an eagle with an eye at once 'supercilious' and far-sighted, that sweeps the ground beneath as he 'ranges' (v. G.) aloft. Cf. note 1.1. 76–9.

119. *by lottery* by chance, i.e. acc. to the tyrant's whim.

these Cf. l. 116.

120–1. *bear fire...kindle* Cf. 4.3. 111 'the flint bears fire'. The tinder-box then suggests 'steel', and Sh. glances at an image from the forge.

122. *women, then* (edd.) F. 'women. Then'.

123. *What* why.

123–4. *spur...To prick* Cf. *Macb.* 1.7. 25–6

125. *secret* See G. and Plut. cited note l. 114.

136. *oath; when* (Cap.) F. 'oath. When'.

144–5. *for his...opinion* Cf. note 1.3. 158–60.

silver 'suggests "purchase" and "buy" in ll. 145–6' (Clar.).

148–9. *Our youths...gravity* Reminiscent of *2 Hen. IV*, 5. 2. 123–4, *Hen. V*, 1. 1. 24–7.

150–2. *let us not...begin* Cf. 1. 2. 185–8 (note). 'Sh. had read Cic.'s character with consummate skill' (Clar.), though helped thereto by Plut.'s *Life of Cicero*. Cf. 'Tudor Trans.', vol. v, p. 337, 'he did too much boast of him selfe' and had a 'worme of ambition and extreme covetous desire of honor in his head'. Sh. prefers vanity to 'cowardice', which acc. to Plut. (Sk. 114) is the quality which made the conspirators distrust Cic. *break with* v. G.

153. *Indeed...fit* Cf. l. 143. Contrast the sturdy independence of 1. 2.

156–91. *Mark Antony...hereafter* Based on Plut. *Antonius* (Sk. 164; see 2. 1 head-note iv) and *Brutus* (Sk. 119):

All the conspirators but Brut....thought it good also to kill Antonius, because he was a wicked man and that in nature favoured tyranny: besides also for that he was in great estimation with soldiers...and specially having a mind bent to great enterprises....But Brut. would not agree to it. First, for that he said it was not honest [=honourable]; secondly, because he told them there was hope of change in him. For...Antonius being a noble-minded and courageous man, when he should know that Cæsar was dead, would willingly help his country to recover her liberty, having them an example unto him to follow.

Again Plut. (Sk. 121) notes that

the first fault he [Brut.] did was when he would not consent ...that Antonius should be slain; and therefore he was justly accused that thereby he had saved and strengthened a strong and grievous enemy of their conspiracy.

Here 'grievous enemy' comes close to Sh.'s 'shrewd contriver' (l. 158).

160. *annoy* v. G.   164. *envy* v. G.

166. *Let us* (Theob.) F. 'Let's'.

167–8. *spirit…spirit* principles…soul.

169–70. *O, that…Cæsar* Tragic irony; cf. 5. 3. 94–5.

173–4. *Let's carve…hounds* The earliest of several passages likening the murder to the death and 'breaking-up' of a hart at the end of a chase; explicit in 3. 1. 205–11, hinted at in 2. 2. 78–9 ánd 3. 1. 106–11, which are an extension of 3. 1. 207, 'crimsoned in thy Lethe'. The imagery is Eliz.; yet Plut. (Sk. 101) supplies the germ in 'Cæsar…was hacked and mangled among them, as a wild beast taken of hunters'—cf. l. 174.

175–6. *let our hearts…rage* Cf. note 2. 1. 66; 'servants' (here) = 'instruments' (there). For 'subtle masters' etc. cf. *K. John*, 4. 2. 208 ff., *Ric. II*, 5. 6. 34 ff.

177. *make* v. G.

180. *purgers* surgeons who treat a patient by bleeding; v. *Macb.* 5. 2. 28 (note and G.).

184. *Cæsar*—(Rowe) F. 'Cæſar.'

185. *Alas, good Cassius* Hunter notes the 'assumption of affectionate superiority' and the pained surprise at his remaining unconvinced. But 'good Cassius' is in the right.

186. *all* i.e. all the harm.

187. *take thought* v. G.

188. *that…should* that would be going a long way for him.

189. *sports…company* Cf. notes 2. 2. 116; 5. 1. 62.

191. S.D. From F. Striking clocks, unknown before the late Middle Ages, became very fashionable in Sh.'s time.

195–7. *superstitious…ceremonies* Plut. gives no ground either for 'superstitious grown of late' or for the earlier Epicureanism, and it seems that Sh. decided to represent Cæs. as one who 'takes to religion' in later life (cf. note 1. 2. 1–11). The hist. Cæs. was a free-thinker who conformed to the State religion and actually became *pontifex maximus,* which North translates 'Bishop of Rome'.

197. *ceremonies* v. G. (ii).

204–6. *unicorns...toils* All great and dangerous beasts, easily trapped or hoodwinked.

betrayed with trees i.e. by getting its horn stuck into a tree behind which its prey had suddenly skipped.

glasses i.e. mirrors, which bamboozle it.

212. *all of us* Cf. 2. 2. 107, S.D., and 'Note on the Copy', pp. 95–6.

215. *bear...hard* v. G.

216. *rated...Pompey* Another perversion of Plut. to the discredit of Cæs. Lig. 'had been accused unto Cæs. for taking part with Pompey and Cæs. discharged [=acquitted] him. But Lig. thanked not Cæs. so much for his discharge as he was offended with him for that he was brought in danger by his tyrannical power' (Sk. 113); in which account the honours are all with Cæs.

218. *go...him* call on him as you pass.

224–5. *look fresh...purposes* Cf. *Macb.* 1. 5. 64–5, 'look like th'innocent flower' etc., and Plut. (Sk. 115), cited 2. 1 head-note (v): Brut. 'did so frame and fashion his countenance and looks that no man could discern he had anything to trouble his mind'.

226–7. *bear it...constancy* i.e. play the part with consistent decorum. Little was known of actors like Roscius and Aesopus (v. Quintilian, XI, 3, 111), but they were reputed to have been models of excellence; and Sh. attributes to them that fidelity to their parts which Hamlet enjoins upon his players (*Ham.* 3. 2. 1–44).

230. *honey-heavy dew* Cf. *Ric. III,* 4. 1. 83 'the golden dew of sleep'; *1 Hen. IV,* 2. 3. 43 'golden sleep'; *dew* =refreshment; v. G. 'honey-heavy'.

231. *figures* pictures of the mind or imagination.
Cf. *M.W.W.* 4. 2. 211 'scrape the figures out of your
husband's brains', which suggests a physiological conception borne out by Th. Wright, *Passions of the
Minde* (1601), p. 62: 'the brayne fitteth best for the
softnesse and moysture to receive the formes and prints
of obiects of understanding.'

233–308. *Brutus, my lord!...sad brows* See 2.1
head-note (v).

237. *You've ungently* etc. Cf. *1 Hen. IV*, 2. 3. 39 ff.
Much in common between the attitudes of the wives
and husbands. *You've* (Rowe) F. 'Y'haue'.

ungently discourteously.

240. *across* Denoting melancholy preoccupation;
cf. *Lucr.* 1662; *Tit.* 3. 2. 4; *L.L.L.* 3. 1. 180; *Temp.*
1. 2. 224.

246. *wafture* (Rowe) F. 'wafter'.

255. *know you Brutus* (F.) recognize you as Brutus.
Edd. follow F4 'know you, Brutus'.

256. *your cause of grief* Cf. *Ham.* 3. 2. 338 'your
cause of distemper'.

261. *physical* healthy.   262. *unbracèd* Cf. 1.
3. 48.

262–6. *suck up...unpurgèd air* The fear of fogs
and of night air was universal at this period; cf. *M.N.D.*
2. 1. 89.

266. *unpurgèd* not purified, i.e. by the sun, cf.
Temp. 2. 2. 1.

267. *his* (F 2) F. 'hit'.

268. *sick...mind* sickness of the mind that troubles
you.

270. S.D. After Collier. F. omits.

271. *charm* v. G.

272. *that great vow* In the Christian marriage service!

273. *incorporate* Cf. Matt. xix, 5, 'they twain shall
be one flesh'; and Eph. v, 31.

274. *your self* (F.) Edd. 'yourself'. The words are gen. printed separately in Sh.'s day and still should be here and in l. 282.

275. *heavy—* F. 'heauy:' The colon is significant.
280. *the* (F2) F. 'tho'.

281–3. *excepted...in sort or limitation* v. G. Legal terms of land-tenure, suggested by 'bond' (l. 280).

285. *suburbs* Furness cites *Arcadia* (1590, II, ch. 20, p. 192 [Feuillerat, p. 279]):

she listed no longer stay in the suburbs of her foolish desires but directly entered upon them.

But Sh. gets it from Plut., who makes Portia say, 'I was married unto thee, not to be thy bed-fellow and companion in bed and at board only, like a harlot' (Sk. 115). The stews in Eliz. London were mostly located in the Southwark suburb. Cf. *Meas.* 1. 2. 93, 98; 2. 1. 63.

289–90. *the ruddy drops...heart* Cf. *Cor.* 1. 1. 140. In the Galenic physiology, only superseded after Harvey's *De Motu Cordis* (1628), the blood, made by the liver, flowed thence to the heart where it received the vital spirits and bodily heat, and so along the arteries to the rest of the body. But the heart needed the blood too, esp. in time of trouble and sadness, the tendency of which was to drain it of blood. Cf. Sherrington, *Jean Fernel*, 1946, pp. 71–7.

295. *Cato's daughter* Cf. *Merch.* 1. 1. 165. Her father, Marcus Porcius Cato, who had been the most obstinate and disinterested of Cæsar's opponents, killed himself in Utica in order to escape being captured by him; cf. 5. 1. 101 (note), and 5. 4. 4.

299–302. *I have...secrets* In Plut. (Sk. 115–16) she wounds herself in the thigh to convince herself that she could 'constantly bear a secret mischance or grief ...which requireth secrecy and fidelity' before asking to share that of her husband. 303. S.D. F. 'Knocke.'

309. S.D. F. 'Enter Lucius with Ligarius'. For 'his head muffled' and 'casts the kerchief off' (l. 321) see l. 315 and cf. *2 Hen. IV*, 1. 1. 147–9; and for the episode see 2. 1 head-note (vi).

324. *mortified* dead or deadened. Cf. *Macb.* 5. 2. 5, 'Excite the mortified man' (i.e. the corpse).

330–1. *going To* (Craik) F. 'going, To'.

332. *new-fired* rekindled. The heart was the source of life, heat, and courage; cf. note ll. 289–90. The incident of Ligarius, derived from Plut. (Sk. 113), skilfully concludes a long and solemn sc. on a note of vigour and hope.

334. S.D. F. 'Thunder. | Exeunt'. The 'thunder' clearly relates to the S.D. at the head of 2. 2 and is prob. a prompter's marginal note; cf. 'Note on the Copy', p. 92.

2. 2.

PLUTARCH. The scene is based on the following in *Cæsar* (Sk. 97–9): 'Cæsar [him]self also doing sacrifice unto the gods found that one of the beasts which was sacrificed had no heart: and that was a strange thing in nature, how a beast could live without a heart.... Then going to bed the same night as his manner was, and lying with his wife Calpurnia, all the windows and doors of his chamber flying open, the noise awoke him, and made him afraid when he saw such light: but more, when he heard his wife Calpurnia, being fast asleep, weep and sigh, and put forth many fumbling lamentable speeches: for she dreamed that Cæsar was slain, and that she had him in her arms.... Insomuch that, Cæsar rising in the morning, she prayed him, if it were possible, not to go out of the doors that day, but to adjourn the session of the Senate until another day. And if that he made no reckoning of her dream, yet that he would search further of the soothsayers by their sacrifices, to know what should happen him that day. Thereby it seemed that Cæsar likewise did fear and suspect somewhat, because his wife Calpurnia until that time was never given to any fear or superstition: and then for that he saw her so troubled in mind with this dream she had. But much more afterwards, when the soothsayers having sacrificed many beasts one after another, told him that none did like them: then he determined to send Antonius to adjourn the session of the Senate.

'But in the mean time came Decius Brutus, surnamed Albinus, in whom Cæsar put such confidence, that in his last will and testament he had appointed him to be his next heir, and yet was of the conspiracy with Cassius and Brutus: he, fearing that if Cæsar did adjourn the session that day, the conspiracy would out, laughed the soothsayers to scorn, and reproved Cæsar, saying, "that he gave the Senate occasion to mislike with him, and that they might think he mocked them, considering that by his commandment they were assembled, and that they were ready willingly to grant him all things, and to proclaim him king of all his provinces of the Empire of Rome out of Italy, and that he should wear his diadem in all other places both by sea and land. And, furthermore, that if any man should tell them from him they should depart for that present time, and return again when Calpurnia should have better dreams, what would his enemies and ill-willers say, and how could they like of his friends' words? And who could persuade them otherwise, but that they would think his dominion a slavery unto them and tyrannical in himself? And yet if it be so," said he, "that you utterly mislike of this day, it is better that you go yourself in person, and, saluting the Senate, to dismiss them till another time." Therewithal he took Cæsar by the hand, and brought him out of his house.'

S.D. 'Cæsar's house' from Camb.; the rest from F. For 'night-gown' v. G., and cf. *Oth.* (Q.) 1. 1. 86, 160 S.D. with *Oth.* (F.) 4. 3. 16, 34. [I owe these references to Dr Simpson.]

6. *success* v. G.

8. *What mean you* etc. Cæs. and Cal. make an interesting contrast with Brut. and Portia; the two

women being as different as the men. The present
speech. would be imposs. to Portia; but I cannot feel
with Barker (p. 85) that Cal. is 'a nervous, fear-haunted
creature'; l. 9 suggests a wife capable of ordering
'immortal Cæsar' about; while in l. 13 speaks one not
usually timid.

10. *Cæsar shall forth* He uses the pompous 3rd
pers. even in private talk with his wife; cf. ll. 29, 42–8.

13. *I never... .ceremonies* Cf. Plut. (Sk. 98) 'Cal.
until that time was never given to any fear and superstition'. For 'stood on' and 'ceremonies' v. G.

16. *horrid* v. G.   *watch* A London institution.

17–25. *A lioness...all use* Cf. the parallel description in *Ham.* 1. 1. 113–25. Having used up all Plut.'s
portents etc. in 1. 3. 10–28, Sh. is obliged to invent
some for himself. The 'lioness' seems a development
of 1. 3. 20–1 suggested·by 'at night wild beasts were
seen | Leaving the woods, lodge in the streets of Rome'
(Marlowe, *Lucan*, bk. 1, 557–8). With ll. 18–24
cf. Marlowe (*ibid.*), ll. 566–8 'Souls quiet and appeas'd
sigh'd from their graves; | Clashing of arms was heard;
in untrod woods | Shrill voices shright; and ghosts
encounter men'; and *Cæsar's Revenge* (Mal. Soc.)
ll. 1646–7 'Sad ghastly sights and raiséd ghosts appear
| Which fill the silent woods with groaning cries'. Ll. 19–
20 give us the time-honoured interpretation of the
Aurora Borealis, which perhaps echoes Tacitus ('Visae
per caelum concurrere acies, rutulantia arma et subito
nubium igne conlucere templum'; *Hist.* bk. v, c. 13),
and is used by Marlowe (*2 Tamb.* 4. 1. 201–6). L. 21
'drizzled blood' (cf. 'dews of blood' in *Ham.* and
'showers of blood', *Cæsar's Revenge*, l. 355) refers to
the 'blood-rain' common in S. Europe. And l. 22 once
again echoes *Lucan*, ll. 577–9: 'with what noise | An
arméd battle joins, such and more strange | Black night
brought forth in secret.'

19. *fought* (Grant White; Clar.) F. 'fight'.

23. *did neigh* (Mal.) F. 'do neigh'. Compositors are very liable to small tense changes.

24. *shriek and squeal* Cf. *Ham.* 'squeak and gibber'. The natural idea that ghosts had thin squeaking voices, like bats, is found in Homer (*Odyss.* xxiv, 5–9). Cf. *Aen.* vi, 492–3 and Horace *Sat.* 1, 8. 41.

25. *beyond all use* quite abnormal; v. G. 'use'.

30–1. *When beggars...princes* Portents and prodigies are reserved for national issues and great persons; v. G. 'blaze'.

32–3. *Cowards...but once* Based on Cæs.'s famous saying, thus reported in Plut. (Sk. 92):

And when some of his friends did counsel him to have a guard for the safety of his person...he would never consent to it, but said it was better to die once than always to be afraid of death.

Sh. as usual scales the point down. For 'taste of death' cf. Mark ix, 1, and Noble, pp. 28, 190.

34–7. *Of all the...come* 'Is there not a hint of the theatrical in this overstrained statement?...If anything could make us suspicious it would be his constant harping on his flawless valour' (MacCallum, p. 221). Cf. Brut.'s unemphatic and therefore convincing statement of the same sentiment (3. 1. 100–1), and Hamlet's, as he too 'defies augury' (*Ham.* 5. 2. 217–20).

37. S.D. F. 'Enter a Seruant.'

39–40. *Plucking...beast* In Plut. (Sk. 97–8) Cæs. himself makes the sacrifice and discovers this omen.

41–8. *The gods...forth* More posturing, with some boasting (as others whistle) to keep up his courage.

42–3. *should...should* i.e. would...would.

without a heart i.e. without the organ of courage; cf. note 2. 1. 332.

44–5. *Danger...than he* This and what follows is a good example of what Hazlitt calls Cæs.'s 'vapouring'.

46. *We are* (Upton; mod. edd.) F. 'We heaṛe'—
wh. looks like an 'intelligent' correction with reference
to ll. 15–7.

47. *the elder* Cf. *Ant.* 3. 10. 13, where 'the elder'
also means 'the stronger' [Hunter].

55–6. *Mark Antony...home* Palmer (p. 40) observes:

> There is no prettier stroke of character in the play. Cæs.
> has declared himself immovable. But...'Call it *my* fear
> that keeps you in the house', suggests the tactful wife, and
> Cæs. complies immediately.

65. *Say he is sick* Cal. overreaches herself: he had
been ready to send that lie by Ant.—a friend of the
family; but with this Decius, who moreover can see
that he is perfectly well, the matter is different.

76–9. *She dreamt...in it* In Plut. (Sk. 98) she
dreams that a decorative pinnacle on the house, con-
ferred as an honour upon Cæs., has broken down. This
being nothing to Sh.'s purpose, he invents a far better
dream, perhaps after first writing 3. 2. 133–4 and
190, which last is a misinterpretation of a phrase in
Plut.

76. *to-night* last night (freq. sense in Sh.). Cf. 3. 3.
1 and contrast 5. 5. 78.

statua (Steev.) F. 'Statue' Camb. 'statuë'. O.E.D.
('statua'), finding 'no evidence of trisyllabic pronunciation of "statue"', supports Steev. Cf. 3. 2. 191, *Ric.
III*, 3. 7. 25, and *2 Hen. VI*, 3. 2. 80, where the word
is also trisyllabic.

78–9. *lusty Romans...bathe...in it* Unlike the rest
of the dream, this connects with the deer-slaying image,
for which see note 2. 1. 173–4 and *K. John*, 2. 1.
321 ff.

> And like a jolly troop of huntsmen came
> Our lusty English all with purpled hands
> Dyed in the dying slaughter of their foes.

80. *And these...portents.* Alexandrine with central pause. Cf. 2. 4. 31. *portents* has the Lat. accent: 'porténts'; cf. 'aspéct' [Dr Percy Simpson].

83. *This dream* etc. Decius now gives Cæs.'s 'humour the true bent' by the application of a little flattery (see 2. 1. 202–10); and Cæs., taken with the notion of his blood being sacred, doesn't notice that it implies his death no less than Cal.'s interpretation. The Bear is dazzled with the mirror.

89. *For tinctures...cognizance* Cf. 3. 2. 131–5. This seems to mean, Verity notes,

that men will dye ('tincture') their handkerchiefs in the blood of Cæs., and keep them as memorials ('relics') and badges of honour ('cognizance').

K. takes 'cognizance' as summing up what precedes: 'for tinctures, stains, relics—in a word for a sign that they are devoted to Cæsar'.

91. *And this...expounded it* Cæs. takes 'suggestion as a cat laps milk' (*Temp.* 2. 1. 285).

96–7. *a mock...rendered* 'an obvious sarcastic rejoinder' (Herford).

102. *dear dear love* Dec. lays it on thick, and Cæs. swallows it all.

103. *your proceeding* 'your career' (Clar.); v. G.

104. *reason...liable* i.e. my love makes me say what reason tells me is too freely spoken; v. G. 'liable'.

105. *now* i.e. after Dec.'s words in ll. 93–4.

107. S.D. From F., wh. however places Publius last; prob. as a substitute for Cass. See pp. 95–6.

109 ff. *Welcome, Publius* etc. Cæs. is at his best in this brief episode, which exhibits 'the great urbanity of his manners and the ease and affability of his conversation' (T. Davies, *Dram. Misc.* 1783, II, 227–8), and 'brings him suddenly to life again. He has a word for everyone and it is the right word. This is the real

Cæsar, courteous and accessible, who has it in him to win hearts and to command respect' (Palmer, p. 43). Add that (i) the affability is an effect of Dec.'s news, (ii) Sh. usually shows us a character at his best shortly before death, (iii) this sc. of a genial host surrounded by his friends is in ironic contrast with 3. 1, in which the same host is surrounded and stabbed by the same friends, (iv) the note of treachery, sounded in different ways by Treb. and Brut., marks a definite point in the ebb and flow of our sympathy with the two causes and their principals (cf. Introd. p. xxxii).

112. *ne'er so…enemy* See note 2. 1. 216.

116. *revels…nights* See note 5. 1. 62.

118. *prepare* i.e. refreshments. Clearly, I think, addressed to Cal., and the cue for her exit.

119. *to blame* (F3). F. 'too blame'.

124–5. *And so near…further* Actually Treb.'s part in 3. 1 is to decoy Ant. away, not to help stab Cæs.

128–9. *That every like…same* Cf. the Lat. proverb 'Omne simile non sit idem'. A play on 'like friends' (l. 127). With this pregnant aside, Sh. preserves our respect for Brut. as he goes in to 'the sacrament of hospitality and trust', as Barker (p. 99) too solemnly calls it.

129. *earns* (F.) Theo. and mod. edd. 'yearns'. Cf. G. and *Hen. V*, 2. 3. 3 (note).

2.3 and 2.4.

PLUTARCH. *Artemidorus*. From *Cæsar* (Sk. 99, following on the last passage quoted in head-note 2. 2): 'And one Artemidorus, of Cnidos, a Doctor of Rhetoric in the Greek tongue, who by means of his profession was very familiar with certain of Brutus' confederates, and therefore knew the most part of all their practices against Cæsar, came and brought him a little bill, written with his own hand, of all that he meant to tell him. He, marking how Cæsar received all the supplications that were offered him, and that he gave them straight to his men that were about him, pressed nearer to him, and said: "Cæsar, read this memorial to yourself, and that quickly, for they be matters of great weight, and touch you nearly." Cæsar took it of him, but could never read it, though he many times attempted it, for the number of people that did salute him; but holding it still in his hand, keeping it to himself, went on withal into the Senate-house.'

Portia. From *Brutus* (Sk. 117–18): 'The weakness of Porcia, not withstanding her former courage.' (Marginal note.) 'Now in the meantime there came one of Brutus' men post-haste unto him, and told him his wife was a-dying. For Porcia, being very careful and pensive for that which was to come, and being too weak to away with so great an inward grief of mind, she could hardly keep within, but was frighted with every little noise and cry she heard, as those that are taken and possessed with the fury of the Bacchantes; asking every man that came from the market-place what Brutus did, and still sent messenger after messenger to know what news. At length Cæsar's coming being prolonged (as you have heard) Porcia's weakness was not able to hold out any longer, and thereupon she suddenly swounded, that she had no leisure to go to her chamber, but was taken in the midst of her house, where her speech and senses failed her. Howbeit she soon came to herself again, and so was laid in her bed, and attended by her women. When Brutus heard these news, it grieved him, as it is to be presupposed: yet he left not off the care of his country and commonwealth, neither went home to his house for any news he heard.'

2. 3.

S.D. Combining 2. 3 and 2. 4 I combine the locality directions of Theo. and Cap. F. 'Enter Artemidorus'. Rowe added 'reading a paper'.

6. *If thou...immortal* A touch of irony here.

7. *look about you* i.e. take care! Cf. *Shrew*, 1. 2. 138, *Rom.* 3. 5. 40, etc.

7. *security...conspiracy* over-confidence gives treason its opportunity.

9. *lover* v. G.

13. *Out...emulation* beyond the reach of envy's
fangs.

2. 4.

Cap. and most edd. begin a new sc. here, unneces-
sarily, as Hunter notes.

S.D. F. 'Enter Portia and Lucius'.

1–3. *I prithee...errand, madam* Portia's agitation,
wh. Sh. uses to increase *our* tension, is due to her knowledge of Brut.'s secret (cf. ll. 9, 15). We take his
promise to impart it (2. 1. 305–6) as having been
fulfilled, although speaking by the book, wh. spectators
cannot do, there has been no opportunity for him to do
so since. Her nervous instability prepares us also for
her suicide later.

6. *constancy* v. G. Cf. 2. 1. 227, 299.

18. *rumour* v. G.

20. S.D. From F.

27–8. *lady: if it...me,* (J.) F. 'Lady, if it...me:'.

41–2. *Brutus hath a suit* etc. An attempt to explain
'enterprise', wh. she thinks Lucius has overheard.

44. *merry* in good heart. Sh.'s Portia is at once
more womanly and more 'constant' than Plut.'s (see
2. 3+4 head-note), the news of whose serious condition
is reported to Brutus on his way to the Senate House—
the story being told in order to illustrate his resolution,
not hers.

3. 1.

PLUTARCH. (i) *The Senate House.* Plut. (*Cæsar*, Sk. 100)
under the marginal heading 'The place where Cæsar was
slain', writes: 'For these things, they may seem to come
by chance; but the place [Pompey's theatre] where the
murther was prepared, and where the Senate were assembled,

and where also there stood up an image of Pompey dedicated by himself amongst other ornaments which he gave unto the theatre, all these were manifest proofs, that it was the ordinance of some god that made this treason to be executed specially in that very place.'

(ii) *The Soothsayer*. See 1. 2 head-note (ii).

(iii) *Artemidorus*. See 2. 3 + 4 head-note.

(iv) *Popilius Lena*. 'Another Senator, called Popilius Laena, after he had saluted Brutus and Cassius more friendly than he was wont to do, he rounded softly in their ears, and told them: "I pray the gods you may go through with that you have taken in hand: but withal despatch, I reade [advise] you, for your enterprise is bewrayed." When he had said, he presently departed from them and left them both afraid that their conspiracy would out.... When Cæsar came out of his litter, Popilius Laena...kept him a long time with a talk. Cæsar gave good ear unto him: wherefore the conspirators (if so they should be called) not hearing what he said to Cæsar, but conjecturing...that his talk was none other but the very discovery of their conspiracy, they were afraid every man of them; and one looking in another's face, it was easy to see that they all were of a mind that it was no tarrying for them till they were apprehended, but rather that they should kill themselves with their own hands. And when Cassius and certain other clapped their hands on their swords under their gowns to draw them, Brutus marking the countenance and gesture of Laena and considering that he did use himself rather like an humble and earnest suitor than like an accuser, he said nothing to his companion (because there were many amongst them that were not of the conspiracy), but with a pleasant countenance encouraged Cassius.. And immediately after, Laena went from Cæsar and kissed his hand; which shewed plainly that it was for some matter concerning himself that he had held him so long in talk.' (*Brutus*, Sk. 117–18.)

(v) *Antony drawn out of the way*. 'Now Antonius that was a faithful friend to Cæsar and a valiant man besides of his hands, him Decius Brutus Albinus entertained out of the Senate-house, having begun a long tale of set purpose.' (*Cæsar*, Sk. 100.)

(vi) *The Assassination* (*Cæsar*, Sk. 100–1). 'So Cæsar
coming into the house, all the Senate stood up on their feet
to do him honour. Then part of Brutus' company and
confederates stood round about Cæsar's chair, and part of
them also came towards him, as though they made suit with
Metellus Cimber, to call home his brother again from banish-
ment: and thus prosecuting still their suit, they followed
Cæsar till he was set in his chair. Who, denying their
petitions, and being offended with them one after another,
because the more they were denied the more they pressed
upon him and were the earnester with him, Metellus, at
length, taking his gown with both his hands, pulled it over
his neck, which was the sign given the confederates to set
upon him. Then Casca, behind him, strake him in the neck
with his sword; howbeit the wound was not great nor mortal,
because it seemed the fear of such a devilish attempt did
amaze him and take his strength from him, that he killed him
not at the first blow. But Cæsar, turning straight unto him,
caught hold of his sword and held it hard; and they both
cried out, Cæsar in Latin: "O vile traitor Casca, what dost
thou?" and Casca, in Greek, to his brother: "Brother,
help me." At the beginning of this stir, they that were
present, not knowing of the conspiracy, were so amazed
with the horrible sight they saw, they had no power to fly,
neither to help him, not so much as once to make an outcry.
They on the other side that had conspired his death compassed him in on every side with their swords drawn in their
hands, that Cæsar turned him no where but he was striken
at by some, and still had naked swords in his face, and was
hacked and mangled among them, as a wild beast taken of
hunters. For it was agreed among them that every man should
give him a wound, because all their parts should be in this
murther; and then Brutus himself gave him one wound about
his privities. Men report also that Cæsar did still defend
himself against the rest, running every way with his body:
but when he saw Brutus with his sword drawn in his hand,
then he pulled his gown over his head, and made no more
resistance, and was driven either casually or purposedly, by
the council of the conspirators, against the base whereupon
Pompey's image stood, which ran all of a gore-blood till

he was slain. Thus it seemed that the image took just revenge of Pompey's enemy, being thrown down on the ground at his feet, and yielding up his ghost there, for the number of wounds he had upon him. For it is reported, that he had three and twenty wounds upon his body: and divers of the conspirators did hurt themselves striking one body with so many blows.'

The account in *Brutus* (Sk. 118–19) is briefer, but adds a little in the concluding sentences which I quote: 'So divers running on a heap together to fly upon Cæsar, he, looking about him to have fled, saw Brutus with a sword drawn in his hand ready to strike at him: then he let Casca's hand go, and casting his gown over his face, suffered every man to strike at him that would. Then the conspirators thronging one upon another, because every man was desirous to have a cut at him, so many swords and daggers lighting upon one body, one of them hurt another, and among them Brutus caught a blow on his hand, because he would make one in murdering of him, and all the rest also were every man of them bloodied.'

(vii) *Antony comes to terms with the conspirators.* Having followed Plut. closely for the assassination, Sh. then begins to manipulate him freely. He takes over a few details, e.g. the panic among the senators and in the city; Antony's flight; the assassins walking the streets, 'having their swords bloody in their hands', with Brutus going 'foremost'; their compact of friendship with Antony. But his Antony is at once bolder and craftier than Plut.'s, who first shows himself next day at a meeting of the Senate which, on a motion of Cicero and himself, not only pardons the conspirators, but confers honours upon them, while Antony himself 'to put them in heart…sent them his son for a pledge', after which 'every man saluted and embraced each other'. (*Brutus*, Sk. 120–1.)

(viii) *Antony begs for Cæsar's body.* Plut. (*Brutus*, Sk. 121) states not this, but that when at a second meeting of the Senate 'they came to talk of Cæsar's will and testament and of his funerals and tomb', Ant. thought good 'his testament should be read openly, and also that his body should be honourably buried, and not in hugger-mugger, lest the

the people might thereby take occasion to be worse offended
if they did otherwise'. This, he says, 'Cassius stoutly spoke
against...but Brutus went with the motion;...wherein it
seemeth he committed a second fault...which indeed marred
all' (v. note l. 232). For Plut.'s account of Ant.'s 'funeral
oration' v. 3. 2 head-note (ii).

(ix) *The return of Octavius* (see 3. 2 head-note (iii)).

S.D. I follow Theo. and J. who locate 'The Street
before the Capitol and the Capitol open', and Barker,
who notes (p. 122) 'the inner stage is disclosed and
Cæsar's "state" is set there. Cæsar, the conspirators,
the Senators and the populace enter upon the main
stage'; but I differ as to 'the Senators', who, as 2.2.59 ff.
and 119 show, are in session awaiting Cæsar. For 'chair
of gold' v. Plut. (Sk. 96, where it is misprinted 'chain
of gold'). I place Pompey's statue just without the
inner stage because Cæs.'s body is borne out at the end
of the scene (v. note l. 298). Cap., Camb. and most
mod. edd. locate 'Rome. Before the Capitol; the
Senate sitting above', which implies action on the
upper-stage from l. 11 onwards, a thing quite impossible.

Sh., like most Eliz.s, identified Capitol with Senate
House (cf. *Titus*, 1. 1, where the Senate sit 'aloft' in
'the Capitol') and though the Senate sometimes met
there, in the temple of Jupiter, it gen. met in the Curia
Hostilia near the Forum, and had assembled, as Plut.'s
vague statements (Sk. 100, 116) imply, on the Ides
of March 44 B.C. in the Curia Pompeiana adjoining
Pompey's Theatre.

The F. entry begins 'Flouriſh. Enter', and includes
Art. and Sooth. but not Popilius.

1–2. *The ides...gone.* Herford notes:

In Plut. these words form a private colloquy between
Cæs. and the Sooth.: Cæs. addresses him 'merrily', and he
'softly' answers. Sh.'s Cæs. does not unbend.

4–5. *Trebonius...suit* Nothing of this in Plut. and we are not told why Treb. does not present his own suit or what it is. Enough that Decius, who has led the unicorn-lion-bear to the slaughter-house, sees danger in Artem. and interposes to forestall him.

8. *What touches...served* No hint of this in Plut. (v. 2. 3 + 4 head-note). 'One of the few utterances... worthy of the great Dictator' (V.). 'Sh. gives Cæs. the plural of modern royalty' (Herford).

10. *give place* This jostling conspirator can hardly be the timid old man addressed in l. 90; cf. 'Note on the Copy', p. 96. 'Sirrah' is a term of contempt.

12. S.D. None in F. Cap.+Camb. 'Cæsar enters the Capitol, the rest following'. Cf. Plut.'s account, head-note (vi).

13–24. *I wish...change* Compare this tense dialogue with Sh.'s source (head-note iv).

15. *What said* etc. These asides follow Cap.

19. *sudden* v. G.

prevention Cf. 2. 1. 85 and *Hen. V*, 2. 2. 158.

21. *turn back* i.e. return alive.

22. *be constant* Brut. is a better leader in a crisis than the excitable Cass., of whom Plut. (*Cæsar*, Sk. 100) writes: 'the instant danger of the present time, taking away his former reason, did suddenly put him into a furious passion, and made him like a man half beside himself.' Ll. 27–9 also reveal Brut.'s tactical handling of the situation.

26. S.D. None in F. North calls the decoy 'Decius ['Decimus' in Amyot] Brutus' in *Cæsar* (Sk. 100) and 'Trebonius' in *Brutus* (Sk. 118); relating (Sk. 100) that he 'entertained' Ant. 'out of the Senate-house' with 'a long tale of set purpose'—a funny story of the 'smoking-room' variety, no doubt, to suit Ant.'s taste.

28. *presently* at once.   29. *addressed* ready.

31. *Are...ready?* F. and most edd. give to Cæs.; Collier, Dyce, Hunter to Casca. The abbrev. sp. headings were easily confused, while the words are apt to Casca, who has just been addressed, and in his mouth add a vivid extra touch to the situation.

S.D. None in F. Cf. head-note (vi), *init.*

32. *Cæsar and his senate* Once again he speaks like a Tudor monarch; cf. note l. 8.

35. *heart—* (Cap.) F. 'heart.' *prevent* v. G. 'Cæs. knows what Met. is about to ask (cf. l. 44) and is determined not to grant his suit.' (Hunter.)

38. *pre-ordinance and first decree* 'What has been pre-ordained and decreed from the beginning' (Clar.). Hunter hesitates to 'impute' to Cæs. 'any such presumptuous arrogance'; but 'first decree' confirms the interpretation and 'pre-ordinate' (v. O.E.D.) is commonly used as a theol. term (=predestinate). Cf. Introd. pp. xxvii ff.

39. *law* (J.) F. 'lane'. *the law of children*='mere fickleness' (Hunter).

40. *rebel blood* lack of self-control.

41–2. *thawed...melteth* Cf. 'fire the blood' (l. 37). 'Blood' is in both cases conceived as 'mettle' (v. G.) in the alchemist's crucible; Cæs.'s resolution or mettle being pure gold, is not to be melted like that of baser natures. Cf. notes 1.1.65; 1.2.309–11.

42–3. *sweet words...fawning* Cf. *Ham.* 3.2.58–60.

46. *spurn...cur* Cf. *Merch.* 1.3.115 and Plut. (*Brutus*, Sk. 119): 'Cæsar at the first simply refused their kindness and entreaties; but afterwards, perceiving they still pressed on him, *he violently thrust them from him*'.

47–8. *Cæsar...satisfied* See pp. 93–4. As written by Sh. and orig. performed, the speech prob. ended abruptly, thus:

> Cæsar did never wrong but with just cause.

52. *not in flattery* 'Sh. takes care to protect the honour and dignity of Brut. here' (K.).

53. *Publius Cimber* Plut. does not give the brother's name. 'Publius' serves again at a pinch in 2.2 (v. 'Note on the Copy', p. 96).

54. *Have...repeal* Be free to return from exile at once.

56. *As low...fall* This extreme hypocrisy makes it difficult to believe that Cass. absented himself from Cæs.'s house owing to scruples of any kind. (See 'Note on the Copy', p. 95.) Such self-abasement, following upon the surprising intervention by Brut. on behalf of a man justly exiled, greatly intensifies the contempt and disgust already visited upon the cringing Met., and so occasions the most inordinate expression of *hubris* we have yet heard from Cæs.—the moment before death comes upon him.

59. *If I could...move me* This is to claim super-divinity, since even the gods are moved by prayer.

60. *the northern star* At once 'the ever-fixéd pole' (*Oth.* 2.1.15), supreme symbol of 'constancy', and the lode-star by which men steer; (v. *Son.* 116.5).

67. *apprehensive* endowed with reason.

69. *unassailable* Ominous word!

70. *Unshaked of motion* 'Unshaken either by his own impulses or by external influence' (K.). Motion was the law of every star but one.

74. *wilt...Olympus?* i.e. will you attempt the impossible? The image chosen once again reveals the ἄτη, the infatuated insolence of the speaker, and this time brings down the thunderbolt upon him through heaven's chosen instruments, the now infuriated 'liberators' who ring him round.

76. *Speak...me!* Let my hands speak for me! S.D. F. 'They ſtab Cæsar'. My S.D. is based upon 3.2.184–89; 5.1.43–4; and Plut. (v. head-note vi),

the source of all. For 'covers his face' etc., cf. the
dying words of Cassius (5. 3. 44) and Brutus (5. 5. 47).
It was not seemly that the last agony of a Roman should
be visible.

77. *Et tu, Brute!* Prob. orig. derived from Suetonius
(*Div. Julius*, 82) —'tradiderunt quidam, Marco Bruto
irruenti dixisse: καὶ σὺ τέκνον...'. The Latin form,
almost certainly post-classical if not renaissance, is
first found in *The True Tragedie of Richard Duke of
York* (1595), a 'reported' text of *3 Hen. VI;* but since
the words are an addition by the 'pirate' (*True Trag.*
5. 1. 53=*3 Hen. VI*, 5. 1. 81) the tag must have then
been familiar to the stage. Mal. conj. that it first
occurred in a Latin play, *Cæsar Interfectus*, by Richard
Edes, acted in 1582 and now lost (*Eliz. Stage*, III, 309).
But if so, its appearance in *True Trag.* suggests that it
reached Sh. through an intermediate source, and one
may note that 'What, Brutus too?', found in *Cæsar's
Revenge* (c. 1594) is virtually a translation of it (v.
Introd. p. xxvi). There is no hint of Brut.'s supposed
sonship to Cæs. in Sh., but that the story was current is
proved by *2 Hen. VI*, 4. 1. 137, which speaks of Cæs.
being stabbed by 'Brutus' bastard hand'.

Jonson employs the tag in an extremely comic
situation in *E.M.O.* (1599) 5. 6. 79, (Jonson, III, p. 585)
wh. suggests contempt for Sh.'s use of it. See 'Jonson
and *Julius Cæsar*' (*Sh. Survey*, II, 1949).

Brute F. 'Brutè'. The accent perhaps indicated the
pronunciation to the actor.

80. *the common pulpits* Cf. Plut. (Sk. 120) 'the
pulpit for orations', i.e. the Rostra of the Forum. But
to Sh.'s audience the phrase would suggest the open-air
pulpits of London, such as that at St Paul's.

81. *enfranchisement* Cf. Plut. (Sk. 120) 'persuading
the Romans...to take their liberty again'. Appian,
Civ. Wars, II, 119 adds that one of the liberators 'bore

a cap [viz. the *pileus*, given to enfranchised slaves] on the end of a spear as a symbol of freedom'.

82–4. *People...Brutus.* Cf. Plut. (*Brutus*, Sk. 119):

Cæsar being slain...Brutus, standing in the middest of the house, would have spoken, and stayed the other Senators that were not of the conspiracy, to have told them the reason why they had done this fact. But they, as men both afraid and amazed, fled one upon another's neck in haste to get out at the door.

86. *Where's Publius?* Cf. 'Note on the Copy', p. 96.

90. *Talk...standing* Any hint of civil strife is shocking to Brut.: the deed has only to be explained to the people and all will be well (cf. ll. 225–7).

97. *to his house* This agrees with Appian (*Civ. Wars*, 11, 118), but Plut. (Sk. 101) relates: 'Ant. and Lepidus...fled into other men's houses and forsook their own.'

98–9. *Men, wives...doomsday* Cf. Plut. (*Brutus*, Sk. 120):

When the murther was newly done there were sudden outcries of people that ran up and down the city, the which indeed did the more increase the fear and tumult.

99. *Fates...pleasures* This Stoic addresses Fate as an Eliz. would address his prince. Cf. *Meas.* 1. 1. 26 'I come to know your pleasure'.

will wish to.

100–1. *That we shall die...upon* Cf. note 2. 2. 34–7, and G. 'stand upon'.

102. *Why, he* etc. Pope and most edd. take this from Casca (F.) and give it to Cass.; Clar. arguing that it belongs to Cass. 'who is a Stoic'. 'But Cass. is an Epicurean' (Hunter); and Hudson notes that the lines resemble what Casc. says at 1. 3. 101–2. After this

Casc. drops out of the play, perhaps because the actor taking the part was required to play Octavius.

106–11. *Stoop...liberty!* Plut. relates that the conspirators in their eagerness to strike at Cæs. so hurt each other that 'every man of them' became 'bloodied' (head-note vi *ad fin.*). This passage, together with that quoted in note 2. 1. 173–4, prob. evoked in Sh.'s mind the image of huntsmen bathing their hands in the slain deer's blood; cf. notes 2. 1. 173–4; 2. 2. 78–9; 3. 1. 205–11, 207.

112–14. *How many ages...unknown* An echo of the following stanza of Daniel's *Musophilus*, 1599:

And who, in time, knows whither we may vent
  The treasure of our tongue, to what strange shores
·This gain of our best glory shall be sent,
  T'enrich unknowing nations with our stores?
What worlds in th'yet unforméd Occident
  May come refined with th'accents that are ours?

(*Oxf. Bk. of 16th Cent. Verse*, p. 534), see Introd. p. x.

114. *states* (F 2) F. 'State'.

116. *lies* (F 2) F. 'lye' *along* cf. G.

121–2. *Brutus...Rome* Cf. Plut. (Sk. 120):

Brutus went foremost, very honourably compassed in round about with the noblest men of the city.

122. S.D. Cf. Moulton, pp. 197–8: 'In the whole Sh. drama there is nowhere such a swift swinging round of a dramatic action.' 'As...the conspirators dip their hands in their victim's blood and make their triumphant appeal to the whole world and all time... the arch has reached its apex.' But with the entry of Ant.'s servant 'the Reaction has begun'.

Plut. (*Antonius*, Sk. p. 165) states that Ant. 'sent his son unto them for a pledge' (i.e. hostage). Sh. prefers to invent. Note the boldness and shrewdness of Ant.'s move. To see Brut. and be accepted by him was to secure his own safety; so far from being 'amazed' (l. 97) he acts with instant decision. And his tactics are equally shrewd: a servant is first sent to test Brut., while Ant. waits round the corner; then, at a signal from his man that all is well, he cuts in before Cass. has time to warn Brut.

127–38. *Brutus is noble…faith* Moulton (p. 198) detects in this

the peculiar tone of subtly-poised sentences…inseparably associated with Ant.'s eloquence; it is like the first announcement of that which is to be a final theme in music, and from this point the tone dominates the scene.

128. *royal* v. G., and 3. 2. 246.

130. *feared* Crafty, suggesting that his loyalty to Cæs. had been partly diplomatic.

145. *a mind* a 'presentiment' (Clar.); cf. *Merch.* 1. 1. 175.

146–7. *still Falls…purpose* 'always turns out to be very much to the purpose' (Clar.).

147. S.D. F. 'Enter Antony'. For 'meeting… nods' v. note l. 122 S.D. (near end) and for the rest cf. Davies *Dram. Misc.* (1783), 11, 241 on Wilks, Betterton's successor, who, as Ant.,

as soon as he entered the stage, without taking any notice of the conspirators, walked swiftly up to the dead body of Cæsar and knelt down; he paused some time before he spoke. [Sprague, p. 322.]

To pretend he had not been, or was no longer, Cæs.'s friend would disgust Brut. and deepen Cass.'s suspicions. Ant. therefore utters his genuine feelings, but slips in from time to time ironical expressions of deep respect for the assassins. And it is this Olympian irony more than anything else which for the time detaches the sympathy of the audience from the conspirators.

150–1. *Are all...measure?* Cf. Nashe: 'He was all to bepoynyarded in the Senate house, and had the dust of his bones in a Brasen urne (no bigger then a boule) barreld up, whom (if he had lyued) all the sea and Earth and ayre woulde haue beene to little for' (ii. 82. 27); below 3. 2. 119–20; and *Ham.* 5. 1. 207–10.

153. *let blood...rank* This is to class them with surgeons or 'purgers' (2. 1. 180) as Brut. claimed they were.

154–64. *If I myself...this age* This 'passionate appeal' (Hunter) is perfectly safe; he has the promise of ll. 141–3; and ll. 165–77 show that his words have their desired effect on the magnaminous Brut.

155. *death hour* (Collier) F. 'deaths houre'. I cannot credit Sh. with a mouthful of sibilants when 'death hour' (cf. 'death-bed') offered so ready an alternative.

158. *bear...hard* v. G.

172. *As fire...fire* Cf. Apperson, 213, and *K. John* 3. 1. 277. The first 'fire' is disyllabic.

175. *in strength of malice* Famous crux. Cap. conj. 'no strength of malice', with a comma at end of l. 174; Singer 'in strength of amity' (sp. 'amitie'). I incline to this last as graphically easy and a close parallel to 'I'll wrestle with you in my strength of love', spoken by Oct. as he embraces Ant. in farewell (*Ant.* 3. 2. 61).

178–9. *Your voice...dignities* Cass. tries a little straight corruption, which he knows is more likely to secure Ant. than Brut.'s sob-stuff. It shows, too, that 'the actual result of the assassination is to transfer the authority of the monarch to a little "knot" of oligarchs' (Hunter). Spoken, I think, so as to be unheard by Brut.

184. *I doubt...wisdom* Perhaps the most ironical of Ant.'s comments.

189. *my valiant Casca* Alluding to the treacherous blow from behind,

191. *all...* F. 'all:' A pause natural after the ordeal of shaking their bloody hands and calling them 'gentlemen'; but nausea is at once cloaked in assumed moral bewilderment, specially directed at Brut.

197. *dearer* v. G.   203. *close* v. G.

205–11. *Here wast thou bayed...here lie!* Cf. notes 2.1.173–4; 2.2.78–9; 3.1.106–11. The culmination and key-image of the previous allusions to the 'baying' and 'breaking-up' of the hart.

207. *spoil* bloody skin stripped from a slain animal, v. G.

lethe 'stream of death' (Delius) i.e. 'life-blood' (Furness, who suggests that Sh. may have imagined Lethe, the river in Hades, to be of blood like Cocytus). This gloss is not inconsistent with Cap.'s: 'a term used by hunters to signify the blood shed by a deer at its fall, with which it is still a custom to mark those who came in at the death' (accepted by Madden, p. 63, note 3); and this remained a custom a century later than Cap. (see 'Mr Briggs in Scotland', *Punch's Almanac*, 1861). Sh. himself provides sufficient proof of the custom in *K. John* 2.1.321, cited above, note 2.2.78–9.

208–9. *O world...of thee* Coleridge (1, 17) suspected these lines (i) 'on account of the rhythm, which is not Sh. but just the very *tune* of some old play', (ii) 'because they interrupt not only the sense and connection, but likewise the flow both of the passion, and (what is with me still more decisive) of the Sh. link of association'.

210. *How...princes* Cf. *Ham.* 5.2.362–5, where the 'many princes' are the quarry.

214. *cold modesty* 'faint praise' (Hunter).

216. *compact* The realist speaks again.

217. *pricked* Cf. 4.1.1, 3, 16.

222. *Upon this hope* The hint that friendship depends on satisfactory reasons being given is too slight

to raise Cass.'s suspicions, but enough to show the
audience Ant. is neither coward nor flatterer.

228. *And...moreover* etc. Personal safety and personal relations with the liberators established, Ant. now
takes the boldest step so far; representing it as a trifling
afterthought.

232. *You shall* Plut. (Sk. 121) notes that 'Brut.
committed two great faults after Cæs.'s death' (i)
'when he would not consent...that Antony should be
slain'; and (ii) 'when he agreed that Cæs.'s funerals
should be as Ant. would have them, the which indeed
marred all'.

232 ff. *Brutus* etc. Rowe first marked these 'asides'.

237. *I will...first* We smile at this,—and are even
reminded of Bottom's proposed prologue, wh. seemed
to say 'we will do no harm with our swords' (*M.N.D.*
3. 1. 16–17); yet we respect the idealist for his indomitable trust in the sweet reasonableness of human
nature.

238. *our Cæsar's* 'Suggests in an indescribable way
the feeling with which Brut. regards his dead friend'
(K.).

243. *advantage* i.e. by displaying our magnanimity.

245. *take...body* Inferred from Plut. (see 3. 2
head-note (ii, *c*)).

253. *I do...no more* He has all he could have
desired—including the unlooked-for last word.

255 ff. *O, pardon me* etc. From this moment 'the
spirit of Cæsar' and the enormity of his murder are
brought before us.

258. *the tide of times* the ebb and flow of history.

259. *hands* (Grant White) F. 'hand'.

261. *dumb mouths* Again at 3. 2. 226. Cf. *Ric. III*,
1. 2. 55–6; *1 Hen. IV*, 1. 3. 96; *Cor.* 2. 3. 6–8.

263–76. *A curse...burial* Cf. Carlisle's prophecy,
Ric. II, 4. 1. 136–49.

263. *limbs* (F.). Many edd. read 'lives' (J.), wh. 'is to forget the physical effects of a curse', familiar to anthropology (J. A. K. Thomson, *Sh. and the Classics*, p. 203). Clar. cites *Tim.* 4. 1. 21 ff. [1955].

271. *ranging* v. G.　　272. *Até* v. G.

273. *a monarch's voice* Only a monarch could order 'no quarter', acc. to milit. custom at this period. 'After all Cæs. will be king' (V.). Cf. *Cor.* 3. 1. 274–5.

276. F. 'Enter Octauio's Seruant'. See note l. 298.

279–80. *Cæsar did write* etc. See 3. 2 head-note (iii).

283. *big* v. G.

284–6. *Passion...water* Cf. *Temp.* 5. 1. 63.

284. *catching,...eyes* (F 2 + edd.) F. 'catching from mine eyes'. A good illustration of scanty punctuation leading to corruption.

290. *Rome* A play on 'room'; cf. 1. 2. 156.

292. *corse* (Pope) F. 'courſe'.

298. *Lend me your hand* Historically Cæs.'s body was left in the Senate House after the murder; theatrically it lies at the base of Pompey's statue just on the outer stage, and must therefore be reverently carried off before the next sc. Hence the entry of the Servant at l. 276; Sh. as ever deftly fitting his dramatic texture to his theatrical frame.

3. 2.

PLUTARCH. (i) *Brutus's speech*. Plut. (*Brutus*, Sk. 120) mentions two speeches by Brutus: (*a*) in the Capitol whither he and the conspirators had gone for refuge after the murder: 'an oration...to win the favour of the people and to justify that they had done'; (*b*) later from 'the pulpit for orations' in 'the market-place':—'When the people saw him in the pulpit, although they were a multitude of rakehells [scoundrels] of all sorts, and had a good will to make some stir; yet, being ashamed to do it for the reverence they bare unto

Brutus, they kept silence to hear what he would say. When
Brutus began to speak, they gave him quiet audience: howbeit immediately after they showed that they were not all
contented with the murther. For when another, called
Cinna, would have spoken and began to accuse Cæsar, they
fell into a great uproar among them and marvellously
reviled him.' All this took place on the day of the murder,
before the first meeting of the Senate (v. 3. 1 head-note vii),
and therefore a day or two before the funeral. For the style
of Brutus in Sh. v. note 3. 2. 14–48, and Introd. p. xix.

(ii) *Antony's speech and the fury of the mob.* Plut. gives
three slightly differing accounts of Cæsar's funeral and Sh.
takes something from each: (*a*) *Cæsar*, Sk. 102. Mentions
the riot of the mob, the burning of the body and the firing
of the conspirators' houses, but says nothing of Antony and
attributes all to the reading of the will and the public
exhibition of Cæsar's body 'all bemangled with gashes of
swords'. (Accounts *b* and *c* speak only of the holes in
Cæsar's 'bloody garments'.) (*b*) *Antonius*, Sk. 165. Makes
no reference to the will in this connexion but attributes
the 'uproar among the people' entirely to Antony. 'When
Cæsar's body was brought to the place where it should be
buried [ἐκκομιζομένου Καίσαρος] he made a funeral oration
in commendation of Cæsar according to the ancient custom
of praising noble men at their funerals. When he saw that
the people were very glad and desirous also to hear Cæsar
spoken of, and his praises uttered, he mingled his oration
with lamentable words; and by amplifying of matters did
greatly move their hearts and affections unto pity and
compassion. In fine, to conclude his oration, he unfolded
before the whole assembly the bloody garments of the dead,
thrust through in many places with their swords, and called
the malefactors cruel and cursed murtherers. With these
words he put the people into such a fury, that they presently
took Cæsar's body, and burnt it in the market place, with
such tables and forms as they could get together. Then
when the fire was kindled, they took firebrands and ran to
the murtherers' houses to set them afire, and to make them
come out to fight.' (*c*) *Brutus*, Sk. 121–2: 'Afterwards
when Cæsar's body was brought into the market place,

Antonius making his funeral oration in praise of the dead, according to the ancient custom of Rome, and perceiving that his words moved the common people to compassion, he framed his eloquence to make their hearts yearn the more; and taking Cæsar's gown all bloody in his hand, he laid it open to the sight of them all, showing what a number of cuts and holes it had upon it. Therewithal the people fell presently into such a rage and mutiny, that there was no more order kept amongst the common people. For some of them cried out, "Kill the murtherers": other plucked up forms, tables, and stalls about the market-place, as they had done before at the funerals of Clodius, and having laid them all on a heap together, they set them on fire, and thereupon did put the body of Cæsar, and burnt it in the middest of the most holy places. And furthermore, when the fire was throughly kindled, some here, some there, took burning firebrands, and ran with them to the murtherers' houses that had killed him, to set them afire. Howbeit, the conspirators, foreseeing the danger before, had wisely provided for themselves and fled.'

Such was the light timber from which Sh. framed one of his finest and most famous scenes. N.B. Plut. notes the effects of the oration, but gives very few hints of its contents. Appian (II. 144) on the other hand, assigns Antony an elaborate and passionate speech: but there is no evidence that it is genuine or that Sh. had read it.

(iii) *The return of Octavius.* In *Brutus* (Sk. 123) Plut. follows up his account of the flight of Brutus and Cassius with: 'Now the state of Rome standing in these terms, there fell out another change and alteration, when the young man Octavius Cæsar came to Rome....When Julius Cæsar, his adopted father, was slain, he was in the city of Apollonia (where he studied) tarrying for him, because he was determined to make war with the Parthians: but when he heard the news of his death he returned again to Rome.' And there is a briefer passage in *Antonius* (Sk. 166) to much the same effect. From these Sh. might naturally infer an early, if not an immediate, return to Rome, but though Oct. actually crossed to Italy directly after the assassination, he did not reach Rome before May, while it was another year or two before he made common cause with Antony, during which, as Plut. makes clear (Sk. 166–9), their relations were strained or hostile. Sh. in the interests of drama foreshortens all this and exhibits the Triumvirate as the immediate sequel of the Assassination.

S.D. 'The Forum' (Rowe) F. 'Enter Brutus and goes into the Pulpit, and Caſſius, with the Plebeians'. As Brut. does not ascend the Rostra before l. 10, this puzzling S.D. is prob. a conflation of two in the copy: at the head of the sc. 'Enter Brutus and Cassius with the Plebeians' and in the margin (added perhaps by the prompter; see p. 92) 'goes into the Pulpit'. N.B. the 'commoners' of 1. 1 are now called 'plebeians'.

1. *satisfied* v. G. To 'satisfy' the consciences as well as the stomachs of the people is the secret of government. Once again (cf. the cobbler in 1. 1.) we see that combination of familiarity and deference characteristic of an English crowd.

10. S.D. Based on Cap., expanding Rowe. None in F.

13–47. *Romans...my death*. For Plut. see head-note (i). Sh. seems also to have taken a hint for Brut.'s style from Plut., who says (Sk. 107) that in some of his Greek epistles 'he counterfeited that brief compendious manner of speech of the Lacedaemonians', and gives examples. Cf. Introd. p. xix.

13, 14. *my cause* i.e. the cause of liberty.

14–16. *believe me...may believe* i.e. accept me as an honest man and remember my reputation that you may do so.

17. *senses* reason (O.E.D. 10); i.e. he appeals to their heads, not (like Ant.) to their hearts.

24. *free men* (J.) F. 'Free-men'. A hyphen often implies an accent on the word that precedes it (Simpson, p. 86). Cf. (F.) *Cymb*. 2. 3. 76 'True-man'.

38. *enrolled in the Capitol* Sh. is prob. thinking of

the Crown records in the Tower of London (cf. p. xxxii, Introd. to *Ric. II*).

40. S.D. F. 'Enter Mark Antony, with Cæfars body. For 'an open coffin' see ll. 107, 159–98, and cf. Ophelia's funeral in *Hamlet*. Cf. Plut. (Sk. 121) 'Cæs.'s body was brought into the market-place, Ant. making his funeral oration'.

50. *ancestors* (F.) Perh. 'ancestor's'; i.e. with that of L. Junius Brutus (cf. 1. 2. 159; 2. 1. 53, note).

51. *Let him be Cæsar* One of those strokes wh. reveal Sh.'s profound political understanding; but not without its hint from Plut., who speaks (*Cæsar*, Sk. 97) of those 'that desired change and wished Brutus only their prince and governor above all other'.

51–2. *Cæsar's...Brutus* i.e. let Brut. be crowned as the better man of the two. Ant. overhears all this.

64. *the public chair* Cf. Plut. (Sk. 128) 'the chair or pulpit for orations'; cf. G. 'chair'.

67. *for Brutus' sake* i.e. in the name of Brut. for whom I am acting.

73. *gentle Romans* Cf. Plut. (Sk. 120) 'a multitude of rakehells of all sorts'.

74. *Friends, Romans*, etc. For Plut. see 3. 2 head-note (ii). Ant. begins very quietly and haltingly—the 'plain blunt man' in sad perplexity. Brut. is 'an honourable man', and when he says Cæs. was ambitious, it must be so; and yet, and yet... such is the note. The voice gives no hint of irony, since the force of the irony 'depends on its being so disguised as to seem perfectly unconscious' (Hudson).

75. *bury* 'Sh. was no doubt thinking of his own time and country' (Clar.). But he found the word 'buried' in North (see beg. of quot. in 3. 2 head-note (ii, *b*)), while l. 257 below and 5. 5. 55 show that he knew the Romans burnt their dead. Prob. 'burial'

(also found 5. 5. 77) covered burning as well as inter-
ment; cf. Lat. 'sepelire', 'sepultura'.

not to praise him He disclaims any intention of
delivering the 'laudatio' Brut. had spoken of (l. 60).

78. *Cæsar....* The speech seems carefully punctuated in F., and I mark the periods throughout as long
pauses due to the stress of emotion.

84. *So are they all* By extending the epithet to cover
the whole 'knot', he greatly reduces its value.

86. *He was my friend* Spoken with a catch in the
voice.

105–6. *O judgement...reason* A sobbing outburst;
cf. 'Bear with me' (l. 106) and 'his eyes are red' etc.
(l. 117). For the meaning, cf. *Ham.* 1. 2. 150 'O God,
a beast that wants discourse of reason | Would have
mourned longer'. Ant. then utters a natural hyperbole,
though one a pedantic follower of Aristotle, who held
that animals were without a 'reasonable soul' (v. note
2. 1. 66), might easily make fun of, as Ben Jonson did
in *E.M.O.* (1599) 3. 4. 33, where 'Reason long since
is fled to animals' is quoted as an illustration of 'fustian
philosophy'. See my article, 'Ben Jonson and *Julius
Cæsar*', in *Sh. Survey*, II (1949).

105. *art fled* (F2) F. 'are fled'.

106. *Bear with me* At this point Ant. thinks it
politic to give way to his (genuine) grief in order that
the crowd may wag their heads a little together. 'He
is acting and not acting' (Hunter) throughout.

111. *Has he, masters?* The line being defective,
Cap. read 'my masters', Craik, 'Has he not', and Hunter
'That he has, masters'.

116. *Poor soul!* A woman's voice. It is a mistake
to assign the Plebeians' speeches 'permanently to four
individuals. There can be as many citizens as there are
lines and they are scattered all over the stage' (Skillan).

119–20. *But yesterday...world* Cf. Appian, II, 118

(end) 'him, who a little before had been master of the earth and sea', and Nashe, cited note 3. 1. 150–1.

121. *so poor*=so mean in rank.

123. *mutiny and rage* Cf. Plut. (Sk. 122): 'the people fell presently into such a rage and mutiny' etc.

126. *I will...wrong* As if resisting a strong temptation. Perplexity now gives way to a struggle between duty to the 'honourable men' and anxiety to tell the people how Cæs. loved them; a theme which greatly excites their curiosity.

130. *his will* In Plut. (Sk. 121) the public reading of the will takes place in the Senate *before* Ant.'s speech, two days after the murder.

134–8. *dip...issue* Sh. translates Plut.'s 'Cæs.'s funerals should be honoured as a god' (Sk. 102) into terms of hagiolatry (cf. 2. 2. 89 note).

143. *not wood...not stones* Cf. 1. 1. 39 'You blocks, you stones'.

146–7. *'Tis good...of it!* 'Observe the slow deliberate rhythm due to the use of monosyllables' (V.). 'In the first line he imparts what he pretends to withhold; in the second he suggests what he feigns to deprecate' (Hunter).

150–3. *Will you...fear it* Perplexity, almost anguished, returns to cloak the first mention of the assassination. It gives the return he plays for: the crowd speak the word 'traitors'; after which he can say it openly too (l. 198).

158. *will?* (Pope) F. 'will:'.

159–60. *Then...the will* Ant. knows his 'common man', and knows that nothing fascinates him more than the sight of a corpse (cf. ll. 199–203).

Then Delicious; an absolute *non sequitur*.

161. *Shall...leave?* Note this deference; cf. l. 73.

163. S.D. After Rowe.

168. *Nay...far off* Acc. to traditional stage-practice

Ant. here indicates that his nose is offended by their proximity (cf. 1. 2. 246–51). Right, I think; though Sh.'s technical purpose is to prevent a crowd obstructing the view of Ant. and the coffin.

174. *That...Nervii* The battle of the Sambre, 57 B.C., one of the greatest of his victories, comparable in the risks run and the slaughter of the enemy to Agincourt itself; 'and further the love of the people unto him made his victory much more famous' (Plut., Sk. 61). Arguing from the old soldiers in a London crowd, Sh. would imagine many of Cæs.'s veterans in the Forum.

175. *Look, in this place* The show-down begins here, leading up to 'bloody Treason' (l. 193) and 'traitors' (l. 198). For the orig. in Plut. see head-note (ii).

178–81. *And as he plucked...or no* One of the few conceits in *Cæs.* A development of *Lucr.* ll. 1734–6, where Sh. is speaking of another Brutus.

181. *unkindly* (*a*) cruelly, (*b*) unnaturally; cf. 'unkindest' with the same quibble in l. 184 and *Ham.* 1. 2. 65.

182. *angel* Some gloss 'darling'; others 'genius' (v. note 2. 1. 66). In a popular speech 'darling' is more likely.

186. *traitors'* A preliminary test, not the direct accusation of l. 198.

189. *statua* (Mal.) F. 'Statue'. Cf. note 2. 2. 76.

190. *Which...ran blood* A miracle, which is susceptible of two interpretations: (i) on the analogy of the 'ordeal by touch' or 'ordeal of the bier', by which a suspect was required to touch the corpse of the murdered man and pronounced guilty if the blood flowed, the statue bleeds because touched by the falling Cæs. who had been guilty of Pompey's death; or (ii) as a miraculous token of sympathy on the part of his former rival and foe for Cæsar thus foully done to death, which,

considering when and by whom the words are spoken, seems the true meaning. This note is indebted to suggestions by Mr A. F. Giles and Mr C. B. Young.

Wyndham (Plut. 'Tudor Trans.' 1, pp. lxxiii–iv) notes this as one of the 'touches of genius' derived from a blunder of North's. In the original (Loeb trans.) Cæs. 'sank...against the pedestal on which the statue of Pompey stood; and the pedestal was drenched with his blood'; in Amyot 'il...fut poussé...contre la base, sur laquelle estoit posée l'image de Pompeius, qui en fut toute ensanglantée'; in North, who takes 'qui' as relative to 'l'image', not to 'la base', he 'was driven... against the base whereupon Pompey's image stood, which ran all of a gore-blood till he was slain'.

194. *O, now you weep* Contrast ll. 103–4.

197. *Look you here* This exposure of the body itself, which occurs as it were by accident in one only of the three accounts of the Forum scene in Plut. (v. 3. 2 head-note (ii, *a*)), Sh. seizes upon as Ant.'s crowning stroke.

205–6. *Revenge!...live!* F. continues this to '2' (='Sec. Pleb.'). 'All' Camb., following Delius, who would also assign ll. 209–10 to 'All'.

211. *Good friends* etc. The irony now becomes palpable sarcasm.

216. *with reasons* 'Intentionally ignoring the fact that Brut. had already shown his "reasons"' (Hunter).

217. *steal...hearts* i.e. as Brutus did.

219. *plain blunt man* Like one of yourselves.

222–4. *neither wit...blood* 'The various gifts which marked the orator' (Hunter, who, I think rightly, omits a F. comma after 'speech'). I take 'worth' as 'a reputation for excellence'.

wit (F2) F. 'writ'; v. G. 'wit'.

233. *The stones* Cf. Luke xix, 40, and *Macb*. 2. 1. 58.

244. *seventy-five drachmas* (Plut., Sk. 121.) A little

under £3. At 4. 1. 8–9 we learn how much respect
Ant. pays to this clause in the will.

246. *royal* v. G.   250. *orchards* v. G.

251. *this side* Actually transtiberine, as Plut. states;
but Amyot mistranslated and North followed.

252. *common pleasures* public parks; v. G. 'pleasure'.

256–61. *We'll burn . . . anything* Cf. head-note (ii, c).

261. *windows* shutters; v. G.

263. S.D. F. 'Enter Seruant'.

264. *Octavius . . . Rome* Cf. 3. 2 head-note (iii).

268. *upon a wish* Cf. K. John, 2. 1. 50.

270. *him* Cap. and others conj. 'them' or ''em'.

3. 3.

PLUTARCH. (i) *Cinna (Cæsar,* Sk. 102). 'There was one
of Cæs.'s friends called Cinna, that had a marvellous strange
and terrible dream the night before. He dreamed that Cæs.
bad him to supper, and that he refused and would not go:
then that Cæs. took him by the hand and led him against
his will.' Next day 'he went into the market place to honour
his funerals. When he came thither one of the mean sort
asked him what his name was . . . so that it ran straight
through them all that he was one of them that murdered
Cæs.: for indeed one of the traitors to Cæs. was also called
Cinna as himself. Wherefore . . . they fell upon him with
such fury that they presently dispatched him in the market
place.' In *Brutus* (Sk. 122) the marginal headings to the
parallel passage run: 'The strange dream of Cinna the
Poet' and 'The murder of Cinna the Poet, being mistaken
for another of that name.'

(ii) *Burning the conspirators' houses (Cæsar,* Sk. 102).
'They took the firebrands and went unto their houses that
had slain Cæsar to set them afire.'

S.D. Rowe continues the sc. Cap. and later edd.
change to 'A street'. F. 'Enter Cinna the Poet and after

him the Plebeians'. Cap. and later edd. give Pleb. their entry at l. 4.

2. *unluckily* (F.) Warb.+many mod. edd. 'unlucky'. For the adv. as adj. see Schmidt, ii, 1418, and *Macb.* 4. 1. 126 'amazedly'.

charge my fantasy In Plut. the dream was 'terrible'; Sh. adopts the common notion of a happy dream boding ill luck (cf. close parallels in *Rom.* 5. 1. 1–5 and *Merch.* 2. 5. 16–8, 36).

4. S.D. Cap. 'Enter Citizens'.

9. *directly* v. G.; cf. 1. 1. 13.

18. *bear me a bang* get a blow from me ('me' is ethical dative).

19. *Proceed;* (Camb.) F. 'proceede' J. 'Proceed'.

30. *Tear...bad verses* A Sh. touch!

34. *turn him going* 'send him packing' (Schmidt).

37. *burn all* etc. See head-note (ii).

4. 1.

PLUTARCH. (i) *The Triumvirate* (*Antonius*, Sk. 169). 'Thereupon all three met together (to wit, Cæsar, Antonius and Lepidus) in an island [Bononia off N. Italy]....Now as touching all other matters they were easily agreed, and did divide all the empire of Rome between them, as if it had been their own inheritance. But yet they could hardly agree whom they would put to death: for every one of them would kill their enemies, and save their kinsmen and friends. Yet at length, giving place to their greedy desire to be revenged of their enemies, they spurned all reverence of blood and holiness of friendship at their feet. For Cæs. left Cicero to Ant.'s will, Ant. also forsook Lucius Cæsar who was his uncle by his mother: and both of them together suffered Lepidus to kill his own brother Paulus.'

Sh. is strikingly vague about all the details of this sc. (v. notes ll. 4–5, 7) prob. because he derived it from the *Life of Antony* with which he was less familiar than with the Lives of Cæsar and Brutus. It is even poss. that he added

it later in order to form a link with *Ant. and Cleo*. Lepidus
does not appear elsewhere in *Cæs*.

(ii) *Brutus and Cassius* 'levy powers' (ll. 41–2). Plut.
(*Brutus*, Sk. 129) relates how Cassius in Syria and Brutus in
Macedon had 'leyied great armies' and then met together
at Smyrna, 'having ships, money and soldiers enough, both
footmen and horsemen, to fight for the empire of Rome'.

S.D. Locality from Cap. Theob. following Plut. and
Appian read 'a small island near Mùtina'; but 'Cæsar's
house' and 'the Capitol' (ll. 7, 11) make Rome certain.
F. 'Entèr Antony, Octavius, and Lepidus', to which
Mal. added 'seated at a table'.

It is a diminished world into which Sh. takes us after the
death of Cæs....In Rome which has lost her master, sits
a group of ruffians dictating who shall live, who shall be
spared, how Cæs.'s testament shall be dishonoured and the
people defrauded (Palmer, p. 46).

3. *consent*—(Knight) F. 'confent'.

4. *Publius* Another Publius! Cf. p. 96. Plut.
(v. head-note (i)) speaks of Lucius Cæsar, Ant.'s uncle.

6. *He shall not live* etc.

Thus by a mere touch [Sh.] alienates the sympathy and
admiration which we may have acquired for Ant. in the
preceding Act. (K.)

Cf. Plut. (Sk. 169):

There never was a more horrible, unnatural, and crueller
change than this was.

7. *Cæsar's house* Sh. forgets (i) that acc. to 3. 2. 266
the triumvirate should be meeting there, (ii) that acc. to
3. 2. 130 Ant. himself had taken the will therefrom.

9. *How...legacies* They had served their turn, in
a speech, and could now be dispensed with. Plut. (Sk.
pp. 165–6) relates that Calp. put Ant. in charge of
Cæs.'s goods, on the strength of which he proceeded to
act as executor.

12. *slight unmeritable man* The Lepidus of *Ant*.

and Cleo., a character Sh. d·duced from Plut.'s *Antonius*.
Cf. Syme, p. 69: 'Lep. had influence, but no party;
ambition, but not the will and the power for achieve-
ment.'

14. *three-fold world* Europe, Africa, Asia. Cf. *Ant.*
4. 6. 6.

18. *I have...you* Cf. Plut. (Sk. p. 166) 'Ant. at
the first made no reckoning of him, because he was very
young; and said he lacked wit and good friends to
advise him.' Sh. perhaps unconsciously remembers
North's Homeric tag reproduced at 4. 3. 129–30 below.

21. *as...gold* Prov. 'An ass is but an ass though
laden with gold' (Apperson, 18). Cf. *Meas.* 3. 1. 26–8.

22. *To groan and sweat* Cf. *Ham.* 3. 1. 76.

26. *shake his ears* The only occupation left to an
ass 'turned off'. Cf. *Tw. Nt*, 2. 3. 131; Maria implies
Malvolio is an ass who should be dismissed.

32–3. *wind...spirit* For this language of the
'manage' cf. *1 Hen. IV*, 4. 1. 109; *Ham.* 4. 7. 84–7.

33. *motion* (Pope) F. 'Motion,' *governed* v. G.

37. *objects, arts* (F.). Theob. and most 18th-c. edd.
'abject orts'; Staunton and most mod. edd. 'abjects,
orts'. K., following Furness, restores F., and points
out that 'Which' (l. 38) refers to all three of the preceding nouns. 'Objects' (v. G.)=curiosities noted in
travel. In *Ant.* 2. 7. 27 ff. we have instances of the
kind of 'objects' Lep. fed upon.

imitations, (Rowe) F. 'Imitations.'

39. Steev. cites Shallow who 'came ever in the
rearward of the fashion' (*2 Hen. IV*, 3. 2. 315).

40. *property* a mere accessory on the stage of life,
or a mere tool for other men to handle; cf. 'Vice's
dagger', *2 Hen. IV*, 3. 2. 318.

44. *Our...stretched* Most agree that something
has been omitted and F 2 reads 'our best meanes stretcht
out'. It is anybody's guess; mine being 'Our best

friends made our means and our means stretched',
which is pregnant, while such repetition might easily
give rise to omission.

48–9. *at the stake...bayed about* Cf. *Macb.* 5. 7.
1–2 and above 3. 1. 205. See also G. 'bay' and *M.N.D.*
4. 1. 112.

4. 2 and 4. 3.

PLUTARCH. For these two scenes, which are really one,
Sh. drew on a number of passages from the *Life of Brutus*.
The main events up to the exit of the cynic poet were
furnished by the following:

'About that time Brut. sent to pray Cass. to come to the
city of Sardis, and so he did. Brut. understanding of his
coming went to meet him with all his friends. There both
their armies being armed, they called them both Emperors.
Now as it commonly happeneth in great affairs between two
persons, both of them having many friends and so many
captains under them, there ran tales and complaints betwixt
them. Therefore, before they fell in hand with any other
matter, they went into a little chamber together, and bad
every man avoid, and did shut the doors to them. Then
they began to pour out their complaints one to the other,
and grew hot and loud, earnestly accusing one another, and
at length fell both a-weeping. Their friends that were without
the chamber hearing them loud within and angry between
themselves, they were both amazed and afraid also, lest it
should grow to further matter: but yet they were commanded
that no man should come to them. Notwithstanding, one
Marcus Phaonius, that had been a friend and follower of
Cato while he lived, and took upon him to counterfeit a
philosopher, not with wisdom and discretion, but with a
certain bedlam and frantic motion...in despite of the door-
keepers came into the chamber, and with a certain scoffing
and mocking gesture, which he counterfeited of purpose, he
rehearsed the verses which old Nestor said in Homer:

My lords, I pray you hearken both to me,
For I have seen mo years than suchie three.

Cass. fell a-laughing at him: but Brut. thrust him out of the chamber, and called him dog, and counterfeit cynic. Howbeit his coming in brake their strife at that time, and so they left each other.' (Sk. 134–5.)

In Plut. the quarrel is renewed next day over the condemnation of Lucius Pella, which Sh. makes the original cause and represents as the punishment of one of Cass.'s friends. Apart from this Sh. follows his source very closely at this point, as my italics show:

'The next day after, Brut., upon complaint of the Sardians, did *condemn and note Lucius Pella* for a defamed person, that had been a Praetor of the Romans, and whom Brut. had given charge unto; for that he was accused and convicted of robbery and pilfery in his office. This judgment much misliked Cass., because he himself had secretly (not many days before) warned two of his friends, attainted and convicted of the like offences, and openly had cleared them: but yet he did not therefore leave [=cease] to employ them in any manner of service as he did before. And therefore he greatly reproved Brut. for that he would show himself so straight and severe, *in such a time as was meeter* to bear a little than to take things at the worst. Brut. in contrary manner answered that he should *remember the Ides of March*, at which time they slew Julius Cæsar, who neither pilled nor polled the country, but *only was a favourer and suborner of all them that did rob* and spoil, by his countenance and authority.' (Sk. 135). See also *Antonius* (Sk. 159): 'Cæsar's friends, that governed under him, were cause why they hated Cæsar's government (which indeed in respect of himself was no less than a tyranny) by reason of the great insolencies and outrageous parts that were committed: amongst whom Antonius, that was of greatest power, and that also committed greatest faults, deserved most blame.'

Sh.'s references to the 'itching palm' (4. 3. 10) and the passage about Cass.'s refusal to lend Brut. 'certain sums of gold' (4. 3. 69–82) derive from earlier passages in *Brutus*, in which (i) 'the extreme covetousness and cruelty of Cass. to the Rhodians' is compared with 'Brut.'s clemency unto the Lycians' (Sk. 133), and (ii) it is related that on one occasion Brut. 'prayed Cass. to let him have some part of his money whereof he had great store'; that 'Cass.'s friends...earnestly dissuaded him', urging 'that it was no reason that Brut. should have the money which Cass. had gotten together by sparing, and levied with great evil will of the people their subjects'; but that, 'this notwithstanding, Cass. gave him the third part of his total sum' (Sk. 130–1).

As to Portia, Plut. concludes his *Life of Brutus* with this account of her killing herself: she 'took hot burning coals and cast them into her mouth, and kept her mouth so close that she choked herself' (Sk. p. 151).

Other points from Plut. will be dealt with as they arise in the text.

4. 2.

S.D. Locality from Rowe (v.l. 28) F. 'Drum. Enter Brutus, Lucillius, and the Army. Titinius and Pindarus meet them.' This cannot represent Sh.'s intentions: (i) we are before Brut.'s tent (l. 51) and Brut. clearly enters therefrom when the drum announces the arrival of his troops, since he greets Lucilius who leads them (l. 3) and asks for news of Cass.; (ii) Pindarus, who is Cass.'s bondman (5. 3. 56), does not 'meet' Lucilius but arrives with him, both of them having come from Cass.; (iii) lastly, Titinius, an officer of Cass.'s, who is given nothing to say and is not addressed before l. 52, should enter with Cass. and his army at l. 31, since his presence could not have been ignored earlier.

6. *He greets me well* i.e. 'by a man from whom I am glad to receive it. Brut. is always courteous to... subordinates' (K.).

7. *change* Cf. l. 19.　　*ill officers* e.g. Lucius Pella (4. 3. 2).

10. *satisfied* v. G.

12. *full of regard* Cf. 3. 1. 225.

13–14. *Lucilius;* | *How...you, let* (Mal. Globe, etc.) F., Camb. 'Lucillius | How...you: let'.

16. *familiar instances* marks of friendship; v. G. 'instance'.

23. *hot at hand* frisky at the start. O.E.D. ('hand' sb. 25 c) shows it to be a common phrase.

27. *Sink in the trial* founder when put to the test.

30. S.D. F. 'Low march within', i.e. drums faintly heard from the tiring-house to denote the approaching army. In F. at l. 24, but 'Hark' (l. 30) is clearly a response to the drums. Prob. therefore a marginal prompter's note. Cf. F. 'Low Alarums' at 5. 3. 90; 5. 5. 23.

31. S.D. F. 'Enter Caſsius and his Powers' after 'Cassius' in l. 30. See G. 'power'. Quite a stirring spectacle: massed troops with ensigns flying, sharp words of command passing down the lines, and two generals between whom trouble is brewing.

34–6. F. gives no prefixes. Cap. assigns to '1, 2, 3 officer'.

38. *you gods;* (F.) Edd. 'you gods!' But Brut. keeps 'sober form', l. 40 (v. G.)—exasperatingly so.

41. *be content* don't get excited.

42. *griefs* v. G. *I do...well.* i.e. we are old friends and needn't shout at each other.

46. *enlarge...griefs* v. G. for both words.

50–2. *Lucius...Lucilius* (Craik, Herford) F. 'Lucillius... Let Lucius'. These names are liable to confusion, esp. if abridged in the MS. Objections to F. are: (i) the shorter name is more suitable metrically to l. 50; (ii) the boy 'Lucius' pairs ill with the officer Titinius, well with the slave Pindarus; (iii) at 4. 3. 126 we find Lucilius guarding the tent door with Titinius, and at 4. 3. 137 the two are given an order by Brut. Craik suggests that 'Let' (l. 52) was repeated from l. 50 for the sake of the metre by the compositor.

4. 3.

S.D. F. 'Manet Brutus and Caffius'. Pope first changed the sc. and all edd. have followed, though Hunter notes that no change took place on the Eliz. stage. There the two 'armies' marched out through the doors to L. and R.; Luc. and Tit. drew aside the curtains concealing the inner stage (Brut.'s tent); Brut. and Cass. proceeded c. to symbolize entry into the tent; and Luc. and Tit. as if to stand sentry then exited by the stage doors, through one of which the mad Poet forces an entrance at l. 126.

2–5. *condemned and noted* Cf. North (v. head-note 4. 2 + 3).

noted...slighted off v. G.

5. *was* (F.) Mal. and mod. edd. 'were'. But 'letters' (litterae) = an epistle. Cf. *Oth.* 4. 1. 286 and O.E.D. 4 b.

8. *nice* v. G.

bear his comment come in for its criticism. Cf. *Son.* 89. 2 and *K. John* 4. 2. 263.

10. *itching palm* v. G. 'Itchie palmes' in *Cynthia's Revels* (1600) 3. 4. 39 (Jonson, IV, p. 90).

18–28. *Remember...Roman* See quotation from Plut. (Sk. p. 135) in head-note to 4. 2 + 3. Critics note that this account is quite unsupported by anything earlier in the play. Brut. never hints at 'justice' as a motive at 2. 1. 10–34; so far indeed from accusing him of 'supporting robbers', he confesses that 'the quarrel' would 'bear no colour for the thing he is'. But the point is necessary to Sh.'s purpose here (v. Introd. p. xx); and, as Goethe observes (*Conv. with Eckermann*, Ap. 18, 1827, trans. Oxenford, 1883, p. 250), 'he regarded his plays as a lively and moving scene, that would pass rapidly before the eyes and ears upon the stage, not as one that was to be held firmly and carped at in detail'.

20. *What villain...stab* i.e. who was such a villain as to stab.

28. *bay* (Theob., Globe and many edd.) F. 'baite'. J., Camb., Herford, Hunter follow F. But had Sh. used 'bait', which echoes the sound of 'bay' (l. 27), he must have written 'bait me not', i.e. he would have avoided repeating rhythm as well as sound at the same point in the line. Further, 'bay' (=not only 'bark at' but 'dam in'—v. O.E.D. sb.⁵ vb.⁴) is supported by 'hedge in' (l. 30). F 2 reads 'baite' in both lines.

30. *hedge me in* limit me; cf. *Merch.* 2. 1. 18.

31. *Older* Cf. Plut. (Sk. 129) 'he was the elder man'.

39–45. See G. for *give way...rash...stares... budge...observe.*

47. *You shall digest* I'll make you swallow down your poisonous temper in silence.

49–50. *I'll use you...waspish* The coldness and superiority of this reveal the worst side of Brut.'s character. The warmer-hearted Cass. finds it terribly wounding; cf. ll. 112–14.

54. *noble* (F.) Singer conj. 'able', wh. after the 'vaunting' in l. 52 is, I believe, correct. What is in question is not 'nobility' but generalship. F. 'noble' may be a press correction of some misprint, e.g. 'oble' for 'able'.

69–75. *I did send...indirection* Many critics find this inconsistent with ll. 9–28, if not dishonest: 'Brutus, though he will not stain his own honour by extorting money from peasants, is perfectly willing to profit by Cass.'s "indirection"' (Hunter). But this is to read Plut. into Sh. Plut. tells us that Cass. extorted money from the countries he occupied; Sh. that he was suspected of taking bribes, a very different thing. Nowhere does Sh. say that the money Brut. asks to share had been got 'by vile means', though he might have avoided giving this impression, had he phrased ll. 71–5 more carefully. MacCallum notes (p. 264, n.) that Sh. also suppresses the fact (Plut., *Brutus*; Sk. pp. 130–1) that Brut. was 'neither so scrupulous nor so unsuccessful' in raising supplies as he is here represented. For the ruthless extortions of the historical Brutus v. *C.A.H.* x, 23.

80. *rascal counters* The Stoic's contempt.

95. *braved* v. G.

101. *Pluto's* (F.) Pope+subs. edd. (except Hunter and K.) 'Plutus''.

The identification of Plutus, the god of wealth, with Pluto, the god of the nether world [and of all underground minerals], occurs in classical writers, and their names are the same in origin. Eliz. writers often identify the two deities; cf. Webster, *Duchess of Malfi*, 3. 2. 283 (V.).

Cf. also *Troil.* 3. 3. 197 (F.) and Simpson in *Notes and Queries*, 9th ser. IV, 265.

103. *gold...heart* Cf. notes 1. 1. 65; 1. 2. 309–11; 3. 1. 41–2.

108. *dishonour...humour* 'insult coming from you shall seem mere caprice' (V.).

110–12. *carries...again* Cf. 1. 2. 177, 2 *Hen. IV*, 4. 4. 33, *Troil.* 3. 3. 257 and *Lucr.* 181.

113. '*mirth*' *and* '*laughter*' The words (v. 1. 49) which Cass. could not forget.

114, 115. *ill-tempered* Used with some reference to its physiol. sense of 'ill-mixed'; cf. note 5. 5. 73–5.

117. *What's the matter?* This suggests neither triviality nor indifference, as it would on mod. lips.

122. *leave you so* 'let it go at that' (K.).

123. *Let me go in* Here F. gives S.D. 'Enter a Poet' and heads ll. 123–5 '*Poet*'. Dyce and Theob. added 'within' S.D. at ll. 125, 126. On the Globe stage the audience could watch the man struggling with Lucil. at one of the side doors out of sight of Brut. and Cass. Cf. head-note S.D.

126. S.D. From Dyce after Theob. Plut. (see head-note 4. 2 + 3) calls the intruder a counterfeit philosopher. 'North's doggerel doubtless suggested to Sh. the idea of making Phaonius...a miserable rhymester' (Hunter); v. next note. In Plut. this incident puts an end to the quarrel for the time; Sh. uses it 'as preparation for the sudden drop to the deep still note struck by the revelation of Portia's death' (Barker, p. 113).

129–30. *Love...than ye* A slight improvement on North's doggerel (v. head-note 4. 2 + 3). Plut. of course gives the orig. line from Homer (*Iliad*, 1, 259):

$$\text{ἀλλὰ πίθεσθ' ἄμφω δὲ νεωτέρω ἐστὸν ἐμεῖο}$$

('But hearken, for you are both younger than I am'). Sh. puts this matter to strange use. Had he realized that Plut.'s 'old Nestor' was intervening in the quarrel between Achilles and Agamemnon he would surely have made some dramatic capital out of it; and he must have realized it had he read Chapman's *Seven Books of the the Iliad* (1598).

134. *I'll know...time* I'll put up with his whims when he keeps them for suitable occasions.

136. *Companion* v. G.

140. S.D. F. gives no exits. Lucius, I think, goes through the door at the back of the inner stage; the other two through one of the side stage doors.

149. *touching* v. G.

150–4. *Impatient...fire* Plut. (v. Sk. pp. 151–2) mentions the manner of her death, but not in connexion with the quarrel, while he assumes that it was one worthy of Cato's daughter and the wife of a Brutus, as his *Life of Cato Utican* ('Tudor Trans.' v, p. 179) proves. While he says (v. head-note) she choked herself by casting hot coals into her mouth, Valerius Maximus (as K. notes) writes 'she *swallowed* burning coals'.

150. *Impatient* (F.) Cap. conj. 'Impatience'. Sh.

often omitted mute *e* after *c* and 'impatienc' might be
misread 'impatient' (cf. *Sh.'s Hand in 'Sir Th. More'*,
p. 133) though (K. notes) 'it would make a harsh
collision of sound' with 'absence'.

155. S.D. F. 'Enter Boy with Wine, and Tapers'.

157. S.D. From F.

160. S.D. 'drinks' from Cap.; 'Lucius goes' from
Camb. ('Exit Lucius'); the rest from F.

163. *call in question* v. G.

167–8. *Come down... Philippi* This, taken with ll.
195, 220, 223, imply that both armies are bearing down
upon Philippi, though in fact Sardis (v. 4. 2. 28) and
Philippi are very far apart. Sh. altered his map, like
his clock and his calendar, to suit his own convenience.

171–6. *That by...being one* Here Sh. borrows
verbally from Plut. (Sk. p. 128):

After that these three, *Octavius* Cæsar, *Antonius* and
Lepidus...did set up *bills of proscription and outlawry*, con-
demning the kindred of the noblest men of Rome to suffer
death, and among the number *Cicero was one.*

171. *outlawry* (F4) F. 'Outlarie'.

177. *Cicero one!* E. E. Kellett suggests that this
emphasis is due to the fact that Plut. makes much of it
(*Suggestions*, pp. 36–8). But surely the fame of Cicero,
esp. great with the Eliz.s, is enough to account for it.

179–93. *Had you letters...bear it so* Most (following Resch, 1882; v. Furness) agree that this passage.
represents Sh.'s orig. treatment of the Portia episode,
which he later rejected, but omitted to delete (see
'Note on the Copy', p. 95), in favour of that in ll. 141–
56 (cf. 'Speak no more of her', ll. 156 and 164). See
esp. Barker, pp. 130–2; Chambers, *Wm. Sh.* 1, pp. 396–
7; Furness, p. 225; K. p. xv. Those who believe Sh.
wished both passages to stand have to explain why, if
so, Brut. tells a deliberate lie to Messala at l. 182
(though three lines later adjuring him to speak the

truth as a Roman), and, what is far worse, acts the pharisee. The explanation Hunter (p. 288) offers, that

> what Messala takes for stoical fortitude is in reality a sensitive shrinking from a wound which is too recent and too painful to be laid bare in the presence of any but the most intimate friends,

is met by the fact that what Messala (and Cass.) 'take' will be taken by the audience also, unless Sh. gives them a strong hint to the contrary, wh. he does not. On the face of it the actor would have to act the stoical pharisee; for anything else there is no evidence whatever.

Barker (p. 130) seems to speak the last word:

> Surely it is clear that a mere corruption of text is involved, not the degeneracy of Brut.'s character.... That his [Sh.'s] final intention was to give us a Brut. wantonly 'showing off' to Messala or indulging at this moment in a super-subtle defence of his grief, I would take leave to dispute against the weightiest opinion in the world.

189. *once* some time. Cf. *Macb.* 5. 5. 17; the same, but how different!

192. *in art* v. G. 'art'. Cf. ll. 143–4.

194. *Well...alive* Note how aptly this follows l. 178.

194–223. *What do you think...Philippi* Cf. Plut. (Sk. 138–9):

> Cass. was of opinion not to try this war at one battle, but rather to delay time and to draw it out in length, considering that they were the stronger in money, and the weaker in men and armour. But Brut., in contrary manner, did alway before, and at that time also, desire nothing more than to put all to the hazard of battle, as soon as might be possible: to the end he might either quickly restore his country to her former liberty, or rid him forthwith of this miserable world, being still troubled in following and maintaining of such great armies together.... Thereupon it was presently determined they should fight battle the next day.

208. *off* (Rowe) F. 'off.'

211. *Under your pardon* Cf. 3. 1. 236. Once again
Cass. yields against his better judgement (cf. 5. 1. 73–5);
this time 'from personal affection' (Hunter).

216–22. *There is a tide...ventures* Cf. *2 Hen. IV*,
1. 1. 180–6 for this extended metaphor of merchant-
venturing; and for another series of different images,
illustrating the same idea of taking 'the instant way',
see *Troil.* 3. 3. 145–79.

218–19. *life...in miseries* Cf. 'this miserable
world' cited from Plut. in note ll. 194–223.

222. *with your will* as you wish it.

224. *The deep of night* Cf. *M.W.W.* 4. 4. 40;
Ham. 1. 2. 198 (note).

229. *Lucius...Messala* (Camb. arrangement) F.
'*Enter Lucius.* | *Bru.* Lucius my Gowne: farewell
good Meſſala'.

235. *my lord* Kolbe (1896, v. Furness) notes this
'wonderful touch', and Hunter that 'in reply ("good
brother") Brut. affectionately disclaims the title of
superiority'.

236. S.D. F. 'Enter Lucius with the Gowne' at
l. 234.

237. *instrument* a lute (Barker, p. 127).

240. *Claudius* (Rowe) F. 'Claudio'.

242. *Varro and Claudius* (Rowe) F. 'Varrus and
Claudio'.

S.D. F. 'Enter Varrus and Claudio'. See p. 94.

247. *watch* v. G.

250. *here's the book* etc. Plut. (*Brutus*, Sk. 136)
notes that Brut. 'slept very little', and that in time of war

after he had slumbered a little after supper, he spent all the
rest of the night in dispatching of his weightiest causes; and
after he had taken order for them, if he had any leisure left
him, he would read some book till the third watch of the
night, at what time the captains...did use to come to him.

Cf. the earlier account of the campaign of Pharsalus
(Sk. 108):

> Brutus, being in Pompey's camp, did nothing but study
> all day long....Furthermore, when others slept, or thought
> what would happen the morrow after, he fell to his book.

251. S.D. From Camb.

264. S.D. From F. Acc. to stage-tradition the song
used is 'Orpheus with his lute' from *Hen. VIII*, 3. 1,
the words of wh. are 'very appropriate' (Barker, p. 130).
This music (not in Plut.) is 'designed by Sh. to give
repose and attune our minds to what follows', i.e. the
apparition (V.).

265. *slumber* (F3) F. 'flumbler'.

266. *Lay'st...mace* Cf. *Faerie Queene*, 1. iv. 44:
'whenas Morpheus had with leaden mace | Arrested
all that courtly company'. Alluding to the sergeant or
bailiff who touched the shoulder with his mace when
making an arrest. Cf. *Err.* 4. 3. 27; 4. 2. 37.

leaden Cf. *Lucr.* 124 'leaden slumbers'.

270. S.D. Cap. 'lays the Instrument by, and sits
down'.

271. *the leaf turned down* An anachronism, of course,
since the 'liber' was a 'volumen' or roll.

272. S.D. From F. The Apparition is thus described in Plut. *Brutus* (Sk. 136):

> One night very late (when all the camp took quiet rest)
> as he was in his tent with a little light, thinking of weighty
> matters, he thought he heard one come in to him, and
> casting his eye towards the door of his tent, that he saw a
> wonderful strange and monstruous shape of a body coming
> towards him, and said never a word. So Brut. boldly asked
> what he was, a god or a man, and what cause brought him
> thither. The spirit answered him, 'I am thy evil spirit,
> Brutus: and thou shalt see me by the city of Philippes.'
> Brut., being no otherwise afraid, replied again unto it: 'Well,
> then I shall see thee again.' The spirit presently vanished

away: and Brut. called his men unto him, who told him
that they heard no noise, nor saw anything at all.

It is only in the dialogue at 5. 5. 17 we learn that the
apparition is Cæsar's Ghost, but the audience would of
course recognize him as they do Banquo's Ghost in
Macb. Edd. assume the identification of Plut.'s 'evil
spirit' with Cæsar's Ghost to have been Sh.'s invention;
but in fact it was traditional on the Eliz. stage, e.g. we
find it in *Cæsar's Revenge*, written between 1592 and
1596 (v. Mal. Soc. *Collections*, 1, Parts iv and v,
pp. 290–2). Cf. Introd. p. xxvi and above 2. 1. 167–70.

273. *How ill...burns* Plut. *Cæsar* (Sk. 103) speaks
of 'the light of the lamp that waxed very dim'. Cf.
Ric. III, 5. 3. 180. A common superstition.

274–5. *I think...apparition* Cf. *Macb*. 2. 1. 48–9.
For 'monstrous' and 'shapes' see quotation from Plut.
in note l. 272 S.D.

276. *comes upon* Cf. l. 167.

277. *god...angel...devil* Sh. translates Plut.'s 'a
god or a man' into the terms of Eliz. ghost-lore; cf. my
What Happens in 'Hamlet', pp. 60 ff.

278. *stare* v. G. and cf. *Ham*. 3. 4. 121–2.

280. *Thy evil spirit, Brutus* From Plut., v. above.

284. *I will* 'I am quite ready to' (Hunter). In
l. 282 'shall'=must.

284. S.D. None in F. Rowe 'Exit Ghost'.

285. *Now...vanishest* L. 286 and 5. 5. 17, apart
from the visibility to the audience (cf. end of note
l. 272 S.D.) show that the Ghost is not, as some suppose,
subjective. Cf. *Macb*. 3. 4. 106–8, and 3. 4. 37 (note).

287–8. *Varro! Claudius!...Claudius!* (Rowe) F.
'Varrus, Claudio,...Claudio'.

293. *Lucius* (F 2) F. 'Lucus'.

297. *Claudius* F. 'Claudio'.

5. 1.–5. 5.

PLUTARCH (*Brutus*, Sk. 137–51) describes the two battles of Philippi in considerable detail. Sh. follows him in the main, but treats the two battles as one, and only avails himself of certain episodes, Plut.'s account of which will be quoted below as they occur.

5. 1.

S.D. 'The plains of Philippi' (Cap.) Cap. also introduced the (quite unnecessary) scene-divisions into the Act. For 'rocks' see 5. 5. 1 and for the 'hill' see 5. 3. 12 ff. Entry from F. Barker (pp. 113–20) reconstructs the Eliz. staging of the whole act.

1–20. *Now, Antony,...do so* Intended to bring out the relations between Oct. and Ant., in preparation perhaps for *Ant. and Cleo*. Note on the one hand Oct.'s use of the royal 'our' in l. 1; his greater prescience (ll. 1–6); and stronger will (l. 20); on the other, Ant.'s tolerant air of superiority towards a youngster (l. 7); cf. 4. 1. 18. To effect all this Sh. freely manipulates or suppresses Plut.'s facts, one of them being the sickness of Oct. which prevented him being present at the battle in person.

1. *answerèd*   **4.** *battles*   **6.** *Answering* v. G.

7. *I...bosoms* Cf. 2. 1. 305 and *Lear*, 4. 5. 26.

8–9. *content...places* glad to be elsewhere.

9–10. *places; and...bravery*, (Pope) F. 'places, and ...bravery:'.

10. *fearful bravery* Cf. G. 'bravery', *Ham*. 5. 2. 79 'the bravery of his grief', and Plut. (Sk. 137):

In truth Brutus's army was inferior to Oct. Cæs.'s in number of men; but for bravery and rich furniture, Brutus' army far excelled Cæs.'s. For the most part of their armours were silver and gilt, which Brutus had bountifully given them.

14. *Their bloody sign* Cf. Plut. (Sk. 139):

The next morning, by break of day, the signal of battle was set out in Brutus' and Cassius' camp, which was an arming scarlet coat [ὁ φοινικοῦς χιτών, Plut.'s usual Greek for 'vexillum'].

18. *Upon the right hand I* Clar. notes that in Plut. (Sk. 140):

Cass., although more experienced as a soldier, allowed Brut. to lead the right wing of the army. Sh. made use of this incident, but transferred to the opposite camp, in order to bring out the character of Oct.

20. S.D. F. 'Drum...Army'. Cap. added 'Lucilius ...others'. F. also prints 'March' in margin of l. 20, but as this merely duplicates 'Drum' it is prob. a prompter's note. See p. 92.

21–66. *They stand...stomachs* This 'parley' is of Sh.'s invention. K. notes that such 'flytings' before a fight are common in Eliz. drama, and instances *1 Hen. VI*, 1. 3; 3. 2. 41–70; *3 Hen. VI*, 1. 4. 27–64; 2. 2. 81– 177; *Cor.* 1. 8; *Rom.* 1. 1. 46–70; *Cymb.* 4. 2. 70–100. Was it a practice in 16th-c. warfare?

33. *The posture...unknown* v. G. 'posture'.
are...unknown In the fluid Eliz. syntax 'the posture ...blows' contains the plur. idea of 'your blows and where you mean to plant them'. I owe this note and G. 'posture' to Dr Percy Simpson.

34–5. *But...honeyless* Sarcastic allusion to Ant.'s eloquence in the Forum.
Not...too? (Delius) F. 'Not...too.' Alludes to its deadly effect.

36–8. *O yes...sting* The reply is feeble; but Brut. has no skill in word-fence; cf. his *tu quoque* in ll. 56–7.

40. *Hacked...Cæsar* see 3. 1 head-note (vi).

41. *showed your teeth* grinned. Cf. *Merch.* 1. 1. 55.
teeth (F 3) F. 'teethes'.

fawned See note 3. 1. 42–3.

45–7. *Now, Brutus...ruled* Alluding to 2. 1. 155–66.

48. *cause* v. G. The quibble is pursued in 'arguing' and 'proof'.

53. *three and thirty* 'Three and twenty' in Plut. and all other authorities. Perhaps 'xxiii' wrongly expanded.

54–5. *till...traitors* i.e. till traitors have slain another Cæsar.

61. *schoolboy* Oct. Cæs. was 21.

worthless unworthy.

62. *a masker...reveller* Cf. 2. 1. 189; 2. 2. 116.

PLUT. *Antonius* (Sk. 161): 'The noblemen (as Cicero saith) did not only mislike him, but also hate him for his naughty life: for they did abhor his banquets and drunken feasts he made at unseasonable times, and his extreme wasteful expenses upon vain light huswives; and then in the daytime he would sleep or walk out his drunkenness, thinking to wear away the fume of the abundance of wine which he had taken over night. In his house they did nothing but feast, dance, and mask: and himself passed away the time in hearing of foolish plays,' etc.

66. *stomachs* Two meanings, v. G.

S.D. F. 'Exit Octauius, Antony, and Army.'.

67–8. *blow...hazard* Cf. *Macb.* 5. 5. 51–2.

69. S.D. F. 'Lucillius and Meſſala ſtand forth'.

70–5. *Messala...liberties* Cf. Plut. *Brutus* (Sk. 139):

But touching Cassius, Messala reporteth that he supped by himself in his tent with a few of his friends...and that after supper he took him by the hand and holding him fast (in token of kindness, as his manner was) told him in Greek: 'Messala, I protest unto thee, and make thee my witness, that I am compelled against my mind and will (as Pompey the Great was) to jeopard the liberty of our country to the hazard of a battle. And yet we must be lively and of good courage'....Having spoken these last words unto him, he bad him farewell, and willed him to come to supper to him the next night following, because it was his birthday.

71. *as* v. G.

74. (*As Pompey was*) i.e. at Pharsalus.

76. *Epicurus* Plut. three times speaks of Cass. as an Epicurean: (i) just before the assassination, when 'though otherwise he did favour the doctrine of Epicurus, beholding the image of Pompey...he did softly call upon it to aid him' (*Cæsar*, Sk. 100); (ii) at Sardis (*Brutus*, Sk. 136–7) when he argues with Brut. that the apparition of the spirit in his tent must have been a creature of imagination; and (iii) in connexion with the 'unlucky signs' before Philippi (see note ll. 84–8) 'the which began somewhat to alter Cass.'s mind from *Epicurus' opinion* [my italics], and had put the soldiers also in a marvellous fear' (Sk. 138). Cf. 1. 3. 46–52 (note).

79–83. *on our...gone* Cf. Plut. (Sk. 137):

When they raised their camp, there came two eagles that, flying with a marvellous force, lighted upon two of the foremost ensigns, and always followed the soldiers, which gave them meat and fed them, until they came near to the city of Philippes: and there, one day only before the battle, they both flew away.

This follows immediately upon Cass.'s elaborate exposition of 'visions' as illusions (v. note l. 76), though, unlike Sh., Plut. does not connect the two. But see note ll. 84–8.

79. *former* v. G.; cf. Plut. 'foremost' (note ll. 79–83).

84–8. *And in their steads...ghost* An elaboration of Plut. (Sk. 138), who mentions, among other 'unlucky signs unto Cass.' before the battle, 'a marvellous number of fowls of prey, that feed upon dead carcases'. See note l. 76 (iii).

87–8. *canopy*...*ghost* Image of a man on his death-bed.

fatal foreboding death.

89–91. *I but*...*constantly* See the end of Cass.'s words to Messala quoted from Plut. in note ll. 70–5.

92–115. *Now, most noble*...*farewell take.* Based on Plut. (Sk. 139–40):

'Brut. and Cass. talk before the battle.' 'And both the chieftains spake together in the midst of their armies. There Cass. began to speak first, and said: "The gods grant us, O Brut., that this day we may win the field, and ever after to live all the rest of our life quietly one with another. But sith the gods have so ordained it, that the greatest and chiefest things amongst men are most uncertain, and that if the battle fall out otherwise to-day than we wish or look for, we shall hardly meet again, what art thou then determined to do, to fly, or die?" Brut. answered him, being yet a young man, and not over greatly experienced in the world: "I trust (I know not how) a certain rule of philosophy, by the which I did greatly blame and reprove Cato for killing himself, as being no lawful nor godly act, touching the gods: nor concerning men, valiant; not to give place and yield to divine providence, and not constantly and patiently to take whatsoever it pleaseth him to send us, but to draw back and fly: but being now in the midst of the danger, I am of a contrary mind. For if it be not the will of God that this battle fall out fortunate for us, I will look no more for hope, neither seek to make any new supply for war again, but will rid me of this miserable world, and content me with my fortune. For I gave up my life for my country in the Ides of March, for the which I shall live in another more glorious world." Cass. fell a-laughing to hear what he said, and embracing him, "Come on then", said he, "let us go and charge our enemies with this mind. For either we shall conquer, or we shall not need to fear the conquerors."'

93. *The gods*...*stand* optative mood.
95. *rest* (Rowe) F. 'reſts'.

100–7. *Even by...us below* Much debated; most take it as inconsistent both with Brut.'s next speech and with his suicide in 5. 5; and suppose Sh. to have been misled by North, who reading the following in Amyot:

Estant encore jeune et non assez experimenté ès affaires de ce monde, je fis, ne sçay comment, un discours de philosophie, par lequel je reprenois et blasmois fort Cato de s'estre deffait soy-mesme. [i.e. 'When I was still but a young man with little experience of life, I wrote (lit. 'made') a philosophical essay, I can't tell why, in which I strongly reprehended Cato for having killed himself.']—

mistranslated 'je fis' by 'I trust' and 'discours' by 'rule' (v. note, ll. 92–115). Yet neither is guilty of inconsistency. North makes Brut. say that though he disapproves of suicide in theory, 'being now in the midst of danger, I am of a contrary mind'; Sh. instead of reporting this change of opinion, shows it actually taking place: i.e. the philosopher condemns suicide (ll. 102–7); the Roman soldier, faced with the prospect of walking in Ant.'s triumph, sees in it the only honourable course (ll. 110–12). Thus in Sh. Cass., who persuades Brut. to kill Cæsar, also persuades him to kill himself, while Brut. finds it no more possible to die by philosophy than to live by it in this rude world.

101. *Cato* the younger, who slew himself at Utica rather than fall into Cæsar's hands and was in fact Brut.'s uncle and hero.

102. *himself, I know not how* F. 'himſelfe, I know not how:' Camb. 'himself: I know not how,'. The 'But' (l. 103) proves that 'I know not how' goes with the principal sentence.

104–5. *prevent...life* anticipate the natural end of life. Cf. the mod. phrase 'die before one's time'.
life; (Theob.) F. 'life,'.

106. *some high powers* Hunter writes:

Notice the indefinite 'some'. In North Brut. speaks with much more confident faith of 'the gods' and 'God'. As Cass. is losing his old belief that 'men are masters of their fate', so Brut. seems to waver in the opposite direction.

108–9. *led in triumph...Rome* 'Sh. prob. did not know that no Roman citizen was ever led in triumph' (Hunter). Cf. Pompey in *Cæsar's Revenge*, ll. 116–17; 'Captive to follow Cæsar's chariot wheels | Riding in triumph to the Capitol.'

114–21. *And whether...well made* With this tragic last farewell contrast 'Cassius fell a-laughing' etc. in North.

122–5. *O, that a man might know...is known* Exactly the mood and sentiment of Hamlet at *Ham.* 5. 2. 218–22.

5. 2.

PLUTARCH (Sk. 140–2): 'Then Brut. prayed Cass. he might have the leading of the right wing....Cass. gave it him, and willed that Messala (who had charge of one of the warlikest legions they had) should be also in that wing with Brut. So Brut. presently sent out his horsemen, who were excellently well appointed, and his footmen also were as willing and ready to give charge. Now Ant.'s men... taking no heed to them that came full upon them to give them battle, marvelled much at the great noise they heard.... In the meantime Brut., that led the right wing, sent little *bills* to the colonels and captains of private bands, in which he wrote the word of the battle; and he himself riding a-horseback by all the troops, did speak to them and encouraged them to stick to it like men. So by this means very few of them understood what was the word of the battle, and besides, the most part of them never tarried to have it told them, but ran with great fury to assail the enemies; whereby, through this disorder, the legions were marvellously scattered and dispersed one from the other....

But that which the conquerors thought not of, occasion [i.e. chance] showed it unto them that were overcome; and that was, the left wing of their enemies left naked and unguarded of them of the right wing, who were strayed too far off, in following of them that were overthrown. So... they brake and overthrew the left wing where Cass. was, by reason of the great disorder among them and also because they had no intelligence how the right wing had sped.... So that Brut. had conquered all of his side, and Cass. had lost all on the other side. For nothing undid them but that Brut. went not to help Cass., thinking he had overcome them as himself had done: and Cass. on the other side tarried not for Brut., thinking he had been overthrown as himself was.'

S.D. F. 'Alarum. Enter Brutus and Meſſala.'— again at l. 2 'Lowd Alarum', which I take as a prompter's marginal note merely duplicating the centred 'Alarum' (v. p. 92). Cf. Barker pp. 114–15:

The talk between Brutus and Cassius over...a chill quiet talk, for they feel they are under the shadow of defeat—the stage is left empty. Then the silence is broken by the clattering *alarum*, the symbol of a battle begun. Then back comes Brut., and a very different Brut....And he is gone as he came. It is a most stirringly dramatic effect.

1. *bills* v. G. and see Plut. (head-note above).
4. *Octavius'* (Pope) F. 'Octauio's'. See pp. 95, 100.

5. 3.

PLUTARCH (Sk. 142–4): [Offended with the sundry errors Brut. and his men committed in battle] 'Cass. found himself compassed in with the right wing of his enemy's army....Furthermore, perceiving his footmen to give ground, he did what he could to keep them from flying, and took an ensign from one of the ensign-bearers that fled, and stuck it fast at his feet; although with much ado he could scant keep his own guard together. So Cass. himself was at length compelled to fly, with a few about him, unto a little hill, from whence they might easily see what was done in all the plain: howbeit Cass. himself saw nothing, for his sight was very bad, saving that he saw (and yet with much ado) how the enemies spoiled his camp before his eyes. He saw also a great troop of horsemen, whom Brut. sent to aid him, and thought that they were his enemies that followed him: but yet he sent Titinnius, one of them that was with him, to go and know what they were. Brut.'s horsemen saw him coming afar off, whom when they knew that he was one of Cass.'s chiefest friends, they shouted out for joy; and they that were familiarly acquainted with him lighted from their horses, and went and embraced him. The rest compassed him in round about a-horseback, with songs of victory and great rushing of their harness, so that they made all the field ring again for joy. But this marred all. For Cassius, thinking indeed that Titinnius was taken of the enemies, he then spake these words: "Desiring too much to live, I have lived to see one of my best friends taken, for my sake, before my face." After that, he got into a tent where nobody was, and took Pindarus with him, one of his freed bondmen whom he reserved ever for such a pinch, since the cursed battle of the Parthians, where Crassus was slain, though he notwithstanding scaped from that overthrow: but then, casting his cloak over his head, and holding out his bare neck unto Pindarus, he gave him his head to be stricken off. So the head was found severed from the body: but after that time Pindarus was never seen more. Whereupon some took occasion to say that he had slain his master without his commandment. By and by they knew the horsemen that came towards them, and might see Titinnius crowned with a garland of triumph, who came before with great speed unto Cass. But when he perceived, by the cries and tears of his friends which tormented themselves, the misfortune that had chanced to his captain Cass. by mistaking, he drew out his sword, cursing himself a thousand times that he had tarried so long, and so slew himself presently in the field. Brut. in the mean time came forward still, and understood also that Cass. had been overthrown: but he knew nothing of his death till he came very near to his camp. So when he was come thither, after he had lamented the death of Cass., calling him the last of all the Romans, being unpossible that Rome should ever breed again so noble and valiant a man as he, he caused his body to be buried, and sent it to the city of Thassos, fearing lest his funerals within his camp should cause great disorder.'

S.D. F. 'Alarums. Enter Caffius and Titinius.'

1. *the villains* His own footmen; see Plut. above.

4. *I slew the coward* 7. *fell to spoil* Sh.'s additions.

8. *enclosed* 'compassed in' (Plut.).

11. *far*=farther. Cf. Franz, §§ 213–14 and *Wint*. 4. 4. 428.

19. *with a thought* v. G. 'thought'. 21. *thick* v. G.

22. S.D. None in F. The meditative lines (23–5) allow the player just time to exit at one of the side-doors and climb the hidden stair to the upper stage.

23–4. *time...I end* Cf. the *impresa* of Mary of Guise: 'a phoenix in flames, the word *En ma fin gît mon commencement*', embroidered 'on a bed of state' by her daughter, Mary Stuart (v. letter of W. Drummond: Jonson 1. 208). Was this in Sh.'s mind, as it was in the mind of T. S. Eliot when writing *East Coker*? [I owe this note to suggestions by Mr Burbidge of the C.U.P. and Dr Sharp, Edinburgh University Librarian.]

32. S.D. From F. 35. S.D. F. 'Enter Pindarus'.

38. *swore* Trans., cf. 2. 1. 129, 131–2.

44. *when...covered* Cf. note 3. 1. 76 S.D. (end).

45. *sword.* F. 'Sword—' No S.D. in F. Camb. 'Pindarus stabs him'. 46. S.D. From Cap.

49–50. *Far...of him* Cf. Plut. (above).

50. S.D. F. 'Enter Titinius and Meffala'.

60. *O setting sun* Contrast l. 109—'three o'clock'; sunset here prob. episodic scene-painting to enhance Tit.'s tragic words (cf. Goethe, quoted in note, 4. 3. 18–28). Cf. *Cæsar's Revenge*, ll. 2399 ff. (Tit. speaks): 'The sun doth hide his face, and fears to see | This

bloody conflict.' That 5. 5 begins at night implies that 5. 4 represents the 'second fight' of some 3 or 4 hours.

61. *to night* into darkness.

65, 66. *success* v. G.　　68. *apt* v. G.

71. *the mother* i.e. melancholy (v. l. 67); hence, by transf., Cass., the embodiment of melancholy.

74–5. *thrusting...ears* Cf. *Temp.* 2. 1. 105–6; *Ant.* 2. 5. 24.

82–5. *Put...brow* This is Sh.'s invention. Cf. Prince Hal's similar gesture towards the dead Hotspur (*1 Hen. IV*, 5. 4. 96).　　88. *regarded* v. G.

89. *By your leave, gods* He asks permission to depart before his appointed hour. Cf. 5. 1. 104–7 [K.].

a Roman's part Cf. *Macb.* 5. 7. 30 and *Ham.* 5. 2. 339. Tit.'s reason here (v. l. 65) is a finer one than Plut.'s 'cursing himself a thousand times that he had tarried so long'.

90. S.D. F. 'Dies. | Alarum. Enter Brutus, Meſſala, yong Cato, Strato, Volumnius, and Lucillius.' And at l. 96, 'Low Alarums.', which once again I take as a prompter's marginal note. See p. 92. Strato and Volumnius do not speak until 5. 5 and edd. generally omit them here; but they stand for Labeo and Flavius who are addressed (following Plut.) at l. 108, and these ought therefore to take their place in the S.D.

94–5. *O Julius...abroad* Cf. Brut.'s words at 2. 1. 167–70 and Ant.'s prophecy 3. 1. 271 ff. 'The last two Acts are closely bound to the first three by this conception.' (K.)　　96. *Brave* v. G.

97. *whe'r* F. 'where', Camb. and mod. edd. 'whether'. Cf. note 1. 1. 65.

99–101. *The last of all the Romans...fellow* Cf. Plut. (cited above) and Jonson cited Introd. p. xxiv.

fare (F 2) F. 'far'. Cf. *MSH*, p. 114.

104. *Thasos* (S. Walker) F. 'Tharsus'. 'Thassos' in North, see above. An island off the coast of Thrace.

105. *funerals* The sing. is more usual with Sh., but here he takes the word from North (cited above).

108. *Labeo and Flavius* (Hanmer+F4) F. 'Labio and Flauio'. See note l. 90 S.D. Plut. (Sk. 150) relates of Brut. that 'naming the friends he had seen slain in battle before his eyes, he fetched a greater sigh than before, specially when he came to name Labeo and Flavius, of whom the one was his lieutenant and the other captain of the pioners of his camp'.

109. *'Tis three o'clock* From Plut.'s account (v. head-note 5. 4) of the second battle twenty days after the first. Sh. combines the two. Cf. note l. 60 above.

5. 4.

PLUTARCH. This brief scene is taken from a long passage in Plut. (*Brutus*, Sk. pp. 144–9), describing the second battle of Philippi. Having recounted Brut.'s troubles after Cass.'s death and Oct.'s still greater difficulties through the destruction at sea of a convoy of men and food, he notes that had Brut. heard of the latter, he would have delayed fighting on land. 'Howbeit the state of Rome (in my opinion) being now brought to that pass that it could no more abide to be governed by many lords, but required one only absolute governor: God, to prevent Brut. that it should not come to his government, kept this victory from his knowledge.' He next tells how the 'evil' and 'monstruous' spirit appeared again to Brut. on the eve of the battle, but 'said never a word'. On the day itself Brut. for various reasons delayed giving the signal for attack until 'past three of the clock', and once joined, the battle went against him. 'There was the son of Marcus Cato slain valiantly fighting amongst the lusty youths. For...telling aloud his name and also his father's name at length he was beaten down.' Plut. then relates 'the fidelity of Lucilius', who proclaimed himself Brut. and when captured 'prayed them to bring him to Antonius', to whom he said, '"Antonius, I dare assure thee, that no enemy hath taken, nor shall take, Marcus Brutus alive, and I beseech God keep him from that fortune: for

wheresoever he be found, alive or dead, he will be found
like himself." Whereupon Ant. turning to those who brought
him, said, "I do assure you, you have taken a better booty
than that you followed. For instead of an enemy you have
brought me a friend: and for my part, if you had brought
me Brut. alive, truly I cannot tell what I should have done
to him. For I had rather have such men my friends as this
man here, than mine enemies." Then he embraced Lucilius
and...Lucilius ever after served him faithfully, even to his
death.' The following, too, is relevant, both to Brut.'s
desperate mood at the opening of 5. 4 and to his decision to
kill himself in 5. 5 (v. note, ll. 17–20): 'The second battle
being at hand this spirit appeared again unto him, but spake
never a word. Thereupon Brut. knowing he should die, did
put himself to all hazard in battle, but yet fighting could not
be slain.' (*Cæsar*, Sk. 104.)

S.D. F. 'Alarum. Enter Brutus, Meſſala, Cato,
Lucillius, and Flauius.' Cap. and subs. edd. omit
Messala and Flavius (v. 5. 3. 90. S. D. note and 108).
They have nothing to say because, I take it, they exit
with Brut. at l. 1. F. also gives at l. 6 the S.D. 'Enter
Souldiers, and fight', another prompter's note (v. p. 92),
for it is obvious that the battle surges on to the stage
with the opening of the scene.

1. S.D. See note ll. 7–8.

2. *What bastard* etc. For the idiom cf. 4. 3. 20;
for the sentiment cf. *Hen. V*, 3. 1. 22–3.

4. *son...Cato* Therefore brother of Brut.'s wife.
Cf. note 2. 1. 295.

7–8. *And I am...Brutus* F. no speech-heading; edd.
to '*Brut.*', except Macmillan (Arden), who gives to
'*Lucil.*'; and argues that (*a*) it is strange the well-known
Brut. should tell his name with such emphasis, taking
his cue, too, from young Cato; (*b*) the iteration suggests
pretence; (*c*) Lucil.'s speaking here elucidates l. 14,
obscure to the audience otherwise. 'Prob.', he adds,
'the printer of F. by mistake put the heading *Luc.* two

lines too low down.' This appears to me convincing and seems supported by Plut.'s account of Lucil.'s action in diverting attention from Brut.; v. head-note.

8. S.D. Condenses a long S.D. from Cap.

11. *being Cato's son* i.e. as worthy son of a worthy father.

13. *There is so much* Hanmer and subsequent edd. add S.D. 'Giving [or 'offering'] money'. But, as Macmillan suggests, l. 13 is merely introductory to l. 14; note the F. colon after 'straight'. I paraphrase: 'This will make you kill me forthwith: it is Brutus you kill!'

15. *We must not* etc. Because 'noble prisoners' were worth a large ransom.

17. *tell the news* (Pope) F. 'tell thee newes'. S.D. F. gives the entry at l. 15.

20-9. *Safe...enemies* Here Sh. follows Plut. very closely; see head-note.

25. *like himself* From Plut. Cf. 5. 5. 58-9 and *Hen. V*, 1 Prol. 5 (note).

30. *whe'r* (Cap.) F. 'where' Camb. etc. 'whether'. Cf. note 5. 3. 97.

5. 5.

PLUTARCH (Sk. 149): 'Now Brut. having passed a little river, walled in on either side with high rocks and shadowed with great trees, being then dark night, he went no further, but stayed at the foot of a rock with certain of his captains and friends that followed him.'

(Sk. 150-1): 'Furthermore, Brut. thought that there was no great number of men slain in battle: and to know the truth of it, there was one called Statilius, that promised to go through his enemies (for otherwise it was impossible to go see their camp) and from thence, if all were well, that he would lift up a torch-light in the air, and then return again with speed to him. The torch-light was lift up as he had promised, for Statilius went thither. Now Brut. seeing Statilius tarry long after that, and that he came not again, he said: "If Statilius be alive, he will come again." But his evil fortune was such that, as he came back, he lighted in his enemies' hands and was slain. Now the night being far spent, Brut., as he sat, bowed towards Clitus, one of his men, and told him somewhat in his ear: the other answered him not, but fell a-weeping. Thereupon he proved Dardanus, and said somewhat also to him: at length he came to Volumnius himself, and speaking to him in Greek, prayed him for the studies' sake which brought them acquainted together, that he would help him to put his hand to his sword, to thrust it in him to kill him. Volumnius denied his request, and so did many others: and amongst the rest, one of them said, there was no tarrying for them there, but that they must needs fly. Then Brut., rising up, "We must fly indeed", said he, "but it must be with our hands, not with our feet." Then taking every man by the hand, he said these words unto them with a cheerful countenance: "It rejoiceth my heart, that not one of my friends hath failed me at my need, and I do not complain of my fortune, but only for my country's sake: for, as for me, I think myself happier than they that have overcome, considering that I leave a perpetual fame of virtue and honesty, the which our enemies the conquerors shall never attain unto by force nor money, neither can let [hinder] their posterity to say that they, being naughty and unjust men, have slain good men, to usurp tyrannical power not pertaining to them." Having so said, he prayed every man to shift for himself, and then he went a little aside with two or three only, among the which Strato was one, with whom he came first acquainted by the study of rhetoric. He came as near to him as he could, and taking his sword by the hilt with both his hands, and falling down upon the point of it, ran himself through. Others say that not he, but Strato (at his request) held the sword in his hand and turned his head aside, and that Brut. fell down upon it, and so ran himself through, and died presently. Messala, that had been Brut.'s great friend, became afterwards Oct. Cæs.'s friend: so, shortly after, Cæs. being at good leisure, he brought Strato, Brut.'s friend, unto him, and weeping said: "Cæs., behold, here is he that did the last service to my Brut."'

(Sk. 130): 'And in contrary manner his enemies themselves did never reprove Brut. for any such change or desire.
For it was said that Ant. spake it openly divers times, that
he thought, that of all them that had slain Cæs., there was
none but Brut. only that was moved to do it, as thinking
the act commendable of itself: but that all the other conspirators did conspire his death for some private malice or
envy, that they otherwise did bear unto him.

S.D. F. 'Enter Brutus, Dardanius, Clitus, Strato,
and Volumnius'. Cf. Barker, p. 118:

Hard upon the clattering excitement of the fight and the
flattering magnanimity of the triumphant Antony, comes
into sight this little group of beaten and exhausted men,
the torch-light flickering upon their faces.

1. *poor remains* Cf. *Titus*, 1. 1. 81 (note).

2–3. *Statilius...back* A reference to Plut. (see
above) makes this clear. Furness finds it 'an instance
where Sh.'s complete familiarity with his authority
has blinded him to the fact that his auditors have not
the same advantage'. Yet the text is well enough, since
the audience will take Statilius to be a scout who has
been cut off. And the reference to 'torch-light' shows
the time as already night (v. note 5. 3. 60). Whether
Brut., etc. should themselves carry torches as Barker
suggests (v. prev. note) I am doubtful; it would reveal
their presence to the enemy.

5 and 8. S.D. After Rowe and Cap.

13. *vessel full of grief* Cf. *Wint.* 3. 3. 21 'a vessel
of like sorrow | So filled'; and v. G. 'vessel'.

17–20. *The ghost...is come* See Plut., cited 5. 4
head-note (end).

22. *the world...how it goes* i.e. how things are.

23. *pit* v. G.

S.D. F. 'Low Alarums.' Cf. notes 4. 2. 30, S.D.;
5. 3. 90, S.D.

26. *school together* Cf. Plut.: 'Publius Volumnius,

a grave and wise philosopher, that had been with Brut. from the beginning of this war' (Sk. 147); and 'at length he came to Volumnius himself, and speaking to him in Greek, prayed him for the studies' sake' etc. (Sk. 150). 'Sh. makes the appeal more touching by supposing that they were schoolboys together.' (Macmillan.)

29. S.D. F. 'Alarum ſtill.'

31. S.D. After Collier.

32. *asleep* Added by Sh. to show (i) the equanimity of Brut., (ii) that Strato knew nothing of his master's previous attempts at suicide. For Strato as Brut.'s 'man', v. l. 53.

33. *thee too, Strato. Countrymen,* (Theob.) F. 'thee, to Strato. Countrymen:'.

34–8. *My heart...attain unto* Cf. Plut. (head-note).

38. *this vile* Walker 'their vile', which is made likely by 'this' in l. 36.

39. *at once* v. G. 'once'.

40. *life's* (Rowe) F. 'liues'.

42. *That have...hour* 'Brut. makes no such confession of failure in Plut.' (Hunter.) It is also his submission to Fate; cf. what he says at 3. 1. 99–101.

S.D. F. 'Alarum. Cry within, Flye, flye, flye.'

43. S.D. After Cap. F. omits.

45. *of a good respect* v. G. 'respect'.

46. *smatch* Not elsewhere in Sh.; but 'smack' (sb. and vb.) ten times. Perhaps a copyist's form.

47. *turn...face* See notes 3. 1. 76 S.D. (end) and 5. 3. 44.

49. *Give me...first* Cf. Barker, p. 119:

The man's demand for a handshake, the master's response to it;—how much of Sh.'s greatness lies in these little things, and in the love of his art that never found them too little for his care!

50. *Strato.* F. 'Strato.—' (with no S.D.). Cf. 5. 3. 45 (note).

Cæsar, now be still Cf. *Cæsar's Revenge* (Mal. Soc.) ll. 2555–60.

51. S.D. F. 'Dyes', and then, after a break, 'Alarum. Retreat. Enter Antony, Octauius, Meſſala, Lucillius,. and the Army.' 'Retreat' is a technical term for the recall by trumpets of a pursuing force; cf. *2 Hen. IV*, 4. 3. 68 S.D. and 70.

53. *My master's man* Plut. (v. head-note) makes Strato an old fellow-student of Brut.'s, like Volumnius.

60. *entertain* v. G.

68–75. *This was...a man!* Based on two passages in Plut.: (i) cited 5. 5 head-note (end), and (ii) cited in note l. 73 below. Hunter notes:

It is characteristic of Sh.'s Ant. to abandon himself freely to the generous impulse of the moment. His emotional temperament is lightly fired. And yet when other feelings are uppermost he unhesitatingly styles the same Brut. a 'butcher' (3. 1. 256), an ingrate (3. 2. 183 ff.), a 'traitor' (3. 2. 198), and a 'villain' (5. 1. 39).

71–2. *in a general...to all* Here 'in' = (i) under the influence of, (ii) for the sake of.

in a...thought = moved by genuine public spirit. Cf. G. 'general'.

73. *His life was gentle* Cf. Plut. (Sk. 105–6; first paragraph of *Brutus*):

This Marcus Brutus...having framed his manners of life by the rules of virtue and study of philosophy, and having employed his wit, which was *gentle* and constant, in attempting of great things, me thinks he was rightly made and framed unto virtue. So that his very enemies which wish him most hurt, because of his conspiracy against Julius Cæsar, if there were any noble attempt done in all this conspiracy, they refer it wholly unto Brutus.

73–5. *the elements...man* The four elements (earth,

water, air, fire) constituted, when blended together, the
four humours of the body (melancholy, phlegm, blood,
choler); and health, bodily and spiritual, largely depended
upon a just balance or mixture of the humours. Sh.'s
expression of this commonplace appears to have started
a fashion, influencing Jonson's description of the ideal
man in *Cynthia's Revels* (acted 1600) and a stanza in
Drayton's *Barons' Wars* (1603 ed.), which seems to
lean also on Jonson. Cf. my article 'Ben Jonson and
Shakespeare's *Julius Cæsar*' in *Shakespeare Survey*, 11
(1949).

74–5. *that Nature . . . a man!'* Cf. Florio's *Montaigne*,
1, 36 ('Of Cato the Younger'):

This man was truly a pattern, whom nature chose to
show how far human virtue may reach and man's constancy
attain unto.

77. *With all* (F 3) F. 'Withall'.
burial = funeral. 'Sh. did not forget that Brut. was
cremated; see above l. 55' (Hunter). Cf. note 3. 2. 75.
79. *ordered honourably* Cf. Plut. (Sk. 151):

Now Antonius, having found Brutus' body, he caused it
to be wrapped up in one of the richest coat-armours he had.

Acknowledgements. In addition to help received from
various friends upon individual points in the Notes
I have profited much in general from the advice and
encouragement of Dr Percy Simpson, Professor J. A. K.
Thomson, and Mr A. F. Giles, Reader in Ancient
History at Edinburgh. The last named has guided my
steps from the beginning and it was he who chose for
me the remarkable frontispiece to the volume.

GLOSSARY

Note. Where a pun or quibble is intended, the meanings are distinguished as (*a*) and (*b*).

ABIDE, pay the penalty of, atone for (from confusion with 'aby'); 3. 1. 95; 3. 2. 115.

ABUSE (sb.), (i) misuse; 2. 1. 18; (ii) corrupt or evil practice (of. *Meas.* 2. 1. 43); 2. 1. 115.

ADDRESS (vb.), make ready (O.E.D. (vb.) 3); 3. 1. 29.

ADVANTAGE (vb.), benefit, profit; 3. 1. 243.

AFFECTIONS, inclinations, desires; 2. 1. 20.

AIM (sb.), (i) guess; 1. 2. 163; (ii) line or direction (of fire). From shooting at the butts; 1. 3. 52.

ALARUM, lit. summons to battle by trumpet or drum, noise of battle in general (v. notes 5. 3. 90; 5. 4. head; 5. 5. 23, 29); 5. 3 S.D.; 5. 5. 42 S.D.

ALONG, at full length, stretched out (cf. *A.Y.L.* 2. 1. 30; *Rom.* 5. 3. 3; *Cor.* 5. 6. 57); 3. 1. 116.

AMAZE, bewilder, astound; 1. 2. 128; 3. 1. 97.

ANNOY, molest, harm; 1. 3. 22; 2. 1. 160.

ANSWER (vb.), (i) pay the penalty for; 3. 2. 81; (ii) cope with; 4. 1. 47; 5. 1. 24; (iii) 'fulfil', satisfy, (cf. *Meas.* 2. 4. 167); 5. 1. 1; (iv) pay down, discharge (a debt); 5. 1. 6.

APPARENT, manifest, clear, plain; 2. 1. 198.

APPLY (for), explain (as), interpret (as); 2. 2. 80.

APPOINT, supply with, assign (O.E.D. 11, 9); 4. 1. 30.

APT (i) fit; 2. 2. 97; (ii) ready, prepared, willing; 3. 1. 161; (iii) easily impressed, impressionable (cf. *Ham.* 1. 5. 31); 5. 3. 68.

ART, (i) artifice, cunning; 4. 1. 37; (ii) theory; 4. 3. 192.

As, used redundantly in phrases expressing time; 5. 1. 71.

ASTONISH, dismay; 1. 3. 56.

ATÉ, goddess of mischief and of vengeance; 3. 1. 272.

AUGURERS, augurs; 2. 1. 200; 2. 2. 37.

BASIS, pedestal of statue; 3. 1. 116.

BATTLE, force in battle array; 5. 1. 4, 16; 5. 3. 108.

BAY (vb.), (i) bark at; 4. 3. 27, 28; hence (ii) drive to bay like a stag or bear (cf. *M.N. D.* 4. 1. 119); 3. 1. 205; 4. 1. 49 with a quibble on (i).

BEAR, (i) 'bear a hand' = treat in a certain manner. Metaphor from controlling a horse with the rein; 1. 2. 35; (ii) carry off, i.e. win; 1. 2. 131; (iii) 'bear hard' = bear ill-will to; 1. 2. 314; 2. 1. 215; 3. 1. 158; (iv) 'bear it' = conduct oneself, (cf. *2 Hen. IV*, 4. 1.

135; *Oth.* 1. 3. 23); 2. 1. 226; (v) 'bear back' = move back; 3. 2. 169.

BEHOLDING, beholden; 3. 2. 66, 68.

BEND (sb.), inclination of the eye. No other instance in O.E.D.; 1. 2. 123.

BEND (vb.), direct; 2. 3. 6; 4. 3. 168.

BENT (sb.), direction; 2. 1. 210.

BIG, pregnant (with tears; cf. *Merch.* 2. 8. 46); 3. 1. 283.

BILL, (i) decree; 4. 3. 171; (ii) note, memorandum; 5. 2. 1.

BLAZE, (*a*) flame, (*b*) proclaim; 2. 2. 31.

BLOOD, (i) kin, stock; 1. 1. 55; (ii) (*a*) stock, (*b*) disposition; 1. 2. 151; (iii) disposition; 3. 1. 40; 4. 3. 114; 4. 3. 260.

BLUNT, (*a*) slow-witted, dull, (*b*) dull-edged, (*c*) abrupt, rude, harsh (in manner); 1. 2. 296; (*a*) and (*c*) 3. 2. 219.

BRAVE (adj.), noble; 2. 1. 314, 322; 3. 1. 205; 5. 3. 80, 96.

BRAVELY, nobly; 5. 4. 10.

BRAVERY, (*a*) splendour, finery, (*b*) defiance; 5. 1. 10.

BREAK WITH, make a disclosure to, reveal a secret to (cf. *Macb.* 1. 7. 48); 2. 1. 150.

BUSTLING, full of agitation and commotion; 2. 4. 18.

CALCULATE, interpret by astrology, forecast the future; 1. 3. 65.

CALL IN QUESTION, consider, examine; 4. 3. 163.

CANCEL. Legal term: annul; 1. 3. 102.

CAPITOL, the temple to Jupiter Optimus Maximus on the S.W. summit of the Capitoline hill; 1. 3. 20; 2. 1. 201, 211; 2. 2. 21; 2. 4. 11, 18, 23, 25; 3. 1. 12; 3. 3. 25; 4. 1. 11.

CARPENTER, one who makes the wooden framework of houses; 1. 1. 6.

CARRION (adj.), dead and rotting; 3. 1. 276.

CARRION (sb.), lifeless creature, used contemptuously of living people (cf. *Hen. V*, 4. 2. 39, etc.); 2. 1. 130.

CAST, put (or cause to fall) into a state or condition (O.E.D. 33); 1. 3. 60.

CAUSE, (*a*) matter in hand, (*b*) thesis to be argued; 5. 1. 48.

CAUTELOUS, crafty, deceitful (cf. *Cor.* 4. 1. 33); 2. 1. 129.

CENSURE (vb.), judge; 3. 2. 16.

CEREMONY, (i) 'external accessory or symbolical attribute of worship, state, or pomp' (O.E.D. 4, citing Strype, 1709, 'The ceremonies of cap and surplice'); 1. 1. 69; (ii) prescribed rite; 1. 2. 11; (iii) either 'the ceremonial or sacerdotal interpretation of prodigies and omens' (H. N. Hudson), or 'a portent, or omen (drawn from the performance of some rite)', O.E.D. 5; 2. 1. 197; 2. 2. 13.

CHAFE (with), fret, rage (against); 1. 2. 101.

CHAIR, pulpit, Rostra in Forum from which speeches made. A word from North (v. note). (O.E.D. 4b cites Milton: 'mounting twice into the chair with a formal preachment', and Hunter *Cor.* 4. 7. 52; cf. Fr. 'chaire'.) 3. 2. 64.

CHANGE (sb.), exchange (cf. *Hen. V*, 4. 8. 31); 5. 3. 51.

CHANGE (vb.), change colour, turn pale (cf.*Ado*, 5. 1. 138); 3. 1. 24.

CHARACTERY, 'expression of thought by symbols or characters' (O.E.D.). Here the wrinkles on his brow (cf. *Lucr.* 808, 'charáctered in my brow'); 2. 1. 308.

CHARGE (sb.), (i) expense; 4. 1. 9; (ii) military command, and so body of troops under command; 4. 2. 48.

CHARGE (vb.), load, burden; 3. 3. 2.

CHARM (vb.), 'entreat or conjure by some potent invocation' (Onions); 2. 1. 271.

CHASE (sb.), race; 1. 2. 8.

CHECK, rebuke, reprove; 4. 3. 96.

CHOPPED, chapt (cf. 'choppy', *Macb.* 1. 3. 44); 1. 2. 246.

CLIMATE, region, country. Astrol. term = zone of the earth controlled by a particular constellation or planet (cf. *Ham.* 1. 1. 121); 1. 3. 32.

CLOSE (vb.), come to terms; 3. 1. 203.

CLOSET, (i) private room; 2. 1. 35; (ii) 'repository or cabinet for papers' (cf. *Macb.* 5. 1. 6; *Lear*, 3. 3. 12) (Onions); 3. 2. 130.

COBBLER, (*a*) mender of shoes, (*b*) botcher, unskilled workman (V.); 1. 1. 11.

COGNIZANCE, (*a*) term in heraldry for device or emblem worn by retainers, (*b*) generally 'distinctive badge or mark', that by which something is known or remembered (Schmidt); 2. 2. 89.

COLD, lacking in feeling or enthusiasm, 'half-hearted'; 3. 1. 214, 5. 2. 4.

COLOSSUS, gigantic statue of Apollo, said to have spanned the harbour of Rhodes (cf. *1 Hen. IV*, 5. 1. 123); 1. 2. 136.

COLOUR, (i) (*a*) ordinary sense, (*b*) military 'colours'; 1. 2. 122; (ii) ground or excuse (cf. *2 Hen. IV*, 1. 2. 242); 2. 1. 29.

COMMEND ME TO, remember me kindly to; 2. 4. 43; 4. 3. 304.

COMPANION, fellow, a term of contempt (cf. *Err.* 4. 4. 60, etc.); 4. 3. 136.

COMPASS, 'circuit of time, round, revolution' (O.E.D., citing this; cf. *Oth.* 3. 4. 70); 5. 3. 25.

COMPLEXION, visible aspect; 1. 3. 128.

CONCEIT (vb.), form an opinion of, judge; 1. 3. 162; 3. 1. 193.

CONCEPTION, thought, idea; 1. 2. 41.

CONDITION, (i) constitution (of body); 2. 1. 236; (ii) disposition (of mind); 2. 1. 254; (iii) 'make conditions' = 'manage affairs' (K.); 4. 3. 32.

CONFINES, region; 3. 1. 273.

CONFOUND, stun with dismay; 3. 1. 87.

CONJURE, raise spirits by magic incantations; 1. 2. 146; 2. 1. 323.

CONQUEST, victory; 1. 1. 36; 5. 5. 38.

CONSORT, (vb. tr.), accompany; 5. 1. 82.

CONSTANCY, composure, self-control, resolution; 2. 1. 227; 2. 1. 299; 2. 4. 6.

CONSTANT, controlled, steady, unchanging, steadfast; 3. 1. 22, 60, 72.

CONSTANTLY, steadfastly, firmly; 5. 1. 91.

CONSUMED, destroyed; 2. 2. 49.

CONTAGION, poisonous influence; 2. 1. 265.

CONTENT, easy in mind, calm; 1. 3. 142; 4. 2. 41.

CONTRIVE, conspire; 2. 3. 15.

CONTRIVER, plotter; 2. 1. 158.

CORPORAL, bodily, corporeal; 4. 1. 33.

CORSE, corpse; 3. 1. 200.

COUCHING (sb.), grovelling, obeisance; 3. 1. 36.

COUNSEL, secret thought or purpose; 2. 1. 298; 2. 4. 9.

COUNTENANCE, sanction, approval, favour; 1. 3. 159.

COUNTER (sb.), debased coin. Here contemptuously; 4. 3. 80.

COURSE, race; 1. 2. 4.

CRAVE, require, necessitate; 2. 1. 15.

CREST, ridge of horse's neck (cf. *V. & A.*, 272); 4. 2. 26.

CROSS (adj.), forked, of lightning; 1. 3. 50.

CULL (out), pick out, 1. 1. 53.

CUMBER, harass, trouble (cf. *Tim.* 3. 6. 52); 3. 1. 265.

CURTSY, bow, a variant of *courtesy*; 3. 1. 43.

CYNIC, rude fellow; 4. 3. 131.

DAMN, condemn; 4. 1. 6.

DANGER, harm, mischief (cf. *Merch.* 4. 1. 38); 2. 1. 17.

DEAR (adv.), keenly; to the heart; 3. 1. 197, 3. 2. 115.

DEEP (sb.), depth ('deep of night' again in *M.W.W.* 4. 4. 40). Cf. 'waste' (*Ham.* 1. 2. 198) or 'vast' (*Temp.* 1. 2. 327) of night; 4. 3. 224.

DEGREE, (*a*) (lit.) step, rung of ladder, (*b*) (fig.) stage in ascent, rank; 2. 1. 26.

DELIVER, declare or communicate to; 3. 1. 182.

DENY, refuse; 4. 3. 70, 77, 82, 103.

DEW. A symbol of beneficent refreshment; 2. 1. 230.

DIFFERENCE, conflict; 1. 2. 40.

DINT (fig.), force, onset (lit. blow with a sword, or mark made by a blow); 3. 2. 195.

DIRECTLY, to the point; 1. 1. 13; 3. 3. 9, 15, 19, 20, 23.

DISCOMFORT, discourage (cf. *Troil.* 5. 10. 10); 5. 3. 106.

DISCOVER, reveal; 1. 2. 69.

DISPOSED (of persons or substances) inclined to; 1. 2. 311.

DISTRACT, insane; 4. 3. 153.

DOUBLET, close-fitting coat with detachable sleeves (v. Linthicum, p. 197); 1. 2. 266.

DOUBT, suspect (cf. *Ham.* 1. 2. 256); 2. 1. 132.

DRACHMA, Greek silver coin, worth about 8*d.* or 9*d.* (fr. Plutarch, who uses Greek terms for coins); 3. 2. 244; 4. 3. 73.

DRAW, gather, assemble; 1. 3. 22.

DROP, shed; 4. 3. 73.

DULL, spiritless, lacking mettle; 1. 3. 57.

EARN, grieve (cf. *Hen. V*, 2. 3. 3, 6); 2. 2. 129.

ELDER, i.e. stronger (v. note); 2. 2. 47.

ELEMENT, (i) sky (cf. *Tw. Nt.* 1. 1. 26; freq. in Sh. and contemporaries); 1. 3. 128; (ii) (pl.) constituent parts (v. note); 5. 5. 73.

EMBRACE, either 'welcome' (freq. in Sh.) or 'cling to', 'devote oneself to' (cf. *A.Y.L.* 1. 2. 168); 2. 1. 259.

EMULATION, envy, jealous rivalry (cf. *Troil.* 1. 3. 134); 2. 3. 13.

ENFORCE, (i) exaggerate; 3. 2. 41; (ii) (*a*) strike, (*b*) provoke; 4. 3. 111.

ENFORCED, forced, strained; 4. 2. 21.

ENFRANCHISEMENT, (i) recall (from exile), cf. *Ric. II*, 3. 3. 114; 3. 1. 57; (ii) release from servitude; 3. 1. 81.

ENGAGE, pledge (word or honour); 2. 1. 127.

ENGAGEMENT, commitment; 2. 1. 307.

ENLARGE, give free scope to, give vent to; 4. 2. 46.

ENSIGN, (i) standard; 5. 1. 79; (ii) standard-bearer; 5. 3. 3.

ENTERTAIN, take into one's service; 5. 5. 60.

ENVIOUS, malicious; 2. 1. 178; 3. 2. 176.

ENVY, malice, hatred; 2. 1. 164; 5. 5. 70.

EREBUS, place of darkness; in Eliz. Engl. generally =Hell; 2. 1. 84.

ERUPTION, unnatural calamity, lit. a bursting forth from the bounds of nature (cf. *Ham.* 1. 1. 69); 1. 3. 78.

ESTABLISH, appoint by decree (cf. *Cor.* 3. 1. 201); 1. 3. 86.

ETERNAL, used to express extreme abhorrence (Schmidt, O.E.D. 7), perh. by confusion with 'infernal' (cf. 'eternal villain' *Oth.* 4. 2. 130; 'eternal cell' *Ham.* 5. 2. 363); 1. 2. 160.

EVEN, (i) honest, straightforward (cf. *Hen. VIII*, 3. 1. 37); 2. 1. 133; (ii) level; 5. 1. 17.

EXCEPTED, in ref. to the legal phrase 'exceptis excipiendis' found in leases (cf. note *Tw. Nt.* 1. 3. 7); 2. 1. 281.

EXHALATION, meteor (cf. *1 Hen. IV*, 2. 4. 352); 2. 1. 44.

EXIGENT (sb.), exigency, 'critical moment' (K.); 5. 1. 19.

EXPEDITION, rapid march (cf. *Ric. III*, 4. 4. 136); 4. 3. 168.

EXTENUATE, understate; 3. 2. 39.

EXTREMITY, act of extreme violence or cruelty (cf. *Oth.* 5. 2. 137); 2. 1. 31.

FACE, bold front; 5. 1. 10.

FACTION, adherents (not necessarily in a bad sense); 2. 1. 77.

FACTIOUS, 'be factious' =get together a party (cf. *faction*); 1. 3. 118.

FAIN (adv.), gladly; 1. 2. 241.

FALL (vb.), let fall, lower; 4. 2. 26.

FALLING SICKNESS, epilepsy. From North; 1. 2. 255, 257.

FALSE, out of tune; 4. 3. 289.

FANTASY, imagination, fancy; 2. 1. 197; 2. 1. 231; 3. 3. 2.

FASHION (vb.), (i) put (a case); 2. 1. 30; (ii) shape according to one's will or purpose; 2. 1. 220.

FAVOUR, appearance (esp. of the face), aspect; 1. 2. 91; 1. 3. 129; 2. 1. 76.

FEARFUL, (a) timorous, (b) intimidating (both senses freq.); 5. 1. 10.

FELLOW, (i) a form of address to servants or inferiors; 2. 4. 20; 3. 2. 263; 5. 5. 45; (ii) equal; 3. 1. 62; 5. 3. 101.

FIELD, army in the field of battle; 5. 5. 80.

FIT (sb.), shivering fit in malaria; 1. 2. 120.

FLEER, grin, sneer; 1. 3. 117.

FLOOD, the Deluge of Deucalion (cf. Ovid, *Metamorphoses*, 1. 244 ff. and *Cor.* 2. 1. 91–3); 1. 2. 152.

FLOURISH (sb.), fanfare of trumpets to announce a royal person's approach; 3. 1, init. S.D.

FLOURISH (vb.), brandish a sword in triumph (O.E.D. 9), swagger (O.E.D. 10 b); 3. 2. 193.

FORM, appearance, manner; 1. 2. 300; 4. 2. 40.

FORMAL, in accordance with propriety, dignified (cf. *2 Hen. IV*, 5. 2. 133); 2. 1. 227.

FORMER, foremost, forward, front (cf. Adlington's *Golden Asse of Apuleius*, 1566, bk. x, ch. 45, 'holding of my former feet'); 5. 1. 79.

FRET, 'chequer' (Onions); lit. decorate (a ceiling) with a pattern (cf. *Cymb.* 2. 4. 88); 2. 1. 104.

FUNERALS, (pl.), funeral rites (v. note); 5. 3. 105.

GAMESOME, (a) fond of sport, (b) merry; 1. 2. 28.

GENERAL (adj.), public; 3. 2. 90; 5. 5. 71.

GENERAL (sb.), common weal, republic (cf. *Ham.* 2. 2. 442, 'caviare to the general' =above the head of the general public); 2. 1. 12.

GENIUS, tutelary spirit (cf. *Troil.* 4. 4. 52); or 'reasonable soul' (v. note); 2. 1. 66.

GENTLE, good, kind (in complimentary address); 3. 2. 73; 4. 3. 267; noble; 5. 5. 73.

GHASTLY, looking like ghosts, pale with terror; 1. 3. 23.

GIVEN, disposed (cf. 'lewdly given', *1 Hen. IV*, 2. 4. 418, 'virtuously given', *ibid.* 3. 3. 14); 1. 2. 197.

GIVE PLACE, give in, yield; 4. 3. 144.

GIVE WAY TO, give scope for (cf. *2 Hen. IV*, G. 'give'); 2. 3. 7; 4. 3. 39.

GLAZE, stare, glare (v. note); 1. 3. 21.

GO, walk (cf. *Temp.* 2. 2. 63); 1. 1. 30.

GOVERN, control, direct. Often used in astrol. or magical sense; 1. 3. 83; 4. 1. 33.

Gown, (v. *nightgown*); 4. 3. 229, 237, 251.

Grace (sb.), honour; 3. 2. 58.

Grace (vb.), do honour to; 1. 1. 38; 3. 1. 121; 3. 2. 58.

Gracious, virtuous, holy; 3. 2. 196.

Gravity, reputation for stability of character; 2. 1. 149.

Grief, grievance; 1. 3. 118; 3. 2. 214; 4. 2. 42, 46.

Grudge, ill-will; 4. 3. 124.

Hand, (i) hand-writing; 1. 2. 317; (ii) 'at hand' = at the start (v. note); 4. 2. 23.

Hasty, very transient; 4. 3. 111.

Havoc, the command that no quarter should be given; 3. 1. 274.

Hazard, 'on the hazard' = at stake; the word 'hazard' orig. meaning a game of dice where the uncertainty is increased by complicated rules; 5. 1. 68.

Head, armed force, or poss., successful resistance; 4. 1. 42.

Health, welfare, safety; 4. 3. 36.

Heap, great company ('upon a heap' = in a crowd; cf. *Hen. V*, 4. 5. 18); 1. 3. 23.

Hearse, coffin (the only Sh. sense); 3. 2. 166.

Heavy, sad; 2. 1. 275.

Hedge in, limit (one's authority); 4. 3. 30.

Hie, hasten; 1. 3. 150; 3. 1. 291; 5. 3. 78.

High, exact, ('high east' = due east); 2. 1. 110.

High-sighted, (a) supercilious,

'arrogant' (O.E.D.), (b) looking downwards (like a falcon soaring high—cf. *range*); 2. 1. 118.

Hilts (pl.), hilt. Pl. because in three parts; 5. 3. 43; 5. 5. 28.

Hind, (a) female deer, (b) peasant, (c) servant; 1. 3. 106.

Hold, (i) (imper.) here!, take!; 1. 3. 117; 5. 3. 85; (ii) 'hold on', keep; 3. 1. 69.

Honest, honourable, of good character; 1. 3. 43; 3. 1. 127; 5. 5. 71.

Honesty, honour, uprightness, integrity; 2. 1. 127; 4. 3. 67.

Honey-heavy, overpoweringly sweet, laden with sweetness (of sleep); 2. 1. 230.

Honour (sb.), integrity, uprightness; 3. 2. 15.

Honourable (adj.), upright, honest; 3, 2. 83, 84, etc.

Honourable (adv.), honourably; 5. 1. 60.

Hoot, shout (cf. *L.L.L.* 4. 2. 61); 1. 2. 245.

Horrid, horrible, terrible; 2. 2. 16.

However, notwithstanding that, although; 1. 2. 300.

Humour (sb.). See note 5. 5. 73–5; (i) mood, disposition; 2. 1. 210; 4. 3. 46, 120; (ii) whim, caprice; 1. 2. 250; 2. 2. 56; 4. 3. 108, 134; (iii) damp air, moisture; 2. 1. 262.

Humour (vb.), influence (a person) by playing on his inclinations; 1. 2. 316.

Hurtle, clatter, crash; 2. 2. 22.

Hybla, town in Sicily, famous for its honey (cf. Virgil, *Ecl.* VII. 37); 5. 1. 34.

IDES, 13th or 15th day of the month (15th in March) in the Roman calendar; 1. 2. 18; 2. 1. 40; 3. 1. 1; 4. 3. 18; 5. 1. 113.

IMITATION, following of fashion (cf. *Ric. II*, 2. 1. 23, 'base imitation'); 4. 1. 37.

IMPATIENT OF, unable to bear (cf. *2 Hen. IV*, 1. 1. 142); 4. 3. 150.

IMPROVE, 'make good use of', (O.E.D.); 2. 1. 159.

INCORPORATE TO, intimately bound up with; 1. 3. 135.

INDIFFERENTLY, without concern; 1. 2. 87.

INDIRECTION, malpractice; 4. 3. 75.

INFUSE, imbue (cf. *Merch.* 4. 1. 137); 1. 3. 69.

INGRAFTED, firmly rooted, implanted; 2. 1. 184.

INSTANCE, proof, evidence, sign (cf. *Lucr.* 1511, 'guilty instance'); 4. 2. 16.

INSTRUMENT, agent; 1. 3. 70; 2. 1. 66.

INSUPPRESSIVE, indomitable (app. not pre-Sh.); 2. 1. 134.

INTERMIT, delay, stay; 1. 1. 58.

ISSUE, action (cf. *Meas.* 1. 1. 36); 3. 1. 295.

ITCHING PALM, 'hankering after gain' (O.E.D.); 4. 3. 10.

JADE, poor, or vicious horse; 4. 2. 26.

JEALOUS, (i) suspicious; 1. 2. 71; (ii) doubtful; 1. 2. 162.

JIGGING, rhyming. Contemptuous; 4. 3. 135.

JUST, right, exact; 1. 2. 54.

KEEP (intr.), (i) associate; 1. 2. 312; (ii) stay; 2. 1. 284.

KERCHIEF, linen head-cloth regularly worn by women; and by men in time of sickness, to keep the head warm. K. cites G. Fletcher—'Pale sickness with his kerchered head upwound' (*Christ's Victory*, 1610, st. 12); 2. 1. 315.

KIND, (i) nature; 1. 3. 64; (ii) species; 2. 1. 33.

KNAVE, term used of menials and inferiors, not abusive; 1. 1. 17; 4. 3. 239, 267.

KNOT, company, group; 3. 1. 118.

KNOTTY, gnarled (cf. *Temp.* 1. 2. 295); 1. 3. 6.

KNOW, 'admit the claims or authority of' (O.E.D.); 4. 3. 134.

LAUGHTER, object of laughter, laughing-stock; 1.2. 72 (F.); 4. 3. 113.

LAY OFF, take off; 1. 2. 243.

LIABLE (to), subject to, at the command of (cf. *K. John*, 2. 1. 490); 2. 2. 104.

LIE, lodge (for the night); 3. 1. 287.

LIGHT, alight, fall, dismount; 1. 1. 59; 3. 1. 263; 5. 3. 31.

LIKE, likely; 1. 2. 175, 255.

LIMITATION. Legal term = 'the period specified for the continuance of · an estate' (O.E.D.); 2. 1. 283.

LOOK ABOUT, be wary; 2. 3. 7.

LOTTERY, 'by lottery' = by chance; 2. 1. 119.

LOVER, friend (common use in Sh.'s time); 2. 3. 9; 3. 2. 18, 46; 5. 1. 94.

Low-crooked, bending low; 3. 1. 43.

Lupercal, the Lupercalia, ancient fertility festival in honour of Pan, conducted with rites of purification; the procession started from the Lupercal, a cave in which a wolf was said to have suckled Romulus and Remus; 1. 1. 71; 3. 2. 97.

Mace, sergeant's staff (v. note); 4. 3. 266.

Main, strong; 2. 1. 196.

Make, make out, make to seem; 2. 1. 177.

Make head, raise an armed force (v. *head*); 4. 1. 42.

Make to, make for, approach; 3. 1. 18; 5. 1. 25; 5. 3. 29.

Mart (vb.), traffic in; 4. 3. 11.

Masker, one who takes part in masques; 5. 1. 62.

Mean (sb.), (i) means; 3. 1. 162; (ii) 'by means whereof' = in consequence of which; 1. 2. 49.

Mechanical (adj.), of the working classes (cf. *2 Hen. IV*, 5. 5. 39); 1. 1. 3.

Merely, entirely; 1. 2. 39.

Mettle or metal, (i) the 'stuff' or life-force of which man, or beast, is made (cf. O.E.D. 'metal' 1f) 1. 1. 65; 1. 2. 297, 310; 4. 2. 24; hence (ii) courage; 2. 1. 134.

Mo (adj. as sb.), more; 2. 1. 72.

Modestly, without exaggeration or flattery; 1. 2. 69.

Monstrous, abnormal, contrary to nature; 1. 3. 68, 71; 2. 1. 81.

Mortal, (v. note); 2. 1. 66.

Motion, (i) inward prompting, impulse (i.e. of the soul); 2. 1. 64; (ii) (*a*) external influence, (*b*) impulse (v. note); 3. 1. 70.

Mutiny (sb. and vb.), riot, revolt (of any kind); 3. 1. 86; 3. 2. 123, 211, 231, 232.

Napkin, handkerchief (the only sense in Sh.); 3. 2. 134.

Native, natural; 2. 1. 83.

Nature, 'the nature of' = something like, a kind of; 2. 1. 69.

Naughty, 'good-for-nothing, rascally' (K.); 1. 1. 17.

Neat's-leather, ox-hide; 1. 1 29.

New-added reinforced; 4. 3. 207.

Nice, trivial; 4. 3. 8.

Niggard (vb. tr.), 'supply sparingly' (Schmidt) (cf. intrans. use in *Son.* 1. 12; no other inst. of trans. use in O.E.D.); 4. 3. 226.

Nightgown, dressing-gown (cf. *Macb.* G. and *Gown*); 2. 2. init. S.D.

Note (vb.), brand, stigmatize. From North (v. Sk. p. 135); 4. 3. 2.

Nothing (adv.), not at all; 1. 2. 162.

Notice, information, news; 3. 2. 272.

Object, sight, spectacle, gazing-stock (O.E.D. 3 b). (Cf. *Gent.* 1. 1. 13, *Ham.* 3. 1. 180); 4. 1. 37.

Observe, pay obsequious respect to (cf. *2 Hen. IV*, G.); 4. 3. 45.

OCCUPATION, (*a*) handicraft, trade (cf. *Cor.* 4. 1. 14; 4. 6. 98); (*b*) business, action; 1. 2. 267.

O'ERSHOOT (refl.), go further than one meant to. Term of archery; 3. 2. 151.

O'ERSWAY, prevail upon, induce to change a resolution; 2. 1. 203.

O'ERWATCHED, tired out by being kept awake (cf. *Lear*, 2. 2. 177); 4. 3. 240.

OFFAL, refuse, rubbish (here fig., scum of the human race, cf. O.E.D. 5); 1. 3. 109.

OFFENCE, hurt, harm (to body or mind); 2. 1. 268; 4. 3. 200.

OFFEND, injure; 3. 2. 30, 31, 33, 36.

OMIT, miss, neglect (cf. *Meas.* 4. 3. 71; *2 Hen. IV*, 4. 4. 27); 4. 3. 218.

ONCE, (i) at some time; 4. 3. 189; (ii) 'at once' =without further ado; 5. 5. 39.

OPINION, (i) reputation; 2. 1. 145; (ii) view of life; 5. 1. 77.

OR, either ('or...or' =either ...or) (freq.); 2. 1. 135; 5. 5. 3.

ORCHARD. Generally ='garden' in Sh.; 2. 1. 1. S.D.; 3. 2. 250.

ORDER (sb.), way in which a thing takes place, arrangements; 1. 2. 25; 3. 1. 231.

ORDER (vb.), regulate (the only Sh. sense); 'ordered honourably' =treated with due honour; 5. 5. 79.

ORDINANCE, natural behaviour as decreed by God; 1. 3. 66.

OUT, (*a*) at variance; 1. 1. 19; (*b*) 'out at heel'; 1. 1. 20.

PALM, emblem of victory; 1. 2. 131.

PALTER, shuffle, equivocate (cf. *Macb.* 5. 8. 20); 2. 1. 126.

PART (sb.), function, business, duty; 1. 3. 54; 5. 3. 89.

PART (vb. intr.), (i) depart; 2. 1. 193; (ii) (tr.) divide; 3. 2. 4; 5. 5. 81.

PASSION, (i) emotion; 1. 2. 40; (ii) signs of deep feeling; 1. 2. 48; (iii) mourning; 3. 1. 284.

PATH (vb.), walk, go about (v. note). O.E.D. gives exx. of the vb. in trans., but no other in intrans. sense; 2. 1. 83.

PEEVISH, childish, silly (cf. *Ric. III*, 4. 2. 100 'a little peevish boy'); 5. 1. 61.

PHANTASMA, 'nightmare' (Onions), vision; 2. 1. 65.

PIECE OUT, eke out, fill out, augment; 2. 1. 51.

PIT, (*a*) grave, (*b*) hole into which game is driven; 5. 5. 23.

PITCH. Term of falconry= height to which a falcon soars (cf. *1 Hen. VI*, 2. 4. 11; *2 Hen. VI*, 2. 1. 5; *Ric. II*, 1. 1. 109); 1. 1. 77.

PLEASURE, pleasure-ground; 3. 2. 252.

PLUCK, pull or draw; 2. 1. 73.

POINT UPON, astrol. term= direct a malign influence towards (cf. *Oth.* 5. 2. 46); 1. 3. 32.

POMPEY'S PORCH, portico of the Theatre, built by P. in 55 B.C.; 1. 3. 126.

POST (vb.), ride with speed, hasten; 3. 1. 288.

POSTURE, the motion or position of a weapon in drill or warfare (cf. O.E.D. 'posture-book', citing Jonson's *Devil is an Ass*, acted 1616, 3. 2. 37); 5. 1. 33.

POWER, body of armed men, armed force; 4. 1. 42; 4. 3. 167, 305.

PRAETOR, a magistrate subordinate to consul, elected annually to administer justice in Rome and the provinces; 1. 3. 143; 2. 4. 34.

PREFER, (i) put forward, present; 3. 1. 28; (ii) recommend (cf. *Merch.* 2. 2. 155); 5. 5. 62.

PRESENT, immediate; 2. 2. 5.

PRESENTLY, at once, immediately; 3. 1. 28, 143; 4. 1. 45; 4. 3. 195.

PRESS, throng, crowd; 1. 2. 15.

PREVAIL, have effect; 2. 1. 254.

PREVENT, forestall, prevent by some previous action, anticipate; 2. 1. 28, 160; 3. 1. 35; 5. 1. 104.

PREVENTION, forestalling; 2. 1. 85; 3. 1. 19.

PRICK (vb.), (i) incite; 2. 1. 124; (ii) indicate by a 'tick' or mark in a list, mark down; 3. 1. 217; 4. 1. 1, 3, 16.

PROCEEDING, advancement; 2. 2. 103.

PRODIGIOUS, portentous, threateningly ominous; 1. 3. 77.

PRODIGY, ominous phenomenon; 1. 3. 28; 2. 1. 198.

PROFESS ONESELF, make professions or protestations of friendship (cf. *Wint.* 1. 2. 456); 1. 2. 77.

PROFESSION, occupation; 1. 1. 5.

PROOF, (i) experience (cf. *Tw. Nt*, 3. 1. 126); 2. 1. 21; (ii) practical test (with a quibble on log. 'proof'); 5. 1. 49.

PROPER, (i) handsome; 1. 1. 29; (ii) peculiar (to), belonging exclusively (to); 1. 2. 41; 5. 3. 96.

PROPERTY, 'an instrument, a tool' (O.E.D.) or stage property; 4. 1. 40.

PROTEST, publicly assert, proclaim; 3. 1. 239.

PROVIDENCE, decree of Providence; 5. 1. 106.

PULPIT, platform, Rostra (erected for orations in the Forum); 3. 1. 80, 84, 230, 237, 251; 3. 2. init. S.D.

PURPLED, blood-stained; 3. 1. 159.

PURPOSE (sb.), (i) meaning (cf. *Meas.* 2. 4. 148); 1. 3. 35; (ii) 'to the purpose' = to the point, in keeping with the matter in hand (cf. Fr. *à-propos*); 3. 1. 147.

PURPOSE (vb.), predetermine; 2. 2. 27.

PUSH, attack, onslaught; 5. 2. 5.

PUT ON, (i) assume; 1. 2. 300; (ii) disclose by outward appearance (as clothes may rank, profession, or nature of an occasion); 1. 3. 60; 2. 1. 225.

PUT UP, sheathe; 1. 3. 19.

QUALITY, nature, character; 1. 3. 64, 68; 3. 1. 41.

QUARREL. 'In Law an accusation or charge, an action or suit' (O.E.D.); 2. 1. 28.

QUESTION, (i) affair (for the consideration of posterity); 3. 2. 37; (ii) 'call in question' =take up for consideration or discussion (cf. *A.Y.L.* 5. 2. 6); 4. 3. 163.

QUICK, lively; 1. 2. 29, 297.

RAISE, rouse, waken up; 4. 3. 245.

RANGE, rove or fly in search of game (O.E.D. 7a); 2. 1. 118; 3. 1. 271.

RANK, 'corrupt, festering' (O.E.D., citing *2 Hen. IV*, 3. 1. 39. Cf. *Ham.* 3. 4. 147–8); 3. 1. 153.

RASCAL (adj.), of little or no value (fig.; sb. = inferior deer, not worth hunting); 4. 3. 80.

RASH, inflammable, explosive (cf. *2 Hen. IV*, 4. 4. 48); 4. 3. 39.

REASON WITH, come to reasonable terms with, face squarely; 5. 1. 96.

REBEL (adj.), refractory; 3. 1. 40.

RECOVER, (*a*) cure, restore to health, (*b*) re-sole; 1. 1. 28.

REEK, steam; 3. 1. 159.

REGARD (sb.), worth, esteem; 3. 1. 225; 4. 2. 12.

REGARD (vb.), (i) watch; 5. 3. 21; (ii) honour, esteem highly (cf. *Cor.* 5. 6. 144); 5. 3. 88.

REMAINS (pl.), remainder, remnant; 5. 5. 1.

REMORSE, pity; 2. 1. 19.

REPEAL, REPEALING (vb. and sb.), recall from exile; 3. 1. 51, 54.

REPLICATION, reply, (here) reverberation; 1. 1. 50.

REPUTE, think of; 1. 2. 173.

RESOLVE, 'be resolved' = have one's anxiety or curiosity set at rest; 3. 1. 132; 3. 2. 180; 4. 2. 14.

RESPECT (sb.), (i) estimation, regard; 1. 2. 59; 3. 2. 15; 5. 5. 45; (ii) 'in respect of' =in comparison with (cf. *L.L.L.* 5. 2. 635); 1. 1. 10.

RESPECT (vb.), heed; 4. 3. 69.

RESTING, immovable; 3. 1. 61.

RETENTIVE, confining; 1. 3. 95.

RHEUMY, dank; 2. 1. 266.

RIGHT, regular; 2. 2. 20.

RIVE, cleave; 1. 3. 6; 4. 3. 84.

ROYAL, noble, munificent; 3. 1. 128; 3. 2. 246.

RUDE, uncivilized or uncultured; 3. 2. 30.

RUFFLE UP, move to indignation; 3. 2. 229.

RUMOUR, confused noise (cf. *K. John*, 5. 4. 45); 2. 4. 18.

SAD, serious, grave; 1. 2. 218, 277.

SAFE, sound, clear; 1. 1. 15.

SATISFY, content one's reason or sense of justice, give a satisfactory answer or explanation to, remove the doubts of; 3. 1. 48; 3. 1. 142, 227; 3. 2. 1; 4. 2. 10.

SAUCE, (*a*) quibbling on 'saucy' (q.v.), (*b*) piquant flavour (the Eliz.s liked 'eccentric flavourings to their sauces' (*Sh. Eng.* II, 126)); 1. 2. 301.

SAUCY, insolent, insulting (stronger than mod. sense); 1. 3. 12; 4. 3. 132.

SAVAGE, wild, ungoverned (not 'uncivilized' in Sh.— Onions); 3. 1. 224.

SCANDAL (vb.), slander (cf. *Cor.* 3. 1. 43); 1. 2. 76.

SCARF, ceremonial fillet on images; 1. 2. 286.

SCHEDULE, written scroll; 3. 1. 3.

SEARCH, probe, pierce; 5. 3. 42.

SECRET, able· to hold one's tongue (cf. *Rom.* 2. 4. 208; *Ado*, 1. 1. 212); 2. 1. 125.

SENNET, trumpet-notes as a signal for a procession; 1. 2. 24 S.D., 214 S.D.

SENSELESS, incapable of feeling; 1. 1. 39.

SENSIBLE, capable of feeling; 1. 3. 18.

SERVE, attend to (at table or in a shop); 3. 1. 7.

SET (upon), stake; 5. 1. 74.

SET ON, (i. intr.) move on, proceed; 1. 2. 11; 5. 2. 3; (ii. tr.), set in motion, send forward; 2. 1. 331; 4. 3. 305; 5. 3. 108.

SEVERAL, (i) various; 1. 2. 318; (ii) separate; 2. 1. 138; 3. 2. 244; 5. 5. 18.

SEVERALLY, separately; 3. 2. 10.

SHADOW, reflected image (cf. *V. & A.* 162); 1. 2. 58.

SHOW (sb.), appearance; 1. 2. 47, 177.

SHREWD, mischievous, malicious; 2. 1. 158.

SHREWDLY, very much (freq.; cf. e.g. *Hen. V*, 3. 7. 169); 3. 1. 147.

SLEEK-HEADED, smooth-haired (cf. North, *Life of Cæsar*, 'smooth-combed'); 1. 2. 193.

SLIGHT, insignificant, of no importance; 4. 1. 12; 4. 3. 37.

SLIGHT OFF (vb.), treat with contempt, put aside as trifling; 4. 3. 5.

SLIP, 'let slip'=unleash; 3. 1. 274.

SMATCH, smack, relish, tincture; 5. 5. 46.

SOBER, calm; 4. 2. 40.

SOFT (interj.), stay, stop; 1. 2. 252; 3. 1. 123.

SOFTLY, slowly; 5. 1. 16.

SOIL, blemish; 1. 2. 42.

SOOTH, truth, for 'in truth'; 2. 4. 20.

SORT, (i) class; 1. 1. 61; (ii) way, manner; 1. 2. 205; 'in sort'=after a fashion; 2. 1. 283.

SOUND (vb.), utter (cf. *Ant.* 2. 2. 38); 1. 2. 143.

SPANIEL-FAWNING, toadying, dog-like, to gain favour; 3. 1. 43.

SPEED, make prosper, give success to (in phrases invoking supernatural assistance) (cf. *M.W.W.* 3. 4. 12); 1. 2. 88; 2. 4. 40.

SPIRIT, soul, reason, intelligence (cf. *Son.* 86. 5); 2. 1. 122, 167 (with quibble on 'spirit' =principles) 168, 169; 4. 1. 33.

SPIRITS, tendencies; 1. 3. 69.

SPLEEN, organ supposed to be seat of the passions; 4. 3. 47.

SPOIL, skin of a slaughtered animal (O.E.D. 5b and Spenser, *Bellay*, vi. 14, 'Soone on a tree uphang'd I saw her [i.e. the wolf's] spoyle'); 3. 1. 207.

SPOT, dot; 4. 1. 6.

SPUR, 'on the s.' = at full speed; 5. 3. 29.

SPURN AT, kick against (cf. *Lucr.* 1026); 2. 1. 11.

STAKE, post to which a 'baited' bear was tied (cf. *Macb.* 5. 7. 12); 4. 1. 48.

STALE (vb.), make stale or common, cheapen; 1. 2. 73; 4. 1. 38.

STAND, (i) (with advl. adjs.), almost = 'be'; 2. 1. 142; 4. 1. 14; 4. 3. 203; 5. 1. 93; (ii) 'stand up' = make a stand; 2. 1. 167; (iii) be particular about, attach importance to; 2. 2. 13; (iv) 'stand upon' (cf. *Err.* 1. 2. 80) = concern oneself about; 3. 1. 101.

STARE, (i) glare; 2. 1. 242; 4. 3. 40; (ii) stand on end (cf. *Temp.* 1. 2. 213); 4. 3. 278.

START (sb.), lead, position in front (metaph. fr. running contests); 1. 2. 130.

START (vb. tr.), startle so as to raise; 1. 2. 147.

STATE, (i) regal magnificence, royal court; 1. 2. 160; (ii) state of affairs; 1. 3. 71; 3. 1. 136; (iii) (*a*) sense (ii), (*b*) (fig.) kingdom, realm; 2. 1. 67.

STAY (intr.), wait; 1. 3. 125, 136, 139; 2. 4. 2, 3; 3. 2. 150, 207.

STAY (tr.), (i) make to stay; 2. 2. 75; (ii) stop, prevent; 4. 3. 126; (iii) await, wait for; 5. 1. 106.

STEM (vb.), breast, plough through (from 'stem', the prow of a ship, *Cor.* 2. 2. 112, *Per.* 4. 1. 63); 1. 2. 109.

STILL, constantly; 1. 2. 244; 3. 1. 146; 5. 1. 95.

STIR (sb.), going out; 1. 3. 127.

STOMACH (fig.), appetite, inclination; 1. 2. 302; 5. 1. 66.

STRAIN, stock, family, race; 5. 1. 59.

STRANGE, distant (as of a stranger), not familiar; 1. 2. 35.

STRANGE-DISPOSED, of an extraordinary character (v. *disposed*); 1. 3. 33.

SUBMIT, expose; 1. 3. 47.

SUBURBS, outskirts (v. note); 2. 1. 285.

SUCCESS, result, (good or bad); 2. 2. 6; 5. 3. 65, 66.

SUDDEN, swift, prompt; 3. 1. 19.

SUFFERANCE, (i) patient endurance; 1. 3. 84; (ii) suffering; 2. 1. 115.

SURE (adv.), securely, safely; 1. 2. 322; 4. 1. 47.

SWAY (sb.), government, dominion (v. note); 1. 3. 3.

SWAY (vb.), (i) (intr.) bear rule, exercise control; 2. 1. 20; (ii) (tr.) 'sway from' = divert, turn aside; 3. 1. 220.

SWEAR, put on oath; 2. 1. 129; 5. 3. 38.

TAG-RAG PEOPLE, rabble. 'Tagrag' = 'odds and ends' (cf. 'tag' = rabble, *Cor.* 3. 1. 247); 1. 2. 259.

TAKE THOUGHT, give way to sorrow (cf. *Ant.* 3. 13. 1, 'think and die'); 2. 1. 187.

TARDY, sluggish, 'foolish' (Herf.); 1. 2. 300.

TARQUIN, Tarquinius Superbus, who outraged Lucretia, and was expelled from Rome by a rising instigated by Lucius Junius Brutus; 2. 1. 54.

TASTE (sb.), 'in some t.' = in some measure; 4. 1. 34.

TEMPER, temperament, disposition (cf. *K. John*, 5. 2. 40; *1 Hen. IV*, 3. 1. 170); 1. 2. 129; 3. 1. 176.

TEMPT, (i) put to the test; 1. 3. 53; 4. 3. 36, 59, 62; (ii) risk; 2. 1. 266.

TENDING TO, relating to, bearing on; 3. 2. 59.

THEREFORE, for that reason; 1. 2. 66; 3. 1. 219.

THEWS, sinews, bodily strength; 1. 3. 81.

THICK, (of sight) dim (cf. *2 Hen. IV*, 3. 2. 311); 5. 3. 21.

THING, being, creature (cf. *All's Well*, 4. 3. 330); 2. 1. 29; 4. 3. 276, 295, 302.

THOROUGH, through; 3. 1. 137; 5. 1. 110.

THOUGHT, (i) sorrow, melancholy (v. *take thought*); 2. 1. 187; (ii) 'with a th.' = 'in a twinkling' (Schmidt) (cf. *Ant.* 4. 14. 9; *1 Hen. IV*, 2. 4. 214); 5. 3. 19.

THUNDER-STONE, thunderbolt; 1. 3. 49.

TIDE, course (of time); 3. 1. 258.

TINCTURE, (*a*) stain, colour, (*b*) technical term in heraldry for a colour ('tincture') in coats of arms (cf. *cognizance*); 2. 2. 89.

TOIL, snare; 2. 1. 206.

TOKENS, signs and wonders; 1. 3. 55.

TOUCH, (i) hurt, injure; 2. 1. 154; 'touching' = wounding, grievous (cf. *Tim.* 3. 5. 19, 'touched to death'); 4. 3. 149; (ii) concern; 3. 1. 78; (iii) play on a musical instrument; 4. 3. 255.

TRADE, craft (in Scotland 'tradesman' still = 'workman'); 1. 1. 5.

TRASH, (i) (*a*) twigs used for fuel, (*b*) rubbish, (*c*) (fig.) worthless thing; 1. 3. 108; (ii) dross; 4. 3. 26, 74.

TRIBUTARY, captive (prince or chief) who will pay tribute; 1. 1. 37.

TRICK, artifice; 4. 2. 22.

TRUE, (i) honest ('true man' proverbial opp. of 'thief'; v. *Ado*, 3. 3. 50); 1. 2. 262; (ii) correct, rightful; 3. 1. 242.

TRUE-FIXED, firmly fixed; 3. 1. 61.

TURN, reflect; 1. 2. 56.

UNBRACED, with clothes unfastened (cf. *Ham.* 2. 1. 72); 1. 3. 48; 2. 1. 262.

UNDERGO, undertake; 1. 3. 123.

UNDONE, not done (cf. General Confession in *Book of Common Prayer*; and *Oth.* 3. 3. 204; 4. 3. 71); 4. 2. 9.

UNFIRM, unsteady, unstable; 1. 3. 4.

UNFOLD, disclose; 2. 1. 274, 330.

UNGENTLE, UNGENTLY, discourteous(ly); 2. 1. 237, 242.

UNLUCKILY, with ill omen; 3. 3. 2.

UNMERITABLE, devoid of merit, undeserving (of respect or high position); 4. 1. 12.

URGE, (i) suggest; 2. 1. 155; (ii) press for an answer; 2. 1. 243; (iii) provoke; 4. 3. 35.

USE (sb.), the natural order of things (cf. *Macb.* 1. 3. 137, 'against the use of nature'); 2. 2. 25; 'in use' =customary; 3. 1. 266.

USE (vb. tr.), (i) practise; 1. 1. 14; (ii) be in the habit of; 1. 2. 72, 261; (iii) treat; 5. 5. 76.

UTTER (vb.), emit (cf. *M.N.D.* 4. 2. 45); 1. 2. 247.

UTTERMOST, latest; 2. 1. 213, 214.

VENTURE (sb.), (*a*) (lit.) merchandise at sea, (*b*) (fig.) anything hazarded; 4. 3. 222.

VESSEL, (fig.) human being, person (as the receptacle of a soul; fr. Biblical use, e.g. in Romans, ix, 21–3 etc.); 5. 5. 13.

VILE, (i) mean, of little worth (Lat. *vilis*); 1. 3. 111; 4. 3. 74; (ii) bad in effect; 2. 1. 265; (iii) mean in rank; 3. 2. 32; (iv) base, evil; 4. 3. 71; 5. 1. 39, 103; 5. 5. 38.

VIRTUE, (i) prerogative, power; 2. 1. 269; (ii) excellence or merit; 1. 1. 90; 2. 1. 133; 5. 5. 76.

VOICE, vote, opinion; 3. 1. 178; 4. 1. 16.

VOID, empty ('more void' = less crowded); 2. 4. 36.

VOUCHSAFE, deign to accept (cf. *K. John*, 3. 1. 394); 2. 1. 313.

VULGAR (sb.), common people; 1. 1. 74.

WAFTURE, waving; 2. 1. 246.

WARN, summon to the fight (cf. *K. John*, 2. 1. 201); 5. 1. 5.

WASTE, spend (time and money); 2. 1. 59; 4. 3. 198.

WATCH (vb. tr.), keep awake and wait for; 4. 3. 247.

WATCHFUL, causing loss of sleep; 2. 1. 98.

WEIGH, consider; 2. 1. 108.

WELL GIVEN, well disposed. From North (v. *given*); 1. 2. 197.

WHAT! (i) exclamation commonly used in calling, addressing, or on seeing, a person; 2. 1. 1; 2. 2. 120; 4. 2. 3; 5. 3. 72; (ii) exclamation of surprise; 2. 1. 263; (iii) (interrog.), why?: 2. 1. 123.

WHEN! exclamation of impatience; 2. 1. 5.

WHE'R, whether; 1. 1. 65; 5. 3. 97; 5. 4. 30.

WHERE. Used loosely, as often in Sh., of time and occasion (cf. *M.N.D.* 5. 1. 95–7); 1. 2. 59.

WHILE, the present time (v. *woe the while*); 1. 3. 82.

WHILES, while; 1. 2. 209.

WILL (sb.), desire, wish; 3. 3. 3; 4. 3. 222; 5. 3. 48.

WIND (vb.), wheel round, turn; 4. 1. 32.

WINDOW, shutter; 3. 2. 261. Not in O.E.D.; but v. the comprehensive and final note by K. Tillotson (*R.E.S.* XVII, 332–4; and G. Tillotson, *Essays*, 1942, 204–7); and cf. *Rom.* 1. 1. 144, 'shuts up his windows, locks fair daylight out'. The Eliz.s and Jacob.s called their shutters 'shuts' or 'wooden windows', or simply 'windows', and the word 'shutter' is not found in this sense before 1683.

WIT, (i) understanding, intelligence; 1. 2. 301; (ii) invention (cf. *L.L.L.* 1. 2. 176); 3. 2. 222.

WITHAL, at the same time, besides; 2. 1. 249, 292, 294.

WOE THE WHILE! alas for the times we live in! 1. 3. 82.

WORD, word of command, order (*not* 'password'); 4. 2. 2, 33; 5. 3. 5.

WORK (vb.), (i) (tr.) move, influence; 1. 2. 163, 310; (ii) (intr.) follow its course, have its full effect; 2. 1. 209; 3. 2. 262.

WORTHY, weighty, important; 1. 2. 50; 3. 1. 49, 117; 4. 2. 8.

WRONG, harm; 3. 1. 243.